9th International Workshop on Finite State Methods and Natural Language Processing 2011

(FSMNLP 2011)

AA004590

Blois, France
12-15 July 2011

ISBN: 978-1-62276-464-8

Printed from e-media with permission by:

Curran Associates, Inc.
57 Morehouse Lane
Red Hook, NY 12571

Some format issues inherent in the e-media version may also appear in this print version.

Printed by Curran Associates, Inc. (2012)

For permission requests, please contact the Association for Computational Linguistics at the address below.

Association for Computational Linguistics
209 N. Eighth Street
Stroudsburg, Pennsylvania 18360

Phone: 1-570-476-8006
Fax: 1-570-476-0860

acl@aclweb.org

Additional copies of this publication are available from:

Curran Associates, Inc.
57 Morehouse Lane
Red Hook, NY 12571 USA
Phone: 845-758-0400
Fax: 845-758-2634
Email: curran@proceedings.com
Web: www.proceedings.com

FSMNLP 2011

Proceedings of the

9th International Workshop Finite State Methods and Natural Language Processing

July 12–15, 2011

Université François Rabelais Tours

Blois, France

Sponsors:

Preface

These proceedings contain the papers presented at the 9th International Workshop on Finite State Methods and Natural Language Processing (FSMNLP 2011), which was held in Blois (France), July 12–15, 2011, jointly with the 16th International Conference on Implementation and Application of Automata (CIAA 2011).

The workshop covers a wide range of topics from morphology to stringology to formal language theory. This volume contains the 14 regular and 3 short papers that were presented at the workshop. In total, 30 papers (25 regular and 5 short papers) were submitted to a doubly blind refereeing process, in which each paper was reviewed by 3 program committee members. The overall acceptance rate was 57%. The program committee was composed of internationally leading researchers and practitioners selected from academia, research labs, and companies.

The organizing committee would like to thank the program committee for their hard work, the referees for their valuable feedback, the invited speakers for their innovative contributions, and the local organizers for their tireless efforts. We are particularly grateful for significant sponsorship from the *Campus de la CCI de Loir-et-Cher*, the *Université François-Rabelais Tours*, the *Centre National de la Recherche Scientifique*, the *Région Centre*, the city of *Blois*, the *Université de Rouen*, the *Université Paris-Est Marne-la-Vallée*, the *Communauté d'Agglomération de Blois* (Agglopolys), the *Ministère de l'Enseignement Supérieur et de la Recherche*, *Humanis*, the *Université d'Orléans* and *MAIF*.

MATTHIEU CONSTANT
ANDREAS MALETTI
AGATA SAVARY

Organizers:

Jean-Yves Antoine, Université François Rabelais Tours (France)
Béatrice Bouchou-Markhoff, Université François Rabelais Tours (France)
Pascal Caron, Université de Rouen (France)
Jean-Marc Champarnaud, Université de Rouen (France)
Matthieu Constant, Université Paris-Est Marne-la-Vallée (France), FSMNLP chair
Nathalie Friburger, Université François Rabelais Tours (France)
Mirian Halfeld Ferrari Alves, Université d'Orléans (France)
Aurore Leroy, Université François Rabelais Tours (France)
Andreas Maletti, University of Stuttgart (Germany)
Patrick Marcel, Université François Rabelais Tours (France)
Denis Maurel, Université François Rabelais Tours (France)
Veronika Peralta, Université François Rabelais Tours (France)
Yacine Sam, Université François Rabelais Tours (France)
Agata Savary, Université François Rabelais Tours (France), CIAA chair

Invited Speakers and Tutorialists:

Eric Laporte, Université Paris-Est Marne-la-Vallée (France)
Sylvain Lombardy, Université Paris-Est Marne-la-Vallée (France)
Mark-Jan Nederhof, University of St Andrews (United Kingdom)
Joachim Niehren, INRIA Lille (France)
Sheng Yu, University of Western Ontario (Canada)

Program Committee:

Cyril Allauzen, Google Inc. (USA)
Francisco Casacuberta, Instituto Tecnológico De Informática (Spain)
David Chiang, ISI, University of Southern California (USA)
Maxime Crochemore, King's College London (United Kingdom)
Jan Daciuk, Gdańsk University of Technology (Poland)
Frank Drewes, Umeå University (Sweden)
Dafydd Gibbon, University of Bielefeld (Germany)
Thomas Hanneforth, University of Potsdam (Germany)
Colin de la Higuera, University of Nantes (France)
Jan Holub, Czech Technical University in Prague (Czech Republic)
André Kempe, CADEGE Technologies & Consulting (France)
András Kornai, Eötvös Loránd University (Hungary)
Derrick Kourie, University of Pretoria (South Africa)
Eric Laporte, Université Paris-Est Marne-la-Vallée (France)
Sylvain Lombardy, Université Paris-Est Marne-la-Vallée (France)
Andreas Maletti, University of Stuttgart (Germany)
Mike Maxwell, University of Maryland (USA)
Kemal Oflazer, Carnegie Mellon University (Qatar)
Jakub Piskorski, Polish Academy of Sciences, Warsaw (Poland)
Laurette Pretorius, University of South Africa (South Africa)
Strahil Ristov, Ruđer Bošković Institute, Zagreb (Croatia)
Jim Rogers, Earlham College, Richmond (USA)
Giorgio Satta, University of Padua (Italy)
Max Silberztein, Université de Franche-Comté (France)
Bruce Watson, Universities of Pretoria and Stellenbosch (South Africa)
Anssi Yli-Jyrä, University of Helsinki (Finland)
Sheng Yu, University of Western Ontario (Canada)
Menno van Zaanen, Tilburg University (Netherlands)
Lynette van Zijl, Stellenbosch University (South Africa)

Additional Reviewers:

Hasan Ibne Akram
Bernd Bohnet
Fabienne Braune
Loek Cleophas
Yuan Gao
Carlos Gómez-Rodríguez
Jan Janousek
Slim Mesfar
Ernest Ngassam
Petr Prochazka
Tinus Strauss

Table of Contents

Conference Program

Tuesday, July 12, 2011

9:00–9:30 Opening

9:30–10:30 *Intersection for Weighted Formalisms*
Mark-Jan Nederhof

11:00–12:00 Tutorial by Sylvain Lombardy

14:00–14:30 *Modularization of Regular Growth Automata*
Christian Wurm

14:30–15:00 *Finite-state Representations Embodying Temporal Relations*
Tim Fernando

15:00–15:30 *Supervised and Semi-Supervised Sequence Learning for Recognition of Requisite Part and Effectuation Part in Law Sentences*
Le-Minh Nguyen, Ngo Xuan Bach and Akira Shimazu

16:00–16:30 *Compiling Simple Context Restrictions with Nondeterministic Automata*
Anssi Yli-Jyrä

16:30–17:00 *Constraint Grammar Parsing with Left and Right Sequential Finite Transducers*
Mans Hulden

17:00–17:30 *E-Dictionaries and Finite-State Automata for the Recognition of Named Entities*
Cvetana Krstev, Duško Vitas, Ivan Obradović and Miloš Utvić

Wednesday, July 13, 2011

9:30–10:30 Invited Talk by Joachim Niehren

11:00–12:00 Tutorial by Sylvain Lombardy

12:30–13:00 FSMNLP business meeting

14:30–15:00 *A Practical Algorithm for Intersecting Weighted Context-free Grammars with Finite-State Automata*
Thomas Hanneforth

15:00–15:30 *Open Source WFST Tools for LVCSR Cascade Development*
Josef R. Novak, Nobuaki Minematsu and Keikichi Hirose

15:30–16:00 *Intersection of Multitape Transducers vs. Cascade of Binary Transducers: The Example of Egyptian Hieroglyphs Transliteration*
François Barthélemy and Serge Rosmorduc

17:00–18:30 Guided Tour

Thursday, July 14, 2011

9:00–10:00 Invited Talk by Sheng Yu

10:00–11:00 Tutorial by Eric Laporte

11:30–12:30 Tutorial by Sylvain Lombardy

15:00–23:15 Excursion and Gala Dinner

Friday, July 15, 2011

9:00–9:20 *A Note on Sequential Rule-Based POS Tagging*
Sylvain Schmitz

9:20–9:40 *FTrace: A Tool for Finite-State Morphology*
James Kilbury, Katina Bontcheva and Younes Samih

9:40–10:00 *Incremental Construction of Millstream Configurations Using Graph Transformation*
Suna Bensch, Frank Drewes, Helmut Jürgensen and Brink van der Merwe

10:00–11:00 Tutorial by Eric Laporte

11:30–12:00 *Stochastic K-TSS Bi-Languages for Machine Translation*
M. Inés Torres and Francisco Casacuberta

12:00–12:30 *Measuring the Confusability of Pronunciations in Speech Recognition*
Panagiota Karanasou, François Yvon and Lori Lamel

14:30–15:00 *Fast Yet Rich Morphological Analysis*
Mohamed Altantawy, Nizar Habash and Owen Rambow

15:00–15:30 *An Open-Source Finite State Morphological Transducer for Modern Standard Arabic*
Mohammed Attia, Pavel Pecina, Antonio Toral, Lamia Tounsi and Josef van Genabith

15:30–16:00 *Recognition and Translation of Arabic Named Entities with NooJ Using a New Representation Model*
Héla Fehri, Kais Haddar and Abdelmajid Ben Hamadou

16:00–16:30 Closing

16:30–18:00 SIGFSM business meeting

Intersection for weighted formalisms

Mark-Jan Nederhof
School of Computer Science
University of St Andrews
North Haugh, St Andrews
Fife, KY16 9SX
United Kingdom

Abstract

The paradigm of parsing as intersection has been used throughout the literature to obtain elegant and general solutions to numerous problems involving grammars and automata. The paradigm has its origins in (Bar-Hillel et al., 1964), where a general construction was used to prove closure of context-free languages under intersection with regular languages. It was pointed out by (Lang, 1994) that such a construction isolates the parsing problem from the recognition problem. The latter can be solved by a reduction of the outcome of intersection.

The paradigm has been extended in various ways, by considering more powerful formalisms, such as tree adjoining grammars (Vijay-Shanker and Weir, 1993), simple RCGs (Bertsch and Nederhof, 2001), tree grammars (Nederhof, 2009), and probabilistic extensions of grammatical formalisms (Nederhof and Satta, 2003). Different applications have been identified, such as computation of distances between languages (Nederhof and Satta, 2008), and parameter estimation of probabilistic models (Nederhof, 2005).

The lecture will focus on another application, namely the computation of prefix probabilities (Nederhof and Satta, 2011c) and infix probabilities (Nederhof and Satta, 2011a) and will address novel generalisations to linear context-free rewriting systems (Nederhof and Satta, 2011b).

References

Y. Bar-Hillel, M. Perles, and E. Shamir. 1964. On formal properties of simple phrase structure grammars. In Y. Bar-Hillel, editor, *Language and Information: Selected Essays on their Theory and Application*, chapter 9, pages 116–150. Addison-Wesley, Reading, Massachusetts.

E. Bertsch and M.-J. Nederhof. 2001. On the complexity of some extensions of RCG parsing. In *Proceedings of the Seventh International Workshop on Parsing Technologies*, pages 66–77, Beijing, China, October.

B. Lang. 1994. Recognition can be harder than parsing. *Computational Intelligence*, 10(4):486–494.

M.-J. Nederhof and G. Satta. 2003. Probabilistic parsing as intersection. In *8th International Workshop on Parsing Technologies*, pages 137–148, LORIA, Nancy, France, April.

M.-J. Nederhof and G. Satta. 2008. Computation of distances for regular and context-free probabilistic languages. *Theoretical Computer Science*, 395:235–254.

M.-J. Nederhof and G. Satta. 2011a. Computation of infix probabilities for probabilistic context-free grammars. In *Conference on Empirical Methods in Natural Language Processing, Proceedings of the Conference*, pages 1213–1221, Edinburgh, Scotland, July.

M.-J. Nederhof and G. Satta. 2011b. Prefix probabilities for linear context-free rewriting systems. In *Proceedings of the 12th International Conference on Parsing Technologies*, Dublin, Ireland, October.

M.-J. Nederhof and G. Satta. 2011c. Prefix probability for probabilistic synchronous context-free grammars. In *49th Annual Meeting of the Association for Computational Linguistics, Proceedings of the Conference*, pages 460–469, Portland, Oregon, June.

M.-J. Nederhof. 2005. A general technique to train language models on language models. *Computational Linguistics*, 31(2):173–185.

M.-J. Nederhof. 2009. Weighted parsing of trees. In *Proceedings of the 11th International Conference on Parsing Technologies*, pages 13–24, Paris, France, October.

K. Vijay-Shanker and D.J. Weir. 1993. The use of shared forests in tree adjoining grammar parsing. In *Sixth*

Proceedings of the 9th International Workshop on Finite State Methods and Natural Language Processing, pages 1–2,
Blois (France), July 12-15, 2011.

Conference of the European Chapter of the Association for Computational Linguistics, Proceedings of the Conference, pages 384–393, Utrecht, The Netherlands, April.

Modularization of Regular Growth Automata

Christian Wurm
Fakultät für Linguistik und Literaturwissenschaften, Universität Bielefeld
CITEC Bielefeld
cwurm@uni-bielefeld.de

Abstract

Regular growth automata form a class of infinite machines, in which all local computations are performed by finite state automata. We present some results which are relevant to application in practice; apart from runtime, the most important one is *modularization*, that is, abstraction over subroutines. We use the new techniques to prove some results on substitution.

1 Introduction

We recently introduced the concept of **regular growth automata** (RGA, we refer the reader to (2) for background, examples and discussion of related work; for some related work see (2),(2)). Whereas previously we focused on mathematical results and provided some formal examples, we will here focus on adapting the concept to make it useful for linguistic application. This will be accomplished via *modularization* of automata; we study how large automata can be reasonably split up into smaller and simpler ones.

Organization is as follows: in the next section, we present definitions and give an overview of the most important formal features of regular growth automata. The third section is about treating regular growth automata in a modular fashion, while preserving determinism, which is a very favorable property of RGA. In our view, this is the key to making the concept applicable on a broader scale. As we argue in the last section, this might also provide new insights in linguistic theory, as it gives us a new perspective on syntactic structures.

2 Formal Concepts

2.1 Definitions

In a sense, regular growth automata are infinite extensions of finite state automata. In FSA, states are atomic symbols like letters;[1] in regular growth automata, the state set $Q \subseteq \Omega^*$ is a *stringset* formed out of a finite alphabet. The most important property of infinite state machines in general is the computability of state transitions. We will require that transition relations on Q be *regular*.[2] The subsequent definitions follow (2).[3]

Definition 1 *Put* $\Sigma_\perp := \Sigma \cup \{\perp\}$, *for* $\perp \notin \Sigma$. *The* ***convolution*** *of a tuple of strings* $\langle \vec{x}_1, \vec{x}_2 \rangle \in (\Sigma^*)^2$, *written as* $\otimes\langle \vec{x}_1, \vec{x}_2 \rangle$ *of length* $max(\{|\vec{x}_i| : i \in \{1,2\}\})$ *is defined as follows: the* k*th component of* $\otimes\langle \vec{x}_1, \vec{x}_2 \rangle$ *is* $\langle \sigma_1, \sigma_2 \rangle$, *where* σ_i *is the* k*-th letter of* $\vec{x}_i$ *provided that* $k \leq |\vec{x}_i|$, *and* $\perp$ *otherwise.*
The ***convolution of a relation*** $R \subseteq (\Sigma^*)^2$, *written* $\otimes R$, *is the the set* $\{\otimes\langle \vec{x}_1, \vec{x}_2 \rangle : \langle \vec{x}_1, \vec{x}_2 \rangle \in R\}$.

Definition 2 *A relation* $R \in (\Sigma^*)^2$ *is called (synchronous)*[4] ***regular****, if there is a finite state automaton over* $(\Sigma_\perp)^2$ *recognizing* $\otimes R$.

[1] For this reason, they have also been called the *internal alphabet* in early work on the topic.

[2] For mathematical background see (2).

[3] We confine ourselves to binary relations, but the concept generalizes without complication.

[4] There is some confusing usage, as some authors use

Proceedings of the 9th International Workshop on Finite State Methods and Natural Language Processing, pages 3–11,
Blois (France), July 12-15, 2011. ©2011 Association for Computational Linguistics

Regular relations as defined here form a proper subset of the relations defined by finite state transducers in general. We use them for three reasons: firstly, they are closed under Boolean operations (contrary to transducer defined relations), secondly, they allow at most a constant growth of strings, a property whose importance will become clear later on, and thirdly, we have not met any case where the additional power provided by transducer relations would have been of any use. We call the class of transducers which computes regular relations **synchronous transducers**. In the sequel we will restrict ourselves to this subclass, so we will omit the adjective, when there is no danger of confusion.

Definition 3 *We define a* ***regular growth automaton*** *(RGA) as a tuple* $\langle \epsilon, Q, F, \delta, \Sigma, Op_\Sigma, \Omega \rangle$, *where* Ω *is a finite set of symbols, the state alphabet,* $Q \subseteq \Omega^*$ *is the state set,* $\epsilon \in Q$ *is the initial state,* $F \subseteq \Omega^*$ *is the set of accepting states,* $\delta \subseteq Q \times \Sigma \times Q$ *the transition relation,* Σ *a finite input alphabet;* Op_Σ *is a set of synchronous transducers, with one* op_x *for each* $x \in \Sigma$, *where* Ω *is the input and output alphabet for all* $op_x \in Op_\Sigma$. *In the sequel, we identify the* $op_x \in Op_\Sigma$ *with the relations they induce on* Ω^*. *In addition, the following hold:*

1. F *is a regular set;*
2. *for every transducer* op_σ, $((q_i, \sigma), q_j) \in \delta$ *exactly if* $q_j \in op_\sigma(q_i)$;
3. Q *is recursively defined as the smallest set such that (i)* ϵ *is in* Q, *(ii) if* α *is in* Q, *then for all* $\sigma \in \Sigma$, $op_\sigma(\alpha)$ *is also in* Q.

We call the transducers in Op_Σ ***letter operators***.

A regular growth automaton is deterministic exactly if the letter operators represent (partial) functions on Ω^*, the RGA is total exactly if the letter operators represent total functions/relations. We can easily totalize RGAs by totalizing the letter operators, sending all previously undefined inputs to a new absorbing state.[5] We strongly conjecture that deterministic and non-deterministic automata are non-equivalent, but still lack a conclusive proof (we will see some evidence later on).[6] We will write *RGA* or regular growth automaton if we make statements valid for both cases; we will write *DGA* for deterministic, *NGA* for non-deterministic automata. We will focus on the deterministic case, which has many favourable properties, as we will see.

Note that there is some redundancy in our presentation, for the letter operators serve to specify the transition function and state set. We keep this redundancy for ease of presentation: if we fix the letter operators, Q and δ are fixed, as well as Σ and Ω. The only additional information we need is the set of accepting states F. When we construct automata, we will thus construct letter operators and an accepting state set, nothing more. We write $\hat{\delta}$ for the transition function generalized from letters to string in the obvious fashion. In case we are handling with several automata, we mark automata and their components with a subscript as in δ_{RGA} to ensure unique reference. Then we have the following:

Definition 4 *A regular growth automaton* RGA *recognizes a language* L, *if* $L = \{\vec{x} : \hat{\delta}_{RGA}(\epsilon, \vec{x}) \in F_{RGA}\}$.

We write $L(RA)$ for the language a given automaton recognizes. There are two ways to conceive of a regular growth automaton: the first one is to think of it as an automaton with an infinite state set which is already specified; alternatively we can think of it as a machine which constructs its own state set only when given an input.

Definition 5 *Two strings* $\vec{x}, \vec{y}$ *are* ***Nerode equivalent*** *in a language* L, *in symbols* $\vec{x} \sim_L \vec{y}$, *if for all* $\vec{z}$, $\vec{x}\vec{z} \in L$ *iff* $\vec{y}\vec{z} \in L$.

---

the term regular for "finite state computable", while others use the term in our sense. We will usually simply say regular, and mean it in the sense defined here.

[5] We call an absorbing a state which is not accepting and from which all transitions point at the state itself.

[6] The classical determinization algorithm via powerset construction does *not* preserve the regularity of the automaton.

From a language theoretic perspective note that, as an ordinary finite state machine, it computes Nerode-equivalences. From a practical perspective, the most remarkable property is that the automaton constructs its state set in runtime; assuming that its input has some upper bound, it will be nothing but a finite state machine. But it is a finite state machine which is constructed *on the fly*, that is, given an input, the necessary states and *only* the necessary states are generated.

In this paper, we will add another property to the one of being dynamic (in the above sense), namely the one of being *modular*: we will show that in regular growth automata, we can *abstract* over certain subsystems of language, factorizing them into modules. This remedies a notorious weakness of classical finite state approaches: the lack of abstraction ((2)).

2.2 Recognizing Power

We call the class of languages recognized by some DGA (NGA) $\mathfrak{L}_{DGA}$ ($\mathfrak{L}_{NGA}$). As we have shown previously, $\mathfrak{L}_{DGA}$ forms a Boolean Algebra. It contains languages which are not context-free, not mildly context sensitive and not semilinear, however there is strong evidence that it does not contain all context-free languages (see below, and contrary to $\mathfrak{L}_{NGA}$, for there is an algorithm which converts any CFG into a NGA). $\mathfrak{L}_{DGA}$ gives thus a true cut across the Chomsky hierarchy, which we judge to be possibly relevant for formal linguistics.

2.3 Runtime

Definition 6 *A finite state transducer T is* ***functional****, if for any given input T computes at most one output. It is* ***deterministic****, if $\delta_T(Q \times \Omega)$ is a (partial) function.*

As is well-known, the latter implies the former, but the former does not imply the latter; for *DGA*, we do require our transducers to be functional, but not to be deterministic.

Lemma 7 *A synchronous functional transducer T computes the output for a given input of length n in $O(n)$ steps.*

Proof. This is obvious, if the transducer is deterministic.[7] If a synchronous transducer is non-deterministic, then there is a constant upper bound to non-determinism: the states $q_i \in \hat{\delta}(q_0, \vec{w}, \vec{v})$ are less than k for all $\vec{w}, \vec{v} \in \Sigma^*$, that is, $|\hat{\delta}(q_0, \vec{w}, \vec{v})| \leq k$. This is obviously due to the fact that T has finitely many states. We show that also the set of *pairs* of states and output strings $\langle \vec{v}, q_i \rangle \in \hat{\delta}(q_0, \vec{w})$ is constantly bounded for any $\vec{w}$, that is, for all $\vec{w}$, $|\hat{\delta}(q_0, \vec{w})| \leq k$. This is because the set of states we can go to is bounded, and for a given input, if we go into one state, we need to write at most one output. For if we have two output words for a prefix by going to a single state, then we can discard both: if it were possible to reach an accepting state from the current one, then the transducer would no longer be functional, contrary to our assumptions. Therefore, for each letter we read, we have to compute at most k transitions and write an output on at most k possible output words. The output word for an input of length n is thus computed in $\leq kn + l$ steps (l is the length of the constantly bounded suffix we might add). ⊣

Theorem 8 *For any string $\vec{w}$, $|\vec{w}| = n$, a given DGA accepts or rejects $\vec{x}$ in $O(n^2)$ steps.*

Proof. As our transducers are synchronous and functional, the length of the states[8] grows (at most) proportionally to the size of the input string. Put $l := max(\{n : n = |op_\sigma(\vec{x})| - |\vec{x}| : \sigma \in \Sigma\})$. For lemma 7, the transducers compute the transitions for states of length m in $\leq km$ steps; as the DGA is deterministic, the letter operators are functional. To calculate the state $\vec{x}$, for $\vec{x} = \hat{\delta}_{DGA}(\epsilon, \vec{w})$ and $|\vec{w}| = n$, we thus have to perform at most $k \times l + k \times 2l + ... + k \times nl = \sum_{i=1}^{n} k(i \times l)$ steps. Checking whether the state is accepting takes at most $l \times n$ steps; so accepting or rejecting takes $O(\sum_{i=1}^{n} kil + ln)$ steps. This is proportional to n^2. ⊣

Note that this is strong evidence for the conjecture that $\mathfrak{L}_{DGA}$ does not contain the context free languages, for it is widely believed that the lowest possible bound for parsing CFLs is higher

[7] A proof of this can be found in (2).

[8] Recall that RGA-states are strings!

than quadratic (see (2)).

For non-deterministic automata, things are much worse: we have to assume that in the worst case runtime is *exponential* in terms of input strings: for in general, a word of length n might lead us to k^n different states, and so we might have to perform exponentially many computations. This is a very good reason to take care that a *DGA* remains deterministic under various transformations.

3 Automaton Construction and Regular Growth Subroutines

3.1 Automaton Construction

For application, the most urgent question is how to construct a regular growth automaton given a language. We have no way of defining directly the state set: we can only define it indirectly via the letter operators, and so we have to be aware of the consequences in the infinite of the interaction of our finite state transducers. Constructing a large set of transducers which interact in the desired way can be a tremendous task.

In this section, we propose a procedure to facilitate the construction of regular growth automata: we will factorize languages into certain *sublanguages*, and adress these by interacting *subroutines*. For example, in natural language, this means that for a given category, say, a NP*[nom]*, we construct a subroutine, which covers all its possible contents regardless of the contexts in which it occurs; and we construct a *matrix automaton* in which it is embedded and which provides its possible contexts, as main clause, complement clause etc. This is not a trivial task, given that we do *not* have an a priori notion of constituency in our approach! We thus have two problems: care for the distribution of an NP*[nom]*, and care for its internal structure. However, each of these seem to be much more feasible problems than both at once.

We will show how to construct transducers out of subroutines, such that the letter operators compute the union of all subroutines they occur in, but where it depends on the context (i.e., the current state) which subroutine is called. We will do this first for simple and then for recursive substitution. If we want to preserve determinism when merging subroutines in the general case, there is however an important condition: there must not be a locally unbounded ambiguity on which subroutine is called at a certain point.

3.2 Regular Growth Subroutines: Equivalence

Definition 9 *A (deterministic)* ***regular growth subroutine*** *is a (D)GA,*

1. *with a regular set of initial states $I \subseteq \Omega^*$ instead of ϵ, and*

2. *for all $op_\sigma \in Op_\Sigma$, all $q_i \in I$ and $\vec{w} \in \Omega^*$, $op_\sigma(q_i\vec{w}) = q_i\vec{v}$ for some $\vec{v} \in \Omega^*$; that is, operators only write and change suffixes to initial states.*

A (deterministic) regular growth subroutine (RGS/DGS) is thus a generalization of a DGA; a DGA is a DGS with the empty string as initial state. A note on the second condition: if subroutines only write suffixes to their initial states, this facilitates their global interaction when we embed them into larger automata. We use prefixes in I to encode global states, and the suffix to encode the state of the subroutine. Importantly, we do not add any additional recognizing power to our automata by generalizing them to subroutines in the above way:

Theorem 10 *For any language L, $L = L(DGS)$ for some DGS exactly if there is a DGA such that $L = L(DGA)$.*

Note that for the nondeterministic case, this result would be trivial, but it is not for the deterministic one. The idea of the proof is quite simple: we use a partition of I to simulate it on a finite tuple. As the proof itself is quite lengthy, we present it in the appendix. The concept of subroutines is very useful from the following perspective: if we merge several DGA into into a single automaton, the resulting automaton will recognize simply the union of their languages. If we merge several DGS with a DGA, this will not be necessarily the case: the initial state sets provide us with a tool to control when a DGS is *called*. We can thus convert DGA into DGS, to be able to merge them in a *controlled* fashion; the equivalence is important for it means we can conceive and check DGA and DGS independently and equivalently. Recall the the definition of $\sim_L$, the Nerode-equivalence in L:

Definition 11 *We say a subroutine S is* ***embedded*** *within a RGA, if*

1. $I_S \cap Q_{RGA} \neq \emptyset$ *and*
2. $F_S \cap Q_{RGA} \neq \emptyset$
3. *if* $\hat{\delta}_{RGA}(q_0, \vec{u}) \in I_S$, *then for all* $\vec{v}$, $\vec{w} \in L(S)$, $\vec{u}\vec{v} \sim_{L(RGA)} \vec{u}\vec{w}$,

that is, S must be reachable, it must lead back into the main automaton, and for all prefixes which call the subroutine, the stringset the subroutine computes forms an equivalence class with respect to the language of the matrix machine.

Note that with this definition, we do not say anything on the internal structure of the automata or the operators, nor of the independent existence of a subroutine in the above sense. Embedded subroutines can be *implicit*, that is, they are computed, but at no point written out as such.

Definition 12 *For a subroutine S embedded within an RGA, if $q \in I_S$, we say that q* ***calls*** *S. If there is a $q \in Q$ such that $op_a(q) \subseteq I_S$, we say that a* ***calls*** *S. A* ***characteristic prefix*** *$\vec{a}$ of a subroutine S, written as $\vec{a} \in cp(S)$, is a word for which holds: for all $q \in Q$, if $\hat{\delta}(q, \vec{a})$ is defined,*[9] *then $\hat{\delta}(q, \vec{a})$ calls S.*

A subroutine S is called ***characteristic*** *if for all $q \in I$, we have $q = \hat{\delta}(q_j, \vec{a})$ for some $\vec{a} \in cp(S)$, where there is a constant k such that for all $\vec{a} \in cp(S)$, $|\vec{a}| \leq k$. A (sub)****language*** *L is characteristic if $L = \{\vec{x}\vec{y} : \vec{x} \in cp(S)$ and $\vec{y} \in L(S)\}$; S (and L) is* ***strictly*** *characteristic if in addition a word in $L(S)$ is not the prefix of another word in $L(S)$.*

[9] And not an absorbing state, we should add, but we leave the issue of total versus partial automata aside; it does not pose any serious problems.

An embedded subroutine is thus characteristic if we always know from a prefix when it is called; it is strictly characteristic if in addition we know when it ends.

Definition 13 *Two subroutines S_1 and S_2 (two languages L_1 and L_2) are called* ***distinct***, *if they are characteristic and have disjoint sets of characteristic prefixes; they are* ***strictly distinct***, *if in addition they are strictly characteristic.*

It is crucial to see that the distinction of subroutines is orthogonal to the distinction between letter operators: if subroutines embedded in a *DGA* share an alphabet, we have different subroutines within *one* letter operator. We write $op_\sigma^{S_i}$ for the function of a subroutine S_i computed by *one* operator. $op_\sigma^{S_i}(\vec{x})$ thus means that op_σ computes its function in S_i on a substring $\vec{x}$.

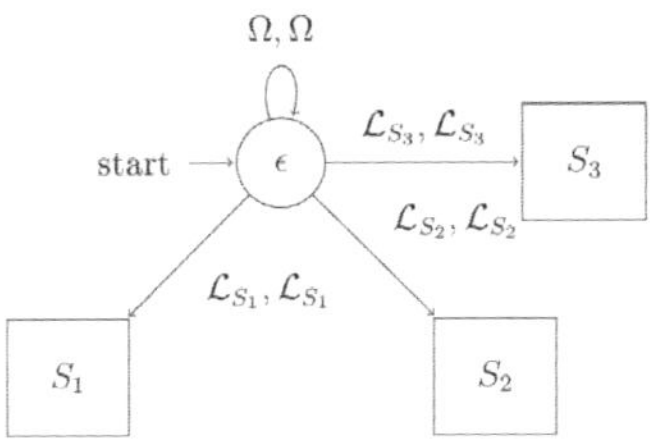

Fig.1: Blueprint of a letter operator computing three subroutines; it computes the identity, until some marker in the input activates a subroutine. Note that these markers are *not* characteristic prefixes; rather, the characteristic prefixes put the marker into the state-string.

3.3 Example I: Simple Substitution

As an example of how to model constituent-like dependencies, we show how to use subroutines for simple letter substitution. Note that inserting subroutines is quite trivial; the problem is to use subroutines *and* preserve determinism of the automaton. The treatment will not be very detailed; in particular, we will not look "inside" the transducers and spell out the operations. This is due to the fact that firstly, we do not really *need* to - which is one of the greatest merits of our approach; and secondly, because transducers quickly result to be large and hard to read. We encourage the skeptical reader to check that all conditions we state below can indeed be checked by synchronous finite state transducers. In the sequel, we will make an abuse of ontology for the sake of readibility and construct regular expressions over languages. Recall that distinct languages have decompositions into a set of bounded prefixes, which call a unique subroutine, and the language of the subroutine itself.

Proposition 14 *Let Σ be an alphabet, and let $\{L_\sigma : \sigma \in \Sigma\}$ be a set of pairwise distinct languages, such that $L_\sigma = cp(DGS_\sigma) \cdot L(DGS_\sigma)$ for all $\sigma \in \Sigma$. Now let $i : \Sigma \to \{L_\sigma : \sigma \in \Sigma\}$ be a one-to-one mapping, where $i(\sigma) = L_\sigma$. For every $L_M \subseteq \Sigma^*$, if there is a DGA_M such that $L(DGA_M) = L_M$, then there is a $DGA_{i(M)}$ such that $L(DGA_{i(M)}) = i[L_M]$.*

Proof. First we change the state alphabet Ω_M of DGA_M to make it disjoint from all other Ω_x, $x \neq M$. The new operators in $Op_\Sigma^{DGA_{i(M)}}$ are constructed as follows: first we take care of the characteristic prefixes; for simplicity we assume they are single letters. If they are not, they are constantly bounded, and so we have some finite amount of non-determinism; this can always be determinized with a tuple construction.[10] To make the treatment more compact, we leave this construction to the reader.

The characteristic prefixes are the letters which compute the interaction of the routines; we add a letter $\mathcal{S}_\sigma$ to $\Omega_{i(M)}$ for each $\sigma \in \Sigma$, where for all $\alpha \neq i(M)$, $\mathcal{S}_\sigma \notin \Omega_\alpha$, and define the operators as follows:

1. For all $a \in cp(S_\sigma) : \sigma \in \Sigma$, $op_a^{i(M)}$ is defined on all and only on states in $(\epsilon|(\Omega_M^*((F_\sigma) : \sigma \in \Sigma)^* \mathcal{S}_x((F_\sigma) : \sigma \in \Sigma))$,
2. If $a \in cp(S_\sigma)$, then $op_a^{i(M)}(\epsilon) = (op_\sigma^M(\epsilon))\mathcal{S}_\sigma(op_a^{S_\sigma}(\epsilon))$,
3. If $a \in cp(S_\sigma)$, then $op_a^{i(M)}(\vec{c}\vec{x}\mathcal{S}_\tau\vec{z}) = op_\sigma^M(\vec{c})\vec{x}\vec{z}\mathcal{S}_\sigma op_a^{S_\sigma}(\epsilon)$, provided it is defined, and where $\vec{c}$ is the longest prefix of the state in Ω_M.

That is, operators for characteristic prefixes (i) only operate on states which consist of a prefix $p_M \in \Omega_M^*$, followed by a (possibly empty) sequence of accepting states F_σ of the subroutines. (ii) They operate on p_M as the letters to for which they are substituted, (iii) they put or change and postpone a distinguished marker $\mathcal{S}_\sigma$ at the end of the string, which marks the beginning of the operating scope of a substitution language, and (iv) then start computing the subroutine.

All other letter operators simply compute their previous function as subroutines, where each subroutine S_σ computes L_σ, and where the initial state set for S_σ is $\Omega^*\mathcal{S}_\sigma$. Before they read the marker, they simply compute the identity, so:

$$(1) \qquad op_a^{i(M)}(\vec{x}\mathcal{S}_\sigma\vec{y}) = \vec{x}\mathcal{S}_\sigma op_a^{S_\sigma}(\vec{y}),$$

Note that our characteristic prefixes make sure there is only one marker $\mathcal{S}_\sigma$ in any state-string. The set of final states $F_{i(L)}$ is now simply the set of all sequences of only accepting states for all languages/subroutines, with possibly a marker $\mathcal{S}_\tau$:

$$(2) \qquad F_{i(L)} := F_M \cdot ((F_\tau) : \tau \in T)^* \mathcal{S}_x((F_\tau) : \tau \in T). \qquad \dashv$$

Note that in this case, we need the condition of distinctness of sublanguages, to make sure we know when to call a subroutine. When we treat recursive substitution, we will see that we need strict distinctness, to also know when we can stop a subroutine.

3.4 Example II: Recursive Substitution

We are surely not only interested in simple substitution, but also *recursive* substitution, that is, we want to be able to call new subroutines during the execution of subroutines. As an example, we will prove the following:

Proposition 15 *Let $P \subseteq \Sigma$; let $(L_\rho) : \rho \in P$ be a set of strictly distinct languages, such that $L_\rho = cp(DGS_\rho) \cdot L(DGS_\rho)$ and $L_\rho \subseteq \Sigma^*$ for all $\rho \in P$. Define $i : P \to (L_\rho) : \rho \in P$ as a one-to-one mapping, where $i(\rho) = L_\rho$. Let $L_M \subseteq \Sigma^*$ be a language such that $L_M = L(DGA_M)$. Then there is a DGA_P which recognizes L_P, which is defined as follows:*

1. *If $\vec{x} \in L_M$, then $\vec{x} \in L_P$.*
2. *If $\vec{x}\rho\vec{y} \in L_P$, then $\vec{x}i(\rho)\vec{y} \in L_P$.*

[10] Alternatively, we can conceive of characteristic prefix strings as *chunks*: as regular relations are closed under composition, we can only let the composition compute the desired function; technically, this amounts to the same, namely a tuple construction.

Proof. We construct DGA_P. First we change the state alphabet Ω_M such that is disjunct from all other Ω_x, $x \neq M$. The new operators $Op_\Sigma^{DGA_P}$ are constructed as follows: first we take care of the characteristic prefixes; for simplicity we assume again they are single letters, and use letters $\mathcal{S}_\rho$ as before.[11]

1. If $a \in cp(S_\rho)$, then $op_a^P(\vec{x}) = op_\rho^M(\vec{x})\mathcal{S}_\rho op_a^{S_\rho}(\epsilon)$, if $\vec{x} \in \Omega_M^*$.

2. If $a \in cp(S_\rho)$, then $op_a^P(\vec{x}\mathcal{S}_\sigma\vec{y}\vec{z}) = \vec{x}\mathcal{S}_\sigma(op_\rho^{S_\sigma}(\vec{y}))\vec{z}\mathcal{S}_\rho(op_a^{S_\rho}(\epsilon))$, where $\vec{z} \in (\epsilon|(S_\rho : \rho \in P)\Omega_P^*)$, and $\vec{y}$ is the *rightmost* substring matching this conditions which does not contain any symbol $\mathcal{S}_\rho$ and is *not* in any $F_{\rho'}$.

Though notation becomes a bit opaque at this point, the concept is quite simple: we simply make sure that in our DGA_P states every subroutine has a clearly distinguished operating scope, where the most deeply embedded subroutine is written as the rightmost one in the state string. We thus translate a structure of the form $[_1[_2[_3]]]$ into a form $[_1][_2][_3]$. This is works because sublanguages are strictly distinct, so we know exactly when a subroutine is completed, and we can ignore all substrings in some F_ρ. The other letters operate as follows:

1. $op_\tau^P(\vec{x}\mathcal{S}_\sigma\vec{y}\vec{z}) = \vec{x}\mathcal{S}_\sigma(op_\tau^{S_\sigma}(\vec{y}))\vec{z}$, where $\vec{z} \in (\epsilon|(S_\rho : \rho \in P)\Omega_P^*)$, and $\vec{y}$ is the rightmost substring which satisfies this conditions which does not contain a $\mathcal{S}_\rho$ and is not in $F_{\rho'}$;

2. $op_\tau^P(\vec{x}\vec{y}) = (op_\tau^M(\vec{x}))\vec{y}$, where $\vec{x} \in \Omega_M^*$ and $\vec{y} \in ((\mathcal{S}_\rho F_\rho) : \rho \in P)^*$

The set of accepting states is

$$F_P := F_M \cdot ((\mathcal{S}_\rho F_\rho) : \rho \in P)^*. \qquad (3)$$

⊣

Note that, while we do not require that any of the languages involved be context-free, this substitution *is* in a precise sense "context-free",[12] as the distribution of the substituted language equals the distribution of a single letter. However, this is of course only one particular case of substitution; recall that the sets of initial states and final states of a subroutine are regular sets; so we can take any substitution point which can be defined by a regular set of states. We see that we can *decouple* the complexity of the substitution/upcalling of subroutines from the complexity of the routines itself. We thus can reasonably encode a difference between local complexity (in the sense of subroutine) and a global complexity (in the sense of substitution conditions), and we can restrict them independently.

4 Outlook: Regular Growth Automata and Linguistic Theory

In the last section we saw how the factorization was useful to find a (quite) simple solution to complex problems of substitution. The main goal was to show that factorization of automata into subautomata makes them easier to handle in application. We want to underline that the reason we think modular treatment is much easier for linguistic application is not only the structure of regular growth automata, but in particular the structure of natural languages. This is partly due to the fact that we often[13] find some kind of constituent structure in natural languages; but there is more to that: we often find very complex local structures, whose scope however is often quite limited. If we look for example at systems of clitic pronouns, we find a very unpredictable behaviour, and a large number of complex rules which possibly even have to take into account segmental and suprasegmental phonology. If we look at constituents which have a (possibly) very complex internal structure, as clausal complements, we find that their distribution is highly regular and follows very simple rules.[14]

This observation is by no means new: for example, the well-known work of John Hawkins is mostly concerned with these and similar ob-

[11]There is a $\mathcal{S}_\rho$ for each $\rho \in P$ and $\mathcal{S}_\rho \notin \Omega_\alpha$, for all $\alpha \neq P$.

[12]More p precisely: deterministic context-free.

[13]Some people say: always.

[14]This asymmetry gets even more striking if we also consider morphology as a part of syntactic structure.

servations. We will not go into detail here, but we think that principles as *early immediate constituents*, *minimize domains* etc. (see (2),(2)) can be roughly restated, with a slightly shifted perspective, in the following way:

(4) The more complex a constituent is, the more regular[15] is its distribution.

We think that this important observation has had unduly little impact on linguistic theory proper. The main reason for this seems to us that usually we posit fully specified constituent structures (of some kind or other) for all utterances: and once we make this step, we are unable to partially redeem it. One could see it as a disadvantage to regular growth automata that they cannot be mapped onto such a constituent structure, contrary to, for example, pushdown automata. However, in this context there is an equal advantage: for a pushdown automaton, the notion of a subroutine does not make much sense, for all configurations are equally well-suited and, in fact, can be easily treated as subroutines. For our automata this is not the case: *because* the notion of a constituent is so problematic, the notion of an embedded subroutine is *truly meaningful*. It allows to capture the asymmetry of local and global structure. This is the reason we think our approach is well suited for natural language descriptions not only from a practical, but also a theoretical point of view: though we give up the notion of a fully specified constituent structure, we can much more easily treat the rich local structure of natural languages with compact local subroutines, and its much more austere global structure by means of very simple interactions of routines. This in turn might facilitate a more realistic view on the organization of linguistic knowledge.

Acknowledgements

The author wants to thank Marcus Kracht and Jens Michaelis for their support, and three anonymous reviewers for their helpful comments.

[15]Here we can read *regular* both in its colloquial and in its technical meaning.

5 Appendix: Proof of Theorem 10

Proof. One direction is immediate. To see the if-direction, we show how to convert a DGS into a DGA. By definition, for the prefixes of states which are in I, the output equals the input, and as we have one output and the transducer is functional, there is a single state we go to (this is the inverse reasoning from lemma 7).[16] Assume without loss of generality that our letter operators are total. We write

(5) $\vec{x} \sim_{op_\sigma} \vec{y}$ if $\hat{\delta}_{op_\sigma}(q_0, \vec{x}) = (\vec{x}', q_i)$ and $\hat{\delta}_{op_\sigma}(q_0, \vec{y}) = (\vec{y}', q_i)$ for some $\vec{x}', \vec{y}'$.

For the above reasons, $\sim_{op_\sigma}$ is an equivalence relation. We form partitions I with the equivalence classes induced by $\sim_{op_\sigma}$, for each $op_\sigma \in Op_\Sigma$: put $P_{op_\sigma} := I/\sim_{op_\sigma}$. As our operators are finite, $|I/\sim_{op_\sigma}| \leq k$ for each $\sigma \in \Sigma$. Next, by intersecting the elements across the different partitions, we construct a more fine-grained partition, which forms a partition (though not maximal) with respect to every $\sim_{op_\sigma}: op_\sigma \in Op_\Sigma$:

(6) $\mathcal{J} := \bigcap_{op_\sigma \in Op_\Sigma} P_{op_\sigma}$.[17]

$\mathcal{J}$ is a partition of I, and for each $J \in \mathcal{J}$ and for each $op_\sigma \in Op_\Sigma$ there is a unique state q such that $\hat{\delta}_{op_\sigma}(q_0, \vec{j}) = (\vec{j}', q)$ for some $\vec{j}'$, and all $\vec{j} \in J$. Crucially, while its elements might be of infinite cardinalitiy, $\mathcal{J}$ itself is of finite cardinality. Put $l = |\mathcal{J}|$. The initial state of our DGA is an l-tupel, where each $\pi_i : i \leq l$ is assigned a $J \in \mathcal{J}$ via a bijection $\phi(\mathcal{J}) \to M$,where $M \subset \mathbb{N}$ and for all $m \in M$, $m \leq l$. We construct the new letter operators op_σ^{DGA}, which operate on $(\Omega^k)^*$, as follows:

(7) $op_\sigma^{DGA}(\langle \vec{x}_1, \vec{x}_2, ..., \vec{x}_l \rangle = \langle op_\sigma^{q_i}(\vec{x}_1), op_\sigma^{q_j}(\vec{x}_2), ..., op_\sigma^{q_m}(\vec{x}_k) \rangle$,

where $op_\sigma^{q_x}$ is op_σ with its initial state changed to q_x; and for every $\pi_i : i \leq l$, we make sure that if $\phi^{-1}(i) = J$, then for all $\vec{j} \in J$, $\hat{\delta}_{op_\sigma}(q_0, \vec{i}) = \langle \vec{w}, q_x \rangle$ for some $\vec{w}$.

We thus simulate the possibly infinite set I with a finite set of tuples, where each projection represents a set of strings for which all op_σ go into a unique state. The operations on projections are still synchronous regular, and as the DGS was deterministic, the tuple size of the DGA remains constant.

[16]Provided the transducer is not redundant; if it is, then the states can be merged.

[17]Note that this is a somewhat sloppy notation, as we do not intersect the partitions, but their elements.

Now to F_{DGA}. Regular languages are closed under projection and cylindrification; so we take as accepting states the set of all l-cylindrifications of F_{DGS}, that is, the set of all l-tuples of which one projection is in F_{DGS}. Call this set $F_{DGS'}$. Finally, we need to take care of the case where a prefix in I has some influence on membership in F. Here we use the fact that regular languages are closed under prefixation: for two languages, L_1, L_2, we put $L_1 \backslash L_2 := \{\vec{v} : \exists \vec{w} \in L_1 : \vec{w}\vec{v} \in L_2\}$. It is well-known that if L_1 and L_2 are regular, then so is $L_1 \backslash L_2$, the set of strings which, given a prefix from L_1, result in a word in L_2. We thus have to put $F_{DGA} := I \backslash F_{DGA'}$. The resulting DGA does the job as required. ⊣

References

Didier Caucal. Synchronization of regular automata. In Rastislav Královic and Damian Niwinski, editors, *MFCS*, volume 5734 of *Lecture Notes in Computer Science*, pages 2–23. Springer, 2009.

Christiane Frougny and Jacques Sakarovitch. Synchronized rational relations of finite and infinite words. *Theor. Comput. Sci.*, 108(1):45–82, 1993.

John A. Hawkins. *A Performance Theory of Order and Constituency*. Cambridge Univ. Pr., Cambridge, 1994.

John A. Hawkins. *Efficiency and Complexity in Grammars*. Oxford Univ. Pr., Oxford, 2004.

Lillian Lee. Fast context-free grammar parsing requires fast boolean matrix multiplication. *J. ACM*, 49(1):1–15, 2002.

Mehryar Mohri. Finite-state transducers in language and speech processing. *Computational Linguistics*, 23(2):269–311, 1997.

Sasha Rubin. Automata presenting structures: A survey of the finite string case. *Bulletin of Symbolic Logic*, 14(2):169–209, 2008.

Shuly Wintner. Strengths and weaknesses of finite-state technology: a case study in morphological grammar development. *Natural Language Engineering*, 14(4):457–469, 2008.

Christian Wurm. Regular growth automata: Properties of a class of finitely induced infinite machines. In *Proceedings of the 12th Mathematics of Language, Springer LNCS*, 2011.

Finite-state representations embodying temporal relations

Tim Fernando
Computer Science Department
Trinity College
Dublin 2, Ireland
Tim.Fernandol@tcd.ie

Abstract

Finite-state methods are applied to the Russell-Wiener-Kamp notion of time (based on events) and developed into an account of interval relations and semi-intervals. Strings are formed and collected in regular languages and regular relations that are argued to embody temporal relations in their various underspecified guises. The regular relations include retractions that reduce computations by projecting strings down to an appropriate level of granularity, and notions of partiality within and across such levels.

1 Introduction

It is a truism that to reason about change, some notion of time is useful to impose order on events. Less clear perhaps is whether or not time is shaped completely by the events it relates. An event-based notion of time going back to Russell and Wiener (Kamp and Reyle, 1993; Lück, 2006) is analyzed in the present work using finite-state methods that extend to interval relations, semi-intervals and granularity; e.g. (Allen, 1983; Freksa, 1992; Mani, 2007). Rather than take for granted some absolute (independent) notion of time (such as the real line), the basic approach is to form strings (from events and generalizations of events described below) and collect them in regular languages and regular relations. The claim is that this leads to a more satisfying account of the partiality of temporal information conveyed (for instance) in everyday speech. In particular, there is a sense (to be explained below) in which the strings, languages and relations of the approach embody a wide range of temporal relations that vary in degrees of underspecification. Those degrees depend on the events under consideration: the more events to relate, the finer grained time becomes.

Two temporal relations between events, called overlap $\bigcirc$ and (complete) precedence $\prec$, are employed in the Russell-Wiener-Kamp construction of time from events. To picture these relations between two events e and e', let us form the three "snapshots"

$$\boxed{e}, \ \boxed{e'} \text{ and } \boxed{e, e'}$$

and arrange them much like a cartoon/film strip (with time progressing from left to right) to produce

$\boxed{e}\boxed{e'}$ as a record of e precedes e' (i.e., $e \prec e'$)

$\boxed{e'}\boxed{e}$ as a record of e' precedes e (i.e., $e' \prec e$)

and finally

$\boxed{e, e'}$ as a record of e overlaps e' (i.e., $e \bigcirc e'$) .

Formally, these strips are strings over the alphabet $Pow(\{e, e'\})$ of subsets of $\{e, e'\}$, with the curly braces in $\{e\}$, $\{e'\}$ and $\{e, e'\}$ redrawn as boxes to reinforce the construal of the subsets as snapshots. As explained in section 2 below, the three strings correspond exactly to the three (Russell-Wiener-Kamp) event structures over the events e and e', with a box in each string identifiable as a (Russell-Wiener-Kamp) temporal moment.[1]

[1] Briefly, $\bigcirc$ is just $\prec$-incomparability, and RWK-moments maximal antichains relative to $\prec$ (Lück, 2006). Details below, where we follow Kamp and Reyle (1993) in foregrounding $\bigcirc$.

Proceedings of the 9th International Workshop on Finite State Methods and Natural Language Processing, pages 12–20, Blois (France), July 12-15, 2011. ©2011 Association for Computational Linguistics

RWK	**Allen**	*Pow*$(\{e,e'\})^*$
$e \bigcirc e'$	$e = e'$	$\boxed{e,e'}$
	$e\ \mathtt{s}\ e'$	$\boxed{e,e'}\boxed{e'}$
	$e\ \mathtt{si}\ e'$	$\boxed{e,e'}\boxed{e}$
	$e\ \mathtt{f}\ e'$	$\boxed{e'}\boxed{e,e'}$
	$e\ \mathtt{fi}\ e'$	$\boxed{e}\boxed{e,e'}$
	$e\ \mathtt{d}\ e'$	$\boxed{e'}\boxed{e,e'}\boxed{e'}$
	$e\ \mathtt{di}\ e'$	$\boxed{e}\boxed{e,e'}\boxed{e}$
	$e\ \mathtt{o}\ e'$	$\boxed{e}\boxed{e,e'}\boxed{e'}$
	$e\ \mathtt{oi}\ e'$	$\boxed{e'}\boxed{e,e'}\boxed{e}$
$e \prec e'$	$e\ \mathtt{m}\ e'$	$\boxed{e}\boxed{e'}$
	$e < e'$	$\boxed{e}\boxed{}\boxed{e'}$
$e' \prec e$	$e\ \mathtt{mi}\ e'$	$\boxed{e'}\boxed{e}$
	$e > e'$	$\boxed{e'}\boxed{}\boxed{e}$

Table 1: From Russell-Wiener-Kamp to Allen

But surely there are more relations than precedence $\prec$ and overlap $\bigcirc$ to consider — not to mention strings in *Pow*$(\{e,e'\})^*$ other than $\boxed{e}\boxed{e'}$, $\boxed{e'}\boxed{e}$ and $\boxed{e,e'}$. Inasmuch as event structures describe intervals, it is natural to ask about the thirteen different interval relations in Allen (1983). Evidently, there are nine ways for e and e' to overlap, and two ways (each) for e to precede e' (and e' to precede e). See Table 1, where strings are associated with Allen relations according to certain constructions presented below. Briefly, under these constructions, granularity can be refined by expanding the set of events related by $\prec$ and $\bigcirc$. In particular, it turns out that all thirteen Allen relations between e and e' fall out of the Russell-Wiener-Kamp construction (RWK) applied to an expansion of $\{e,e'\}$ by markers *pre*(e), *post*(e), *pre*(e'), *post*(e'), of the past and future of e and e', respectively. That is, RWK yields the Allen relations provided that, in McTaggart's terminology (McTaggart, 2008), we first enrich the B-series relations $\prec$ and $\bigcirc$ with A-series ingredients for tense. In the case of the Allen relation $e\ \mathtt{s}\ e'$, for instance, we get the string

$$\boxed{pre(e), pre(e')}\boxed{e,e'}\boxed{post(e),e'}\boxed{post(e),post(e')}$$

which a certain string function $\pi_{\{e,e'\}}$ maps to the Table 1 *Pow*$(\{e,e'\})^*$-entry

$$\boxed{e,e'}\boxed{e'}$$

for $e\ \mathtt{s}\ e'$. The rest of the Allen relations can be obtained similarly. The projection $\pi_{\{e,e\}}$ is one in a family of regular relations π_X that (as will be shown below) correspond to RWK under the aforementioned A-series enhancement. The subscript X indexing that family specifies the ingredients from which strings are formed, and (as a consequence) the granularity of temporal relations the strings embody. By varying that index X, we can overcome the limitations in any choice of finitely many events on which to construct event structures (i.e., $\bigcirc$ and $\prec$). What's more, for any set E (finite or infinite), we can represent every event structure over E in the inverse limit of the system of maps π_X, for X ranging over finite subsets of E.

More precisely, we start in section 2 with a careful presentation of event structures, extracting event structures $\mathbb{E}(\mathsf{s})$ from strings $\mathsf{s} \in$ *Pow*$(X)^*$ (over the alphabet of subsets of X) with A-series extensions $\mathsf{s}_\pm$ to capture the Allen relations in $\mathbb{E}(\mathsf{s}_\pm)$. A function on strings, block compression bc, is defined that gives canonical string representations $bc(\mathsf{s})$ of $\mathbb{E}(\mathsf{s}_\pm)$. In section 3, we transform bc into maps π_X, for different finite sets X of events, forming regular languages representing families of finite event structures, which are subsequently generalized and constrained.

Throughout what follows, strings are formed from subsets of some finite set X. An alternative considered in Karttunen (2005) is to flatten these subsets to strings, introducing brackets [and] to enclose temporal propositions understood to hold at the same period so that, for example, the string $\boxed{e,e'}\boxed{e'}$ of length 2 becomes the string [e e'] [e'] of length 7. It is easy to devise a finite-state transducer translating *Pow*$(X)^*$ to $(X \cup \{[,]\})^*$ in this way. A greater challenge is presented by brackets $[_a$ and $]_a$ decorated with granularities a (such as days or months or years) used in the analysis of calendar expressions in Niemi and Koskenniemi (2009). The approach below of structuring the symbols of the alphabet as sets simplifies many of the finite-state constructions of present interest.[2] An important example is *su-*

[2]As shown in section 3 below, the theme in Niemi and

perposition & (Fernando, 2004), a binary operation on strings over the alphabet *Pow*(X) that forms the componentwise union of strings of the same length

$$\alpha_1 \cdots \alpha_n \,\&\, \alpha'_1 \cdots \alpha'_n \overset{\text{def}}{=} (\alpha_1 \cup \alpha'_1) \cdots (\alpha_n \cup \alpha'_n)$$

(for $\alpha_i, \alpha'_i \subseteq X$). To illustrate,

$$\begin{array}{rcl} \fbox{e, e'} &=& \fbox{e} \,\&\, \fbox{e'} \\ \fbox{e}\fbox{e'} &=& \fbox{e}\square \,\&\, \square\fbox{e'} \\ \fbox{e'}\fbox{e} &=& \fbox{e'}\square \,\&\, \square\fbox{e} . \end{array}$$

A natural notion of containment between strings s and s' can be derived from & as follows. We say s *subsumes* s' and write $\mathsf{s} \trianglerighteq \mathsf{s}'$ if the strings have the same length, and the first is no different from its superposition with the second

$$\mathsf{s} \trianglerighteq \mathsf{s}' \overset{\text{def}}{\iff} \mathsf{s} \text{ and } \mathsf{s}' \text{ have the same length, and } \mathsf{s} = \mathsf{s} \,\&\, \mathsf{s}' .$$

That is, $\trianglerighteq$ is componentwise inclusion $\supseteq$ between strings of the same length,

$$\alpha_1 \cdots \alpha_n \trianglerighteq \alpha'_1 \cdots \alpha'_n \iff \alpha_i \supseteq \alpha'_i \text{ for } 1 \leq i \leq n .$$

To compare strings of different lengths, we *unpad*, stripping off initial and final empty boxes $\square$

$$unpad(\mathsf{s}) \overset{\text{def}}{=} \begin{cases} unpad(\mathsf{s}') & \text{if } \mathsf{s} = \square\mathsf{s}' \text{ or else if } \mathsf{s} = \mathsf{s}'\square \\ \mathsf{s} & \text{otherwise} \end{cases}$$

so that, for example,

$$unpad(\square^n \fbox{e}\square\fbox{e, e'}\square^m) = \fbox{e}\square\fbox{e, e'}$$

for all integers $n, m \geq 0$. Now, using the equivalence $\approx$ between strings that *unpad* maps alike

$$\mathsf{s} \approx \mathsf{s}' \overset{\text{def}}{\iff} unpad(\mathsf{s}) = unpad(\mathsf{s}') ,$$

we generalize subsumption $\trianglerighteq$ to *containment* $\sqsupseteq$, taking $\mathsf{s} \sqsupseteq \mathsf{s}'$ (read: s *contains* s') to mean that s subsumes some string *unpad*-equivalent to s'

$$\mathsf{s} \sqsupseteq \mathsf{s}' \overset{\text{def}}{\iff} (\exists \mathsf{s}'' \approx \mathsf{s}')\, \mathsf{s} \trianglerighteq \mathsf{s}'' .$$

Koskenniemi (2009) of composing finite-state transducers can be developed with symbols structured as sets, and regular relations as retractions.

(A_1)	$e \bigcirc e$ (i.e. $\bigcirc$ is reflexive)
(A_2)	$e \bigcirc e' \implies e' \bigcirc e$
(A_3)	$e \prec e' \implies$ not $e \bigcirc e'$
(A_4)	$e \prec e'$ and $e' \bigcirc e''$ and $e'' \prec e''' \implies e \prec e'''$
(A_5)	$e \prec e'$ or $e \bigcirc e'$ or $e' \prec e$

Table 2: Axioms for (RWK) event structures

Thus, if s contains s' (e.g. if s is s'), then so do $unpad(\mathsf{s})$ and $\mathsf{s}''\mathsf{s}$ and $\mathsf{s}\mathsf{s}''$ (for all s''). It will be convenient to extend $\sqsupseteq$ to languages L, conceived as disjunctions, agreeing that s *contains* L if s contains some element of L

$$\mathsf{s} \sqsupseteq L \overset{\text{def}}{\iff} (\exists \mathsf{s}' \in L)\, \mathsf{s} \sqsupseteq \mathsf{s}'$$

so that $\mathsf{s} \sqsupseteq \mathsf{s}'$ iff $\mathsf{s} \sqsupseteq \{\mathsf{s}'\}$. Containment $\sqsupseteq$ is applied to event structures in section 2, with different sets X of events related by projections π_X in section 3. Containment is also useful when sidestepping completeness assumptions built into event structures and π_X, as we shall see.

2 Event structures from strings

A *(Russell-Wiener-Kamp) event structure* (Kamp and Reyle, 1993) is a triple $\langle E, \bigcirc, \prec \rangle$ consisting of a set E of events, and two binary relations on E, *(temporal) overlap* $\bigcirc$ and *(complete) precedence* $\prec$ satisfying axioms (A_1) to (A_5) in Table 2. To get a sense for what these axioms mean, it is useful to interpret them relative to triples $\langle E^{\mathsf{s}}, \bigcirc^{\mathsf{s}}, \prec^{\mathsf{s}} \rangle$ defined from strings s of sets as follows. We put into E^{s} each e that occurs in s

$$E^{\mathsf{s}} \overset{\text{def}}{=} \{e \mid \mathsf{s} \sqsupseteq \fbox{e}\}$$

and define e to s-*overlap* e' precisely if e and e' share a box in s

$$e \bigcirc^{\mathsf{s}} e' \overset{\text{def}}{\iff} \mathsf{s} \sqsupseteq \fbox{e, e'} .$$

As $\fbox{$e, e$} = \fbox{$e$}$ and $\fbox{$e, e'$} = \fbox{$e', e$}$, it follows that (A_1) and (A_2) are true for $\bigcirc = \bigcirc^{\mathsf{s}}$. Next, we say e s-*precedes* e' if e occurs in s to the left of e' but never in the same box as e' or to the right of e'

$$e \prec^{\mathsf{s}} e' \overset{\text{def}}{\iff} \mathsf{s} \sqsupseteq \fbox{e}\square^*\fbox{e'} \text{ and not } \mathsf{s} \sqsupseteq \fbox{e, e'} \mid \fbox{e'}\square^*\fbox{e}$$

(where $\mid$ is non-deterministic choice, often written $+$). It is easy to see that together $\bigcirc^{\mathsf{s}}$ and $\prec^{\mathsf{s}}$ validate (A3) and (A4). This leaves (A5), a counter-example to which is provided by the string $\boxed{e}\boxed{e'}\boxed{e}$. With this in mind, we define an element $e \in E^{\mathsf{s}}$ to be an s-*interval* if for $\mathsf{s} = \alpha_1 \cdots \alpha_n$,

$$e \in \alpha_i \cap \alpha_j \text{ and } i \leq k \leq j \quad \Longrightarrow \quad e \in \alpha_k$$

for all integers i, j, k from 1 to n. We call s *structural* if every $e \in E^{\mathsf{s}}$ is an s-interval. If s is structural, then

$$e \prec^{\mathsf{s}} e' \quad \Longleftrightarrow \quad \mathsf{s} \sqsupseteq \boxed{e}\boxed{}^{*}\boxed{e'} \text{ and not } \mathsf{s} \sqsupseteq \boxed{e, e'}\,.$$

Moreover, we have

Proposition 1. *If* s *is structural, then* $\langle E^{\mathsf{s}}, \bigcirc^{\mathsf{s}}, \prec^{\mathsf{s}} \rangle$ *is an event structure.*

As a string s need not be structural, it is useful to define the subset $I(\mathsf{s})$ of E^{s} consisting of s-intervals

$$I(\mathsf{s}) \quad \stackrel{\text{def}}{=} \quad \{e \in E^{\mathsf{s}} \mid e \text{ is an } \mathsf{s}\text{-interval}\}\,.$$

For example,

$$I(\boxed{e}\boxed{e'}\boxed{e}) \quad = \quad \{e'\}\,.$$

Next, for any set X, we define the function ρ_X on strings (of sets) to componentwise intersect with X

$$\rho_X(\alpha_1 \cdots \alpha_n) \quad \stackrel{\text{def}}{=} \quad (\alpha_1 \cap X) \cdots (\alpha_n \cap X)$$

so that, for instance, if $\hat{\mathsf{s}}$ is $\boxed{e}\boxed{e'}\boxed{e}$,

$$\rho_{I(\hat{\mathsf{s}})}(\hat{\mathsf{s}}) \quad = \quad \boxed{}\boxed{e'}\boxed{}\,.$$

In general, $\rho_{I(\mathsf{s})}(\mathsf{s})$ is structural for all strings s. Setting $i(\mathsf{s})$ to $\rho_{I(\mathsf{s})}(\mathsf{s})$, and $\mathbb{E}(\mathsf{s})$ to the triple $\langle E^{i(\mathsf{s})}, \bigcirc^{i(\mathsf{s})}, \prec^{i(\mathsf{s})} \rangle$ induced by $i(\mathsf{s})$, we note

Corollary 2. $\mathbb{E}(\mathsf{s})$ *is an event structure for every string* s *of sets.*

An obvious question Corollary 2 raises is: can every event structure over a set E be presented as $\mathbb{E}(\mathsf{s})$ for a suitable string $\mathsf{s} \in Pow(E)^*$? For infinite sets E, more methods are clearly needed — and considered in the next section. As for finite E, an affirmative answer follows from Russell-Wiener-Kamp (RWK, Kamp and Reyle, 1993), which we now briefly recall. Given an event structure $\langle E, \bigcirc, \prec \rangle$, we construct a linear order $\langle T_{\bigcirc}, \prec_T \rangle$ as follows. The set $T_{\bigcirc}$ of *(RWK) temporal moments* consists of subsets t of E that pairwise $\bigcirc$-overlap

$$(\forall e, e' \in t) \qquad e \bigcirc e'$$

and are $\subseteq$-maximal among such subsets

$$(\forall e \in E) \qquad \text{if } (\forall e' \in t)\ e \bigcirc e' \text{ then } e \in t\,.$$

For $t, t' \in T_{\bigcirc}$, we then put $t \prec_T t'$ if some element of t $\prec$-precedes some element of t'

$$t \prec_T t' \quad \stackrel{\text{def}}{\Longleftrightarrow} \quad (\exists e \in t)(\exists e' \in t')\ e \prec e'\,.$$

One can then show that not only does $\prec_T$ linearly order $T_{\bigcirc}$, but that relative to that linear order, every $e \in E$ defines an interval

$$e \in t \qquad \text{whenever } e \in t_1 \text{ and } e \in t_2 \text{ for some } t_1, t_2 \text{ with } t_1 \prec_T t \prec_T t_2$$

and the relations $\bigcirc$ and $\prec$ can be interpreted as overlap

$$e \bigcirc e' \quad \Longleftrightarrow \quad (\exists t \in T_{\bigcirc})\ e \in t \text{ and } e' \in t$$

and complete precedence

$$e \prec e' \quad \Longleftrightarrow \quad (\forall t \in T_{\bigcirc})(\forall t' \in T_{\bigcirc})\ e \in t \text{ and } e' \in t' \text{ implies } t \prec_T t'\,.$$

To illustrate, the three event structures on $E = \{e, e'\}$ yield three linear orders $\langle T_{\bigcirc}, \prec_T \rangle$ that can be pictured as the three strings $\boxed{e, e'}$, $\boxed{e}\boxed{e'}$ and $\boxed{e'}\boxed{e}$.

But then what about the ten other strings in Table 1 and the various Allen relations? Each of these strings violates the $\subseteq$-maximality requirement on $T_{\bigcirc}$ above. We can neutralize that requirement by adjoining pre- and post-events, turning, for instance,

$$\boxed{e}\boxed{e, e'}\boxed{e'} \qquad \text{into} \qquad \boxed{e, \mathit{pre}(e')}\boxed{e, e'}\boxed{e', \mathit{post}(e)}\,.$$

On structural strings, $\mathit{pre}(e)$ and $\mathit{post}(e)$ negate e, whilst preserving structurality. More precisely, given a set E, let

$$E_{\pm} \quad \stackrel{\text{def}}{=} \quad E \cup \{\mathit{pre}(e) \mid e \in E\} \cup \{\mathit{post}(e) \mid e \in E\}$$

and call a string $\mathsf{s} = \alpha_1\alpha_2\cdots\alpha_n$ *E-delimited* if for all $e \in E$ and $i \in \{1,2,\ldots,n\}$,

$$\begin{aligned} \mathit{pre}(e) \in \alpha_i &\iff \mathsf{s} \sqsupseteq \boxed{e} \text{ but } \alpha_1\cdots\alpha_i \not\sqsupseteq \boxed{e} \\ &(\iff e \in (\bigcup_{j=i+1}^{n} \alpha_j) - \bigcup_{j=1}^{i} \alpha_j) \end{aligned}$$

and

$$\begin{aligned} \mathit{post}(e) \in \alpha_i &\iff \mathsf{s} \sqsupseteq \boxed{e} \text{ but } \alpha_i\cdots\alpha_n \not\sqsupseteq \boxed{e} \\ &(\iff e \in (\bigcup_{j=1}^{i-1} \alpha_j) - \bigcup_{j=i}^{n} \alpha_j) . \end{aligned}$$

It is immediate that for every string $\mathsf{s} \in \mathit{Pow}(E)^*$, there is a unique E-delimited string $\mathsf{s}' \in \mathit{Pow}(E_\pm)^*$ such that $\rho_E(\mathsf{s}') = \mathsf{s}$. Let $\mathsf{s}_\pm$ be that unique string.

Proposition 3. *For every finite set E, there is a finite-state transducer that computes the map $\mathsf{s} \mapsto \mathsf{s}_\pm$ from $\mathit{Pow}(E)^*$ to $\mathit{Pow}(E_\pm)^*$.*

If s is structural, then so is $\mathsf{s}_\pm$ — making $\langle E^{\mathsf{s}_\pm}, \bigcirc^{\mathsf{s}_\pm}, \prec^{\mathsf{s}_\pm}\rangle$ an event structure (for structural s). Extending a string $\mathsf{s} \in \mathit{Pow}(\{e,e'\})^*$ to $\mathsf{s}_\pm$ leads to a refinement of $\bigcirc$ and $\prec$ to any of the 13 Allen relations — e.g. whenever e and e' are s-intervals,

$$\begin{aligned} e \;\mathsf{d}^{\mathsf{s}}\; e' &\iff \mathit{pre}(e) \bigcirc^{\mathsf{s}_\pm} e' \text{ and } e \bigcirc^{\mathsf{s}_\pm} e' \\ &\qquad \text{and } \mathit{post}(e) \bigcirc^{\mathsf{s}_\pm} e' \\ e <^{\mathsf{s}} e' &\iff e \prec^{\mathsf{s}_\pm} e' \text{ and} \\ &\qquad \mathit{post}(e) \bigcirc^{\mathsf{s}_\pm} \mathit{pre}(e') . \end{aligned}$$

Given that there is a finite-state transducer for the map $\mathsf{s} \mapsto \mathsf{s}_\pm$, it is tempting to leave out the pre- and post-events for simplicity.

The map $\mathsf{s} \mapsto \mathsf{s}_\pm$ aside, different strings $\mathsf{s} \in \mathit{Pow}(E)^*$ can give the same event structure $\mathbb{E}(\mathsf{s})$. Take, for example, the strings in $\boxed{e}^+\boxed{e'}^+$ (where $L^+ \stackrel{\text{def}}{=} L^*L$), each of which gives the event structure pictured by $\boxed{e}\boxed{e'}$. In general, let us reduce all adjacent identical boxes $\alpha\alpha^n$ to one α in the *block compression* $\mathit{bc}(\mathsf{s})$ *of* a string s

$$\mathit{bc}(\mathsf{s}) \stackrel{\text{def}}{=} \begin{cases} \mathit{bc}(\alpha\mathsf{s}') & \text{if } \mathsf{s} = \alpha\alpha\mathsf{s}' \\ \alpha\,\mathit{bc}(\alpha'\mathsf{s}') & \text{if } \mathsf{s} = \alpha\alpha'\mathsf{s}' \text{ with } \alpha \neq \alpha' \\ \mathsf{s} & \text{otherwise} \end{cases}$$

so that, for example,

$$\mathit{bc}(\mathsf{s}) = \boxed{e}\boxed{e'} \qquad \text{for every } \mathsf{s} \in \boxed{e}^+\boxed{e'}^+ .$$

The map bc is a regular relation, and implements the slogan "no time without change" (Kamp and Reyle 1993, page 674). Clearly, bc does *not* alter the event structure $\mathbb{E}(\mathsf{s})$ represented by a string s

$$\mathbb{E}(\mathit{bc}(\mathsf{s})) \;=\; \mathbb{E}(\mathsf{s}) .$$

Neither does unpadding, which suggests defining a function π that unpads after (or equivalently: before) block compression

$$\pi(\mathsf{s}) \stackrel{\text{def}}{=} \mathit{unpad}(\mathit{bc}(\mathsf{s})) \quad [= \mathit{bc}(\mathit{unpad}(\mathsf{s}))]$$

so that, for example,

$$\pi(\mathsf{s}) = \boxed{e}\boxed{e'} \qquad \text{for every } \mathsf{s} \in \boxed{}^*\boxed{e}^+\boxed{e'}^+\boxed{}^* .$$

Before using π to define the functions π_X in the next section, let us note that on delimited strings $\mathsf{s}_\pm$, π captures what is essential for representing event structures.

Proposition 4. For structural strings s and $\mathsf{s}' \in \mathit{Pow}(E)^*$, the following four conditions, (a) to (d), are equivalent

(a) $\mathit{bc}(\mathsf{s}) = \mathit{bc}(\mathsf{s}')$

(b) $\mathbb{E}(\mathsf{s}_\pm) = \mathbb{E}(\mathsf{s}'_\pm)$

(c) $\mathit{bc}(\mathsf{s}_\pm) = \mathit{bc}(\mathsf{s}'_\pm)$

(d) $\pi(\mathsf{s}_\pm) = \pi(\mathsf{s}'_\pm)$.

It follows from Proposition 4 that for structural $\mathsf{s} \in \mathit{Pow}(E)^*$,

$$\mathbb{E}(\mathsf{s}_\pm) \;=\; \mathbb{E}(\mathit{bc}(\mathsf{s}_\pm)) \;=\; \mathbb{E}(\pi(\mathsf{s}_\pm))$$

as $\mathit{bc}(\mathit{bc}(\mathsf{s}_\pm)) = \mathit{bc}(\mathsf{s}_\pm) = \pi(\mathsf{s}_\pm)$.

3 Varying X with retractions π_X and generalizations

Fix some large set E, and let $\Sigma = \mathit{Pow}(E)$ be the alphabet from which we form strings. Given a language $L \subseteq \Sigma^*$ and a function $f : \Sigma^* \to \Sigma^*$ on strings over Σ, we write $f[L]$ for the f-image of L

$$f[L] \;\stackrel{\text{def}}{=}\; \{f(\mathsf{s}) \mid \mathsf{s} \in L\}$$

and $f^{-1}L$ for the inverse f-image of L

$$f^{-1}L \;\stackrel{\text{def}}{=}\; \{\mathsf{s} \in \Sigma^* \mid f(\mathsf{s}) \in L\} .$$

Applying these constructions in sequence, note that

$$f^{-1}f[L] \quad = \quad \{\mathsf{s} \in \Sigma^* \mid (\exists \mathsf{s}' \in L)\ f(\mathsf{s}) = f(\mathsf{s}')\}$$

which we shall refer to as the *f-closure of L*, L^f

$$L^f \quad \stackrel{\text{def}}{=} \quad f^{-1}f[L]$$

(as $L \subseteq L^f = L^{ff}$ and the operation preserves $\subseteq$-inclusion: $L \subseteq L'$ implies $L^f \subseteq L'^f$). In this section, we form f-closures for different f's computed by finite-state transducers (assuming E is finite), including the functions *unpad*, bc, π, and ρ_X (for subsets X of E; recall $\rho_X(\alpha_1 \cdots \alpha_n) = (\alpha_1 \cap X) \cdots (\alpha_n \cap X)$). Putting these together, let $\pi_X : \mathit{Pow}(E)^* \to \mathit{Pow}(X)^*$ be the composition $\rho_X;\pi$ of ρ_X followed by π

$$\pi_X(\mathsf{s}) \quad \stackrel{\text{def}}{=} \quad \pi(\rho_X(\mathsf{s})) \quad = \quad \mathit{unpad}(\mathit{bc}(\rho_X(\mathsf{s})))$$

so that for every $\mathsf{s} \in \mathit{Pow}(E)^*$ and $e \in E$, e is an s-interval iff $\pi_{\{e\}}(\mathsf{s}) = \boxed{e}$.

To study an event alongside other events, we generalize the superposition operation & (defined in the introduction) from strings of the same length to languages over the alphabet Σ. First, we collect superpositions $\mathsf{s}\ \&\ \mathsf{s}'$ of strings s and s' of the same length from languages L and L' in the *superposition*

$$L \,\&\, L' \quad \stackrel{\text{def}}{=} \quad \bigcup_{n \geq 0} \{\mathsf{s}\ \&\ \mathsf{s}' \mid \mathsf{s} \in L \cap \Sigma^n \text{ and } \mathsf{s}' \in L' \cap \Sigma^n\}$$

(Fernando, 2004). We then form the superposition of the f-closures of L and L', and take its f-image for the *f-superposition* $L \,\&_f\, L'$

$$L \,\&_f\, L' \quad \stackrel{\text{def}}{=} \quad f[L^f \,\&\, L'^f]\,.$$

For example, the π-superposition $\boxed{e} \,\&_\pi\, \boxed{e'}$ consists of the 13 strings in Table 1, which can be divided up as follows. Put the 9 ways for e and e' to overlap (according to Allen) in

$$\begin{aligned}\mathcal{A}(e \bigcirc e') \quad &\stackrel{\text{def}}{=} \quad (\epsilon \mid \boxed{e} \mid \boxed{e'})\boxed{e,e'}(\epsilon \mid \boxed{e} \mid \boxed{e'}) \\ &= \quad \boxed{e,e'} \mid \boxed{e,e'}\boxed{e} \mid \boxed{e,e'}\boxed{e'} \mid \cdots \\ &\qquad \mid \boxed{e'}\boxed{e,e'}\boxed{e'}\end{aligned}$$

(where ϵ is the empty string), and the 2 ways for e to precede e' in

$$\mathcal{A}(e \prec e') \quad \stackrel{\text{def}}{=} \quad \boxed{e}\boxed{e'} \mid \boxed{e}\boxed{\ }\boxed{e'}\,.$$

All 13 strings then end up in

$$\begin{aligned}\boxed{e} \,\&_\pi\, \boxed{e'} \quad = \quad &\mathcal{A}(e \prec e') \mid \mathcal{A}(e \bigcirc e') \mid \\ &\mathcal{A}(e' \prec e)\end{aligned}$$

in accordance with axiom (A_5) in Table 2. Stepping from two to any finite number $n \geq 1$ of events $e_1, \ldots, e_n$ in E (where $\Sigma = \mathit{Pow}(E)$), let us define languages $\mathcal{E}(e_1 \cdots e_n)$ by induction on n as follows

$$\begin{aligned}\mathcal{E}(e_1) \quad &\stackrel{\text{def}}{=} \quad \boxed{e_1} \\ \mathcal{E}(e_1 \cdots e_{n+1}) \quad &\stackrel{\text{def}}{=} \quad \mathcal{E}(e_1 \cdots e_n) \,\&_\pi\, \boxed{e_{n+1}}\end{aligned}$$

(for $n \geq 1$). Recalling that $I(\mathsf{s})$ denotes the set of s-intervals, we can generalize the equation

$$I(\mathsf{s}) \quad = \quad \{e \in E^{\mathsf{s}} \mid \pi_{\{e\}}(\mathsf{s}) = \boxed{e}\}$$

as follows.

Proposition 5. *For every* $\mathsf{s} \in \mathit{Pow}(E)^*$ *and every finite subset* $\{e_1, \ldots, e_n\}$ *of* E*, all* e_i*'s are* s*-intervals iff* $\pi_{\{e_1,\ldots,e_n\}}$ *maps* s *to a string in* $\mathcal{E}(e_1 \cdots e_n)$

$$\{e_1, \ldots, e_n\} \subseteq I(\mathsf{s}) \quad \iff \quad \pi_{\{e_1,\ldots,e_n\}}(\mathsf{s}) \in \mathcal{E}(e_1 \cdots e_n)\,.$$

We can bring out the f-closures behind Proposition 5 by defining a language $L \subseteq \Sigma^*$ to be *f-closed* if its f-closure L^f is a subset of L. As it is always the case that $L \subseteq f^{-1}f[L]$,

$$L \text{ is } f\text{-closed} \quad \iff \quad L^f = L\,.$$

According to Proposition 5, the set $\mathcal{I}(e_1 \cdots e_n)$ of strings s such that each e_i is an s-interval (for $1 \leq i \leq n$) is $\pi_{\{e_1,\ldots,e_n\}}$-closed, and what's more, its $\pi_{\{e_1,\ldots,e_n\}}$-image is a subset of (in fact, identical to) $\mathcal{E}(e_1 \cdots e_n)$. Observe that a language L is f-closed iff for all $\mathsf{s} \in \Sigma^*$,

$$\mathsf{s} \in L \quad \iff \quad f(\mathsf{s}) \in f[L]$$

which constitutes a reduction in the cost of checking membership in L insofar as the f-image $f[L]$ of

L is a reduction of L (and the computational cost of f can be ignored). In the case of Proposition 5, whereas $\mathcal{I}(e_1 \cdots e_n)$ is infinite, $\mathcal{E}(e_1 \cdots e_n)$ is finite. Focusing on the case $n = 2$, note that the relations of overlap $\bigcirc$ and precedence $\prec$ between e and e' are $\pi_{\{e,e'\}}$-closed in that

Proposition 6. *For every* $\mathsf{s} \in Pow(E)^*$ *such that* $e, e' \in E$ *are* s*-intervals,*

$$\begin{aligned} e \bigcirc^{\mathsf{s}} e' &\iff \pi_{\{e,e'\}}(\mathsf{s}) \in \mathcal{A}(e \bigcirc e') \\ e \prec^{\mathsf{s}} e' &\iff \pi_{\{e,e'\}}(\mathsf{s}) \in \mathcal{A}(e \prec e')\,. \end{aligned}$$

Under the appropriate definitions, the 13 Allen relations between e and e' are also $\pi_{\{e,e'\}}$-closed. A notion for which π_X-closedness is problematic, however, is the following. We say $e \in E$ is *left-bounded in* s if s is a non-empty string such that $e \notin \alpha$ where α is the first symbol of s — or equivalently, $pre(e) \in E^{\mathsf{s}\pm}$. Although the set of strings s in which e is left-bounded is not $\pi_{\{e\}}$-closed, the equivalences

$$e \notin \alpha \iff bc(\rho_{\{e\}}(\mathsf{s})) \in (\boxed{\ }\boxed{e})^+(\boxed{\ }\,|\epsilon)$$

(where α is the first symbol of the non-empty string s) and

$$pre(e) \in E^{\mathsf{s}\pm} \iff \pi_{\{pre(e)\}}(\mathsf{s}_\pm) = \boxed{pre(e)}$$

give two different functions f for which the set is f-closed — viz., the composition $\rho_{\{e\}}; bc$ of $\rho_{\{e\}}$ followed by bc, and the composition $\cdot_\pm; \pi_{\{pre(e)\}}$ of the map $\mathsf{s} \mapsto \mathsf{s}_\pm$ followed by $\pi_{\{pre(e)\}} = \rho_{\{pre(e)\}}; bc; unpad$. Note

Proposition 7. *If* $f = g; h$ *where* $g; g = g$ *then every* f*-closed language is* g*-closed.*

The cascade of regular relations above is reminiscent of Niemi and Koskenniemi (2009), with each successive function reducing the input. The case of left-boundedness suggests caution against over-reducing; the map *unpad* (separating bc from π) abstracts away temporal span. To see that $\&_{bc}$ gives us more control than $\&_\pi$, let us reformulate the example (from (Niemi and Koskenniemi, 2009)) of the 12 months of year 2008 in our framework as

$$\begin{aligned} & \boxed{\mathsf{y2008}} \,\&_{bc}\, \boxed{\mathsf{Jan}}\boxed{\mathsf{Feb}}\boxed{\mathsf{Mar}}\cdots\boxed{\mathsf{Dec}} \\ = \; & \boxed{\mathsf{y2008,Jan}}\boxed{\mathsf{y2008,Feb}}\boxed{\mathsf{y2008,Mar}}\cdots \\ & \boxed{\mathsf{y2008,Dec}} \end{aligned}$$

which $\rho_{\{\mathsf{y2008}\}}; bc$ maps back to $\boxed{\mathsf{y2008}}$. Given a function f such that $f; f = f$ and a subset X of E, we may call the composition $f_X \overset{\text{def}}{=} \rho_X; f$ of ρ_X with f a *retraction* insofar as f_X preserves the structure $\&_f$ introduces

$$f_X(\mathsf{s} \,\&_f\, \mathsf{s}') \;=\; f_X(\mathsf{s}) \,\&_f\, f_X(\mathsf{s}')$$

(where a string s is, as usual, conflated with the language $\{\mathsf{s}\}$). Let us say a language L is X-*determined* if L is ρ_X-closed. By Proposition 7, f_X-closed languages are X-determined. Moreover, the totality of finite subsets X of E (partially ordered by $\subseteq$) indexes an inverse system of maps π_X, the inverse limit of which represents every event structure over E. This fact bolsters the claim of embodiment made in the title of the present paper, reinforcing (as it does) the notion that strings are full-blooded semantic entities (familiar already from Linear Temporal Logic, where they can be viewed as Kripke models.; e.g. (Emerson, 1990)). Is the choice of π in the inverse system π_X sacrosanct? Should we not perhaps stop short of π_X at bc_X to capture, for instance, left-bounded events e? Not necessarily. Delimiting $\mathsf{s} \mapsto \mathsf{s}_\pm$ before applying $\pi_{\{e,pre(e)\}}$, we have

$$e \text{ is left-bounded in } \mathsf{s} \iff \pi_{\{e,pre(e)\}}(\mathsf{s}_\pm) \in \boxed{pre(e)}(\boxed{e}\boxed{\ })^*\boxed{e}\,.$$

But should we take it for granted that s amounts to $\mathsf{s}_\pm$?

Not if a string s is to embody underspecification, so that s may represent, relative to some background set C of strings, the set $C[\mathsf{s}]$ of strings in C that $\sqsupseteq$-contain s

$$C[\mathsf{s}] \;\overset{\text{def}}{=}\; \{\mathsf{s}' \in C \mid \mathsf{s}' \sqsupseteq \mathsf{s}\}$$

(a regular language, provided C is). Recall, for instance, the interest in representing cognitively natural disjunctions of Allen relations (Freksa, 1992). Under the present framework, some such disjunctions can be read off strings. For example, overlap between e and e' described by the (disembodied) abstract expression "$e \bigcirc e'$" is embodied by the box $\boxed{e, e'}$. That is, the set of strings s such that $e \bigcirc^{\mathsf{s}} e'$ is $C[\mathsf{s}]$ for $C = \Sigma^*$ and $\mathsf{s} = \boxed{e, e'}$. What about the precedence $e \prec e'$? This is where $pre(e')$ and

$post(e)$ are helpful. Form $C[\mathsf{s}]$ where s is the (non-delimited) string

$$\boxed{e, pre(e')}\boxed{post(e)}$$

and C is the language $\{\mathsf{s}'_{\pm} \mid \mathsf{s}' \in Pow(E)^*\}$. This language C and many more constraints can be formulated in finite-state terms familiar from say, Beesley and Karttunen (1983), as shown in Fernando (2011). Auxiliary constructs such as $pre(e)$ and $post(e)$ (that may later be dropped) have proved enormously useful tools advancing finite-state methods. Rather than claim for these constructs the same ontological status that events in E may enjoy, however, we might reconstrue the elements in boxes not as concrete particulars but rather as temporal propositions with possibly scattered occurrences (instead of the restriction to intervals characteristic of event structures). This would allow us to introduce a negation of e without requiring that the temporal projection of e or its complement be an interval. (Moreover, recalling the calendar example of Jan, Feb, ..., Dec above, we may well want to form a string s such that none of Jan, Feb, ..., Dec are s-intervals.)

That said, the families $\mathcal{E}(e_1 \cdots e_n)$ of regular languages above extend to

$$\mathcal{S}(e) \stackrel{\text{def}}{=} \boxed{pre(e)}(\epsilon \mid \boxed{})\boxed{e}(\epsilon \mid \boxed{})\boxed{post(e)}$$

and for $n \geq 1$,

$$\mathcal{S}(e_1 \cdots e_{n+1}) \stackrel{\text{def}}{=} \mathcal{S}(e_1 \cdots e_n) \ \&_{\pi}\ \mathcal{S}(e_{n+1})$$

with uncertainty injected $\boxed{}$ at the semi-intervals $\boxed{pre(e)}\boxed{e}$ and $\boxed{e}\boxed{post(e)}$, so that strings in $\mathcal{S}(e_1 e_2)$ embody disjunctions of Allen relations between e_1 and e_2. For example, we can represent temporal inclusion of e_1 within e_2 by the string

$$\boxed{pre(e_1), pre(e_2)}\boxed{pre(e_1)}\boxed{e_1, e_2}$$
$$\boxed{post(e_1)}\boxed{post(e_1), post(e_2)}$$

(of length 5) in $\mathcal{S}(e_1 e_2)$, instead of the four strings from $\mathcal{E}(e_1 e_2)$ for $e_1 \ \mathtt{R}\ e_2$, $\mathtt{R} \in \{\mathtt{=}, \mathtt{s}, \mathtt{f}, \mathtt{d}\}$. Resisting the step from s to $\mathsf{s}_{\pm}$ leaves room for a form of underspecification that is natural for strings *qua* extensions (denotations), if not indices (Fernando, 2011).

4 Conclusion

The sense of embodiment claimed by the present paper boils down to reducing chronological order to succession within a string of boxes. But what boxes? That depends on our interests. Were we interested in months, then we might portray a year as the string

$$\mathsf{s}_{yr/mo} \stackrel{\text{def}}{=} \boxed{\mathsf{Jan}}\boxed{\mathsf{Feb}}\boxed{\mathsf{Mar}} \cdots \boxed{\mathsf{Dec}}$$

of length 12. Or were we also interested in days, perhaps the string

$$\mathsf{s}_{yr/mo,dy} \stackrel{\text{def}}{=} \boxed{\mathsf{Jan,d1}}\boxed{\mathsf{Jan,d2}} \cdots \boxed{\mathsf{Dec,d31}}$$

of length 365 (for a non-leap year). Observe that for $X = \{\mathsf{Jan,Feb,\ldots,Dec}\}$,

$$\pi_X(\mathsf{s}_{yr/mo,dy}) = \mathsf{s}_{yr/mo}$$

and that we can picture the $\mathsf{s}_{yr/mo,dy}$-intervalhood of Jan by the equation

$$\pi_{\{\mathsf{Jan}\}}(\mathsf{s}_{yr/mo,dy}) = \boxed{\mathsf{Jan}}$$

in contrast to d1, for which

$$\pi_{\{\mathsf{d1}\}}(\mathsf{s}_{yr/mo,dy}) = (\boxed{\mathsf{d1}}\boxed{})^{11}\boxed{\mathsf{d1}} .$$

In general, e is an s-interval precisely if $\pi_{\{e\}}$ maps s to $\boxed{e}$

$$e \in I(\mathsf{s}) \iff \pi_{\{e\}}(\mathsf{s}) = \boxed{e} .$$

Hence, all of $e_1, e_2, \ldots, e_n$ are s-intervals if $\mathsf{s} \in \mathcal{E}_{\circ}(e_1 \cdots e_n)$ where

$$\mathcal{E}_{\circ}(e_1 \cdots e_n) \stackrel{\text{def}}{=} \bigcap_{i=1}^{n} \pi^{-1}_{\{e_i\}} \boxed{e_i} .$$

That is, we can form the regular languages

$$\mathcal{E}(e_1 \cdots e_n) = \pi_{\{e_1,\ldots,e_n\}}[\mathcal{E}_{\circ}(e_1 \cdots e_n)]$$

starring in Proposition 5, without ever mentioning $\&$ or $\trianglerighteq$. More importantly, the regular relations π_X apply with or without the constraint of intervalhood imposed by RWK event structures. Furthermore, a bounded level of granularity is supported that we can adjust through X, as illustrated by the McTaggart A-series enhancement $X_{\pm}$ for the Allen relations. We can glue together any number of granularities by forming inverse limits, but arguably it is the finite approximations that we can process (and manipulate) — not the infinite objects (such as the real numbers) that arise at the limit.

References

James F. Allen. 1983. Maintaining knowledge about temporal intervals. *Communications of the Association for Computing Machinery* **26** (11):832–843.

Kenneth R. Beesley and Lauri Karttunen. 2003. *Finite State Morphology*. CSLI Publications, Stanford.

E. Allen Emerson. 1990. Temporal and modal logic. In J. van Leeuwen (ed.), *Handbook of Theoretical Computer Science*, volume B: Formal Methods and Semantics, pp. 995–1072. MIT Press.

Tim Fernando. 2004. A finite-state approach to events in natural language semantics. *Journal of Logic and Computation* **14** (1):79–92.

Tim Fernando. 2011. Regular relations for temporal propositions. *Natural Language Engineering* **17** (2):163–184.

Christian Freksa. 1992. Temporal reasoning based on semi-intervals. *Artificial Intelligence* **54** (11):199–227.

Hans Kamp and Uwe Reyle. 1993. *From Discourse to Logic*. Kluwer Academic Publishers, Dordrecht.

Lauri Karttunen. 2005. The Yale Shooting Problem. `http://www.stanford.edu/~laurik/fsmbook/examples/YaleShooting.html`

Uwe Lück. 2006. Continu'ous Time Goes by Russell. *Notre Dame J. Formal Logic* **47** (3):397–434.

Inderjeet Mani. 2007. Chronoscopes: a theory of underspecified temporal representations. In F. Schilder et al. (eds.) *Reasoning about Time and Events*, pp. 127–139. Springer LNAI 4795.

John M.E. McTaggart. 1908. The Unreality of Time. *Mind* **17** 457–473.

Jyrki Niemi and Kimmo Koskenniemi. 2009. Representing and Combining Calendar Information by Using Finite-State Transducers. In J. Piskorski, B. Watson and A. Yli-Jyr (eds.), *Finite-State Methods and Natural Language Processing: Post-proceedings of the 7th International Workshop FSMNLP 2008*, pp. 122–133. IOS Press, Amsterdam.

Supervised and Semi-Supervised Sequence Learning for Recognition of Requisite Part and Effectuation Part in Law Sentences

Le-Minh Nguyen and **Ngo Xuan Bach** and **Akira Shimazu**
Japan Advanced Institute of Science and Technology (JAIST)
Asahidai 1-1, Nomi, Ishikawa, 923-1292 Japan
{nguyenml,bachnx,shimazu}@jaist.ac.jp

Abstract

Analyzing the logical structure of a sentence is important for understanding natural language. In this paper, we present a task of Recognition of Requisite Part and Effectuation Part in Law Sentences, or RRE task for short, which is studied in research on Legal Engineering. The goal of this task is to recognize the structure of a law sentence. We empirically investigate how the RRE task is conducted with respect to various supervised machine learning models. We also compared the impact of unlabeled data to RRE tasks. Experimental results for Japanese legal text domains showed that sequence learning models are suitable for RRE tasks and unlabled data also significantly contribute to the performance of RRE tasks.

1 Introduction

Legal Engineering (Katayama 07) is a new research field which aims to achieve a trustworthy electronic society. There are two important goals of Legal Engineering. The first goal is to help experts make complete and consistent laws, and the other is to design an information system which works based on laws. To achieve this we need to develop a system which can process legal texts automatically.

Legal texts have some specific characteristics that make them different from other daily-use documents. Legal texts are usually long and complicated. They are composed by experts who spent a lot of time to write and check them carefully. One of the most important characteristics of legal texts is that law sentences have some specific structures. In most cases, a law sentence can roughly be divided into two parts: a *requisite part* and an *effectuation part* (Nakamura et al., 07; Tanaka et al., 93). For example, the Hiroshima city provision 13-2 *When the mayor designates a district for promoting beautification, s/he must in advance listen to opinions from the organizations and the administrative agencies which are recognized to be concerned with the district*, includes a requisite part (before the comma) and an effectuation part (after the comma) (Nakamura et al., 07).

The requisite part and the effectuation part of a law sentence are composed from three parts: a *topic part*, an *antecedent part*, and a *consequent part*. There are four cases (illustrated in Figure 1) basing on where the topic part depends on: case 0 (no topic part), case 1 (the topic part depends on the antecedent part), case 2 (the topic part depends on the consequent part), and case 3 (the topic part depends on both the antecedent part and the consequent part). In case 0, the requisite part is the antecedent part and the effectuation part is the consequent part. In case 1, the requisite part is composed from the topic part and the antecedent part, while the effectuation part is the consequent part. In case 2, the requisite part is the antecedent part, while the effectuation part is composed from the topic part and the consequent part. In case 3, the requisite part is composed from the topic part and the antecedent part, while the effectuation part is composed from the topic part and the consequent part. Figure 2 gives examples of law sentences in four cases.

Analyzing the logical structure of law sentences is an important task in Legal Engineering. This task is

Proceedings of the 9th International Workshop on Finite State Methods and Natural Language Processing, pages 21–29,
Blois (France), July 12-15, 2011.

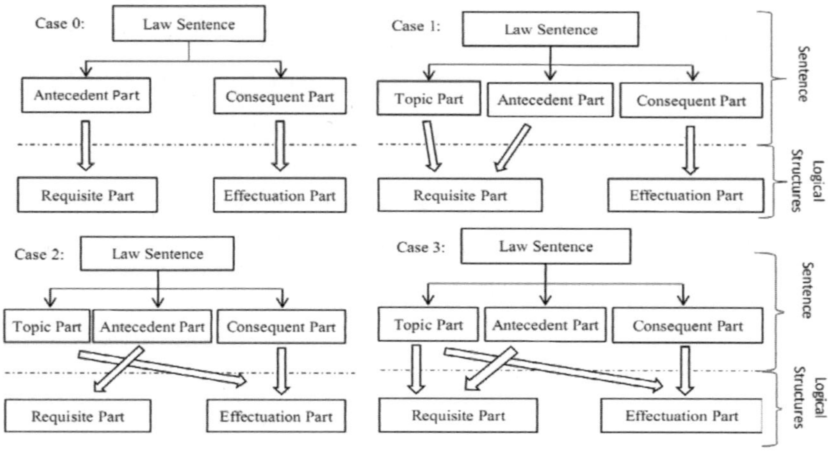

Figure 1: Four cases of the logical structure of a law sentence.

Case 0:
<A>被保険者期間を計算する場合には、</A><C>月によるものとする。</C>
<A>When a period of an insured is calculated,</A><C> it is based on a month.</C>

Case 1:
<A>被保険者の資格を喪失した後、さらにその資格を取得した</A><T1>者については、</T1><C>前後の被保険者期間を合算する。</C>
<T1>For the person</T1>
<A>who is qualified for the insured after s/he was disqualified, </A>
<C>the terms of the insured are added up together. </C>

Case 2:
<T2>この法律による年金の額は、</T2><A>国民の生活水準その他の諸事情に著しい変動が生じた場合には、</A><C>変動後の諸事情に応ずるため、速やかに改定の措置が講ぜられなければならない。</C>
<T2>For the amount of the pension by this law, </T2>
<A>when there is a remarkable change in the living standard of the nation or the other situations, </A>
<C>a revision of the amount of the pension must be taken action promptly to meet the situations. </C>

Case 3:
<T3>政府は、</T3><A>第一項の規定により財政の現況及び見通しを作成したときは、</A><C>遅滞なく、これを公表しなければならない。</C>
<T3> For the Government, </T3>
<A>when it makes a present state and a perspective of the finance, </A>
<C>it must announce it officially without delay.</C>

Figure 2: Examples of four cases of the logical structure of a law sentence. *A* means *antecedent part*, *C* means *consequent part*, and *T1*, *T2*, *T3* mean *topic parts* which correspond to case 1, case 2, and case 3 (the translations keep the ordinal sentence structures).

a preliminary step to support tasks in legal text processing, such as translating legal articles into logical and formal representations and verifying legal documents, legal article retrieval, legal text summarization, question answering in legal domains, etc (Katayama 07; Nakamura et al., 07). In a law sentence, the consequent part usually describes a law provision, and the antecedent part describes cases in which the law provision can be applied. The topic part describes the subjects which are related to the law provision. Hence, the outputs of the RRE task will be very helpful to not only lawyers but also people who want to understand the law sentence. They can easily understand 1) what does a law sentence say? 2) what cases in which the law sentence can be applied? and 3) what subjects are related to the provision described in the law sentence?

In this paper, we present a task of *Recognition of Requisite Part and Effectuation Part in Law Sentences* - the RRE task. We show how to model this task by using sequence learning models. The first one applies Conditional Random Fields (CRFs), a special version of conditionally-trained finite state machines. We studies two different machine learning models for CRFs. The second one focus on discriminative sequence learning models using online learning framework (Crammer et al, 2006). We then empirically investigate several sequence learning models for RRE task. In addition, We depict a simple semi-supervised learning method for the RRE task using the Brown clustering algorithm. We also show experimental results on an annotated corpus of Japanese national pension law sentences. Our models achieved 88.58% (using supervised learning) and 88.84% (using semi-supervised learning) in the $F_{\beta=1}$ score.

The remainder of this paper is organized as follows. First, Section 2 presents how to model the RRE task as a sequence labeling problem, and shows experimental results about the effect of features on the task. Next, we describe another setting for the task based on Bunsetsu (chunks in English) in Section 3. Then, Section 5 describes a simple semi-supervised learning method for the task. Finally, some conclusions are given in Section 6.

2 RRE as a Sequence Learning Problem

2.1 Problem Setting

Let x be an input law sentence in a law sentence space X, then x can be represented by a sequence of words $[w_1, w_2, \ldots, w_n]$. Let P be the set of predefined logical part categories. A logical part $p(s,e)$ is the sequence of consecutive words spanning from word w_s to word w_e with category $p \in P$.

We define two kinds of relationships between two logical parts: *overlapping* and *embedded*. Let $p_1(s_1, e_1)$ and $p_2(s_2, e_2)$ be two different logical parts of one sentence x. We say that $p_1(s_1, e_1)$ and $p_2(s_2, e_2)$ are *overlapping* if and only if $s_1 < s_2 \leq e_1 < e_2$ or $s_2 < s_1 \leq e_2 < e_1$. We denote the *overlapping* relationship by $\sim$. We also say that $p_1(s_1, e_1)$ is *embedded* in $p_2(s_2, e_2)$ if and only if $s_2 \leq s_1 \leq e_1 \leq e_2$, and denote the *embedded* relationship by $\prec$.

In the RRE task, we try to split a source sentence into some *non-overlapping* and *non-embedded* logical parts. Let S be the set of all possible logical parts, $S = \{p(s,e) | 1 \leq s \leq e \leq n, p \in P\}$. A *solution* of the RRE task is a subset $y \subseteq S$ which does not violate the *overlapping* relationship and the *embedded* relationship. Formally, the *solution space* can be described as follows: $Y = \{y \subseteq S | \forall u, v \in y, u \nsim v, u \nprec v\}$. The learning problem in the RRE task is to learn a function $R : X \to Y$ from a set of m training samples $\{(x^i, y^i) | x^i \in X, y^i \in Y, \forall i = 1, 2, \ldots, m\}$.

One important characteristic of our task is that the input sentences are usually very long and complicated, so the logical parts are also long.

We model the RRE task as a sequence labeling problem, in which each sentence is a sequence of words. Figure 3 illustrates an example in IOB notation. In this notation, the first word of a part is tagged by B, the other words of the part are tagged by I, and a word not included in any part is tagged by O. This law sentence consists of an antecedent part (tag A) and a consequent part (tag C) (we will use this example for all the sections of this paper).

In the RRE task, we consider two types of law sentences: *implication type*[1] and *equivalence type*. Figure 4 shows the logical structure of a law sentence in the equivalence type. In this type, a sentence consists of a *left equivalent part* and a *right equivalent part*. The requisite part is the left equivalent part, and the effectuation part is the right equivalent part. In all, we have 7 kinds of parts, as follows:

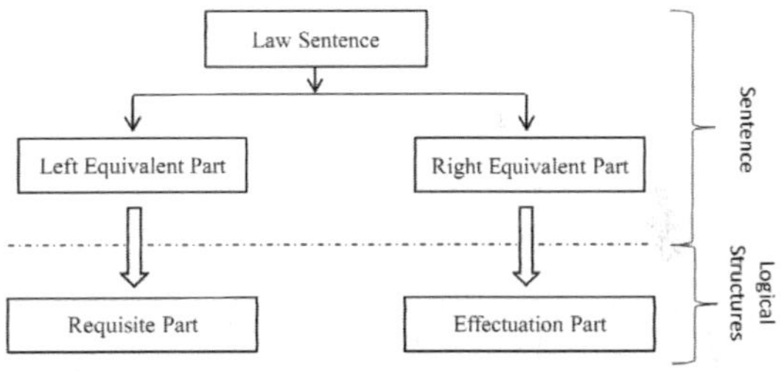

Figure 4: The logical structure of a law sentence in the equivalence type.

1. Implication sentences:
   - Antecedent part (A)
   - Consequent part (C)
   - Three kinds of topic parts T_1, T_2, T_3 (correspond to case 1, case 2, and case 3)
2. Equivalence sentences:
   - The left equivalent part (EL)
   - The right equivalent part (ER)

[1]The logical structure of a law sentence in this type is shown in Figure 1.

Source Sentence	<A>被保険者期間を計算する場合には、</A><C>月によるものとする。</C> *(When a period of an insured is calculated, it is based on a month.)*																
Word Sequence	被 *hi*	保険 *hoken*	者 *sha*	期間 *kikan*	を *wo*	計算 *keisan*	する *suru*	場合 *baai*	に *ni*	は *wa*	、	月 *tsuki*	による *niyoru*	もの *mono*	と *to*	する *suru*	。
Tag Sequence	B-A	I-A	I-A	I-A	I-A	I-A	I-A	I-A	I-A	I-A	I-A	B-C	I-C	I-C	I-C	I-C	I-C

Figure 3: A law sentence in the IOB notation.

In the IOB notation, we will have 15 kinds of tags: B-A, I-A, B-C, I-C, B-T_1, I-T_1, B-T_2, I-T_2, B-T_3, I-T_3, B-EL, I-EL, B-ER, I-ER, and O[2]. For example, an element with tag B-A begins an antecedent part, while an element with tag B-C begins a consequent part.

2.2 Discriminative Sequence Learning Models

In this section, we briefly introduce three discriminative sequence learning models for RRE problems.

2.2.1 Conditional Random Fields

Conditional Random Fields (CRFs) (Lafferty et al., 01) are undirected graphical models used to calculate the conditional probability of values on designated output nodes, given values assigned to other designated input nodes for data sequences. CRFs make a first-order Markov independence assumption among output nodes, and thus correspond to finite state machine (FSMs).

Let $\mathbf{o} = (o_1, o_2, \ldots, o_T)$ be some observed input data sequence, such as a sequence of words in a text (values on T input nodes of the graphical model). Let $\mathbf{S}$ be a finite set of FSM states, each is associated with a label l such as a clause start position. Let $\mathbf{s} = (s_1, s_2, \ldots, s_T)$ be some sequences of states (values on T output nodes). CRFs define the conditional probability of a state sequence given an input sequence to be

$$P_\Lambda(s|o) = \frac{1}{Z_o} exp\left(\sum_{t=1}^{T} F(s, o, t)\right) \qquad (1)$$

where $Z_o = \sum_s exp\left(\sum_{t=1}^{T} F(s, o, t)\right)$ is a normalization factor over all state sequences. We denote δ to be the Kronecker-δ. Let $F(s, o, t)$ be the sum of CRFs features at time position t:

$$\sum_i \lambda_i f_i(s_{t-1}, s_t, t) + \sum_j \lambda_j g_j(o, s_t, t) \qquad (2)$$

[2]Tag O is used for an element not included in any part.

where $f_i(s_{t-1}, s_t, t) = \delta(s_{t-1}, l')\delta(s_t, l)$ is a *transition* feature function which represents sequential dependencies by combining the label l' of the previous state s_{t-1} and the label l of the current state s_t, such as the previous label $l' = B - A$ and the current label $l = I - A$. $g_j(o, s_t, t) = \delta(s_t, l)x_k(o, t)$ is a *per-state* feature function which combines the label l of current state s_t and a context predicate, i.e., the binary function $x_k(o, t)$ that captures a particular property of the observation sequence o at time position t. For instance, the current label is $B - A$ and the current word is *"conditional"*.

Training CRFs is commonly performed by maximizing the likelihood function with respect to the training data using advanced convex optimization techniques like L-BFGS. Recently, several works apply Stochastic Gradient Descent (SGD) for training CRFs models. SGD has been historically associated with back-propagation algorithms in multilayer neural networks.

Inference in CRFs, i.e., searching the most likely output label sequence of an input observation sequence, can be done using the Viterbi algorithm.

2.2.2 Online Passive-Aggressive Learning

Online Passive-Aggressive Learning (PA) was proposed by Crammer (Crammer et al, 2006) as an alternative learning algorithm to the maximize margin algorithm. The PA algorithm has been shown to be successful for many sequence classification tasks. The details of the PA algorithm for RRE task are presented as follows.

Assume that we are given a set of sentences x_i and their labels y_i where $i = 1, ..., n$. Let the feature mapping between a sentence x and a sequence of labels y be: $\Phi(x, y) = \Phi_1(x, y), \Phi_2(x, y), ..., \Phi_d(x, y)$ where each feature mapping Φ_j maps (x, y) to a real value. We assume that each feature $\Phi(x, y)$ is associated with a weight value. The goal of PA learning for sequence learning tasks is to obtain a parameter w that minimizes the

Source Sentence	<A>被保険者期間を計算する場合には、</A><C>月によるものとする。</C> (*When a period of an insured is calculated, it is based on a month.*)																
Original Sequence	被 *hi*	保険 *hoken*	者 *sha*	期間 *kikan*	を *wo*	計算 *keisan*	する *suru*	場合 *baai*	に *ni*	は *wa*	、	月 *tsuki*	による *niyoru*	もの *mono*	と *to*	する *suru*	。
Original Tag	B-A	I-A	I-A	I-A	I-A	I-A	I-A	I-A	I-A	I-A	I-A	B-C	I-C	I-C	I-C	I-C	I-C
Bunsetsu	1					2		3				4		5		6	
New Tag	B-A					I-A		I-A				B-C		I-C		I-C	

Figure 5: New setting for RRE task.

hinge-loss function and the margin of learning data.

1 Input: $S = (x_i; y_i), i = 1, 2, ..., n$ in which x_i is the sentence and y_i is a sequence of labels
2 Output: the model
3 Initialize: $w_1 = (0, 0, ..., 0)$
4 **for** *t=1, 2...* **do**
5 Receive an sentence x_t
6 Predict $y_t^* = \arg\max_{y \in Y}(w_t.\Phi(x_t, y_t))$
Suffer loss: $l_t = w_t.\Phi(x_t, y_t^*) - w_t.\Phi(x_t, y_t) + \sqrt{\rho(y_t, y_t^*)}$
7 Set:$\tau_t = \frac{l_t}{||\Phi(x_t, y_t^*) - \Phi(x_t, y_t)||^2}$
8 Update: $w_{t+1} = w_t + \tau_t(\Phi(x_t, y_t) - \Phi(x_t, y_t^*))$
9 **end**

Algorithm 1: The Passive-Aggressive algorithm for RRE task.

Algorithm 1 shows briefly the Online Learning for sequence learning problem. The detail about this algorithm can be referred to the work of (Crammer et al, 2006). In Line 7, the argmax value is computed by using the Viterbi algorithm. Algorithm 1 is terminated after T rounds [3]

2.2.3 Feature Set

In the previous setting (Ngo et al., 10), we model the RRE task as a sequence labeling problem in which elements of sequences are words. Because a sentence may contain many words, the length of a sequence becomes large. Our idea is that, instead of considering words as elements, we consider each Bunsetsu as an element. This can be done because no Bunsetsu can belong to two different parts in this task. By doing this, we can reduce the length of sequences significantly. The process of obtaining a new setting from the previous one is illustrated in Figure 5.

In this example, the length of the sequence is reduced from 17 to 6. On average, in the Japanese National Pension Law corpus, the length of a sequence with the old setting (words) is **47.3**, while only **17.6** with the new setting (Bunsetsus).

We use features including head words, functional words, punctuations, and the co-occurrence of head words and functional words in a window size 1. A window size 1 in this model will cover three Bunsetsu. So, it is much longer than a window size 2 (which covers five words) in a model based on words. This is the reason why a window size 1 is sufficient in this model. The results show that modeling based on Bunsetsu, an important unit in Japanese sentences, is suitable for the RRE task.

There are two reasons that may explain why the Bunsetsu-based model is better than the word-based model. The first reason is that Bunsetsus are basic units in analyzing Japanese (in fact, dependency parsing of Japanese based on Bunsetsus, not words). Bunsetsus convey the meaning of a sentence better than words. In the Bunsetsu-based model, we only use head words and functional words to represent a Bunsetsu. Hence, the Bunsetsu-based model also take advantages of the model using head words and functional words. The second reason is that the Bunsetsu-based model reduces the length of sequences significantly compared with the word-based models. It helps the Bunsetsu-based model so much in the learning process. We choose the IOE strategy for our RRE task because this representation attained highest results on our development set (Ngo et al., 10).

3 A Simple Semi-Supervised Learning Method for RRE

This section describes a brief survey of semi-supervised learning, and presents a simple semi-supervised method for the RRE task using Brown word clusters (Brown et al., 92).

3.1 Brown Clustering

The Brown clustering algorithm is a word clustering algorithm based on the mutual information of bigrams (Brown et al., 92). The input to the algorithm is a set of words and a text corpus. In the initial step, each word belongs to its own individual clus-

[3] T is set to 10 in our experiments.

ter. The algorithm then gradually groups clusters to build a hierarchical clustering of words.

Figure 6 shows an example of Brown word-cluster hierarchy in a binary tree style. In this tree, each leaf node corresponds to a word, which is uniquely identified by the path from the root node to it. This path can be represented by a bit string, as shown in Figure 6. From the root node, we add bit 0 to the left branch and bit 1 to the right branch. A word-cluster hierarchy is reduced to depth n if all words with the same n-bit prefix are grouped in one cluster. For example, if the word-cluster hierarchy in Figure 6 is reduced to depth 2, we will obtain a new hierarchy in Figure 7.

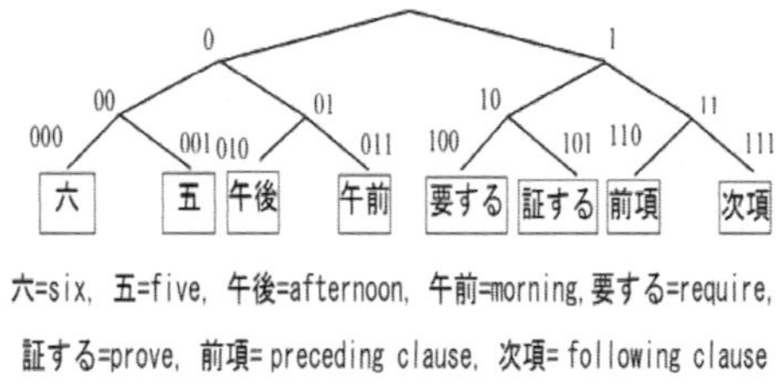

Figure 6: An example of Brown word-cluster hierarchy.

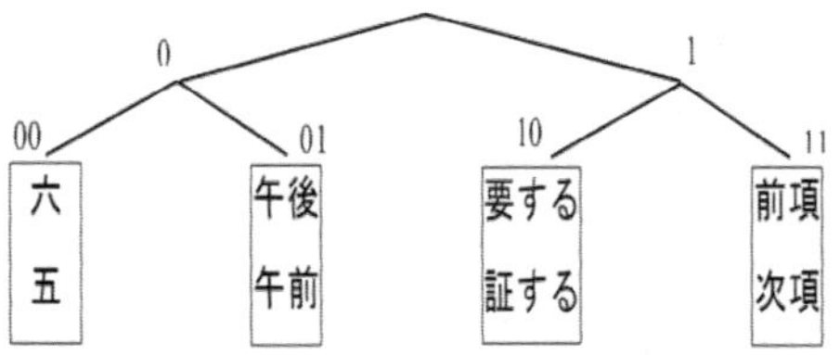

Figure 7: A Brown word-cluster hierarchy after reduction to depth 2.

Features extracted at n-bit depth are binary strings with length n. By reducing the word-cluster tree to different values of depth n, we can group words at various levels, from coarse clusters (small value of n) to fine clusters (large value of n).

3.2 RRE with Extra Word Features

The main idea of our semi-supervised learning method is to use *unsupervised* word representations as extra word features of a *supervised* model. We use Brown word clusters as the word representation method. In this framework, *unlabeled data* are used to produce word clusters. From these word clusters, we extract extra word features, and add these features to a *supervised* model (*labeled data* are used to train this model). Figure 8 shows our semi-supervised learning framework. This framework consists of two phase: *unsupervised* phase with the Brown clustering algorithm, and *supervised* phase with CRFs.

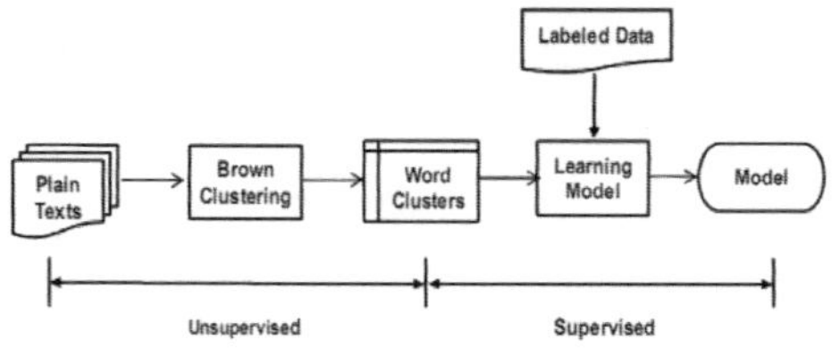

Figure 8: Semi-supervised learning framework.

To produce word representations, we first collected plain text from the address http://www.japaneselawtranslation.go.jp[4]. Our plain text corpus includes more than 13 thousand sentences about Japanese laws. After word segmenting (using Cabocha tool [5]), we conducted the Brown clustering algorithm to cluster words. In our work, we used the implementation of Percy Liang (Liang 05), and the number of clusters was set to 200. Experimental results showed that CRFs-LBFG obtained highest result in both supervised and semi-supervised experiments. In order to consider the impact of learning size to RRE tasks, we do an experiment with various size of training data.

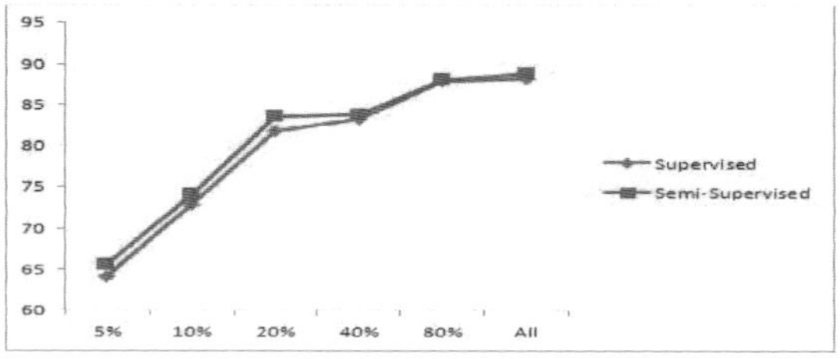

Figure 9: Comparison between the supervised method and the semi-supervised method with respect to the training sizes and F-measure scores.

The result in Fig 9 clearly showed that semi-supervised models are useful for RRE tasks with respect to various size of training data.

[4]This website provides many Japanese law articles in both Japanese and English.

[5]http://chasen.org/ taku/software/cabocha/

4 Experimental Results

We test our system on the corpus of Japanese National Pension Law, using F-measure for evaluation.

4.1 Corpus and Evaluation Method

This sub-section presents our corpus for the RRE task and evaluation method.The Japanese National Pension Law corpus includes 764 annotated Japanese law sentences[6]. Some statistics on this corpus are shown in Table 1. We have some remarks to make here. First, about 98.5% of sentences belong to the implication type, and only 1.5% of sentences belong to the equivalence type. Second, about 83.5% of topic parts are T_2, 15.2% of topic parts are T_3, and only 1.3% of topic parts are T_1. Finally, four main types of parts, C, A, T_2, and T_3 make up more than 98.3% of all types.

4.2 Evaluation Method

We divided the corpus into 10 sets and performed 10-fold cross-validation tests. The results were evaluated using precision, recall, and $F_{\beta=1}$ scores as follows:

$$precision = \frac{\#\text{correct parts}}{\#\text{predicted parts}}, recall = \frac{\#\text{correct parts}}{\#\text{actual parts}} \tag{3}$$

$$F_{\beta=1} = \frac{2 * precision * recall}{precision + recall} \tag{4}$$

A logical part is recognized correctly if and only if it has correct start word, correct end word, and correct part category (kind of logical part).

4.3 Experimental Results

Table 1 shows the comparison of three discriminative learning methods for RRE tasks. Three sequence learning methods include: CRFs using the LBFGS method, CRFs with SGD, and Online Learning. Experiment results show that the CRFs-LBFGS is the best in comparison with others. However, the computational times for training is slower than either SGD or Online Learning. The SGD is faster than CRF-LBFS approximately 6 times.

Note that we used CRF++ [7] for Conditional Random Fields using LBFGS, and for Stochastic Gradient Descent (SGD) we used SGD1.3 which is developed by Leon Bottou [8].

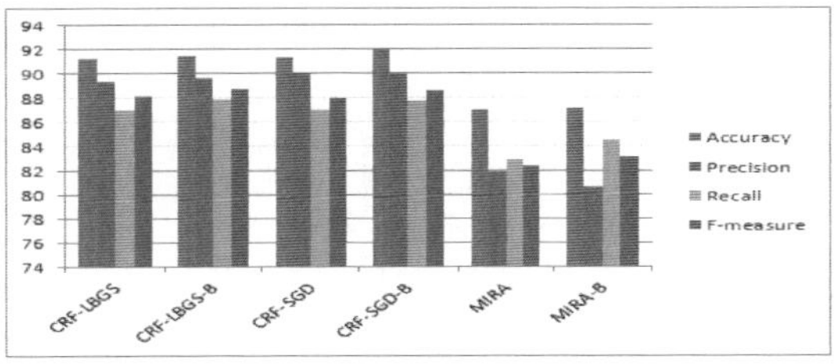

Figure 10: Comparison between the supervised method and the semi-supervised method.

For the RRE task, we extracted features at 4-bit depth and 6-bit depth. We integrated these features into three sequence learning models: CRFs-LBFG, CRF-SGD, and online learning (MIRA). The experimental results of the semi-supervised method with extra word features are shown in Figure 10. In three models, the semi-supervised method outperforms the supervised method. For CRF-LBFG model, the $F_{\beta=1}$ score was 88.80%, compared with 88.18% for the supervised method. The CRF-sgd model got 88.58% in the $F_{\beta=1}$ score, compared with 88.03% for the supervised method. MIRA method got 82.3% and 83.21% for supervised and semi-supervised models. In conclusion, word cluster models significantly improve the performance of sequence learning models for RRE tasks. We believe that word cluster models are also suitable for other sequence learning models.

5 Conclusions

In this paper, we report an investigation of developing a RRE task using discriminative learning models and semi-supervised models. Experimental results using 10 Folds cross-validation test have showed that the discriminative models are well suitable for RRE task. Conditional random fields show a better performance in comparison with other methods. In addition, word cluster models are suitable for improving the performance of sequence learning models for RRE tasks.

[6] The corpus consists of only the first sentence of each article.

[7] http://crfpp.sourceforge.net/

[8] http://leon.bottou.org/projects/sgd

Table 1: Statistics on the Japanese National Pension Law corpus.

Sentence Type	Number	Part Type	Number
Equivalence	11	EL	11
		ER	11
Implication	753	**C**	**745**
		A	**429**
		T_1	9
		$\mathbf{T}_2$	**562**
		$\mathbf{T}_3$	**102**

Table 2: Experimental results with sequence learning models for RRE task.

Methods	Accuracy	Precision	Recall	F-measure
CRF-LBFG	91.27	89.328%	87.039%	88.158
CRF-LBFG-B	91.45	89.708%	87.866%	88.807
CRF-SGD	91.39	90.046%	86.953%	88.023
CRF-SGD-B	92.041	90.011%	87.787%	88.584
MIRA	87.081	81.881%	82.909%	82.339
MIRA-B	87.139	80.679%	84.59%	83.213

There are still room for improving the performance of RRE tasks. For example, more attention on features selection is necessary. We would like to solve this in future work.

Acknowledgments

The work on this paper was partly supported by the grants for Grants-in-Aid for Young Scientific Research 22700139.

References

K. Crammer et al. 2006. Online Passive-Aggressive Algorithm. Journal of Machine Learning Research, 2006

P.F. Brown, P.V. deSouza, R.L. Mercer, V.J.D. Pietra, J.C. Lai. Class-Based n-gram Models of Natural Language. *Computational Linguistics*, Volume 18, Issue 4, pp.467-479, 1992.

X. Carreras, L. Màrquez, J. Castro. Filtering-Ranking Perceptron Learning for Partial Parsing. *Machine Learning*, Volume 60, pp.41-71, 2005.

M. Collins. Discriminative Training Methods for Hidden Markov Models: Theory and Experiments with Perceptron Algorithms. In *Proceedings of EMNLP*, pp.1-8, 2002.

T. Katayama. Legal engineering - an engineering approach to laws in e-society age. In *Proceedings of the 1st International Workshop on JURISIN*, 2007.

T. Kudo, K. Yamamoto, Y. Matsumoto. Applying conditional random fields to Japanese morphological analysis. In *Proceedings of EMNLP*, pp.230-237, 2004.

J. Lafferty, A. McCallum, F. Pereira. Conditional Random Fields: Probabilistic Models for Segmenting and Labeling Sequence Data. In *Proceedings of ICML*, pp.282-289, 2001.

P. Liang. Semi-Supervised Learning for Natural Language. *Master's thesis, Massachusetts Institute of Technology*, 2005.

M. Murata, K. Uchimoto, Q. Ma, H. Isahara. Bunsetsu identification using category-exclusive rules. In *Proceedings of COLING*, pp.565-571, 2000.

Ngo Xuan Bach, Nguyen Le Minh, Akira Shimazu. Recognition of Requisite Part and Effectuation Part in Law Sentences. In Proceedings of (ICCPOL), pp. 29-34, San Francisco California USA, July 2010

M. Nakamura, S. Nobuoka, A. Shimazu. Towards Translation of Legal Sentences into Logical Forms. In *Proceedings of the 1st International Workshop on JURISIN*, 2007.

E.T.K. Sang, S. Buchholz. Introduction to the CoNLL-2000 Shared Task: Chunking. In *Proceedings of CoNLL*, pp.127-132, 2000.

K. Tanaka, I. Kawazoe, H. Narita. Standard structure of legal provisions - for the legal knowledge processing by natural language. In *IPSJ Research Report on Natural Language Processing*, pp.79-86, 1993.

V.N. Vapnik. Statistical learning theory. New York: Wiley, pp.339-371, 1998.

Compiling Simple Context Restrictions with Nondeterministic Automata

Anssi Yli-Jyrä
The Department of Modern Languages, PO Box 3, 00014 University of Helsinki, Finland
anssi.yli-jyra@helsinki.fi

Abstract

This paper describes a non-conventional method for compiling (phonological or morpho-syntactic) context restriction (CR) constraints into non-deterministic automata in finite-state tools and surface parsing systems. The method reduces any CR into a simple one that constraints the occurrences of the empty string and represents right contexts with co-determististic states. In cases where a fully deterministic representation would be exponentially larger, this kind of *inward* determinism in contexts can bring benefits over various De Morgan approaches where full determinization is necessary. In the method, an accepted word gets a unique path that is a projection of a ladder-shaped structure in the context recognizer. This projection is computed in time that is polynomial to the number of context states. However, it may be difficult to take advantage of the method in a finite-state library that coerces intermediate results into canonical automata and whose intersection operation assumes deterministic automata.

1 Introduction

Context restriction (CR) constraints and the related extended regular expression operator ($\Rightarrow$) are included in some widely used finite state compilers (such as XFST, SFST, and FOMA) and is a standard part of Two Level Morphology (Koskenniemi, 1983). In addition, context-sensitive rewriting (e.g. XFST replace rules) have an inherent connection to CR constraints and their implementation can be based on them (Yli-Jyrä, 2008a). Optimized CR compilation methods can thus bring advantage to a wide range of applications.

The current work presents a complement-free method that has some advantages and disadvantages in comparison with the commonly used De Morgan implementations of the inherent universal quantification of CRs. It expresses the universal quantification positively, by recognizing ladder-shaped structures between deterministic left contexts and co-deterministic right contexts and by projecting them to accepted words. The complexity of the method is analyzed here, but a fuller evaluation remains for further work.

1.1 The Use of CR Constraints

Let Σ be the (pair symbol) alphabet over which all the words are defined. A *context restriction (CR)* constraint checks the occurrences of a pattern in the words. For example, a phonological constraint (Koskenniemi, 1983) such as

$$\mathtt{p:m} \Rightarrow \Sigma^*\mathtt{n:m}\_\Sigma^*, \qquad (1)$$

specifies a formal language $L \subseteq \Sigma^*$ where the (pair) symbol $\mathtt{p:m}$ may occur only when immediately preceded by the symbol $\mathtt{n:m}$. The left hand side ($\mathtt{p:m}$) describes the constrained *pattern* while the right hand side ($\Sigma^*\mathtt{n:m}\_\Sigma^*$) specifies the *contexts* to which the pattern occurrences are restricted.

More generally, the CR constraints have the form $\alpha \Rightarrow \lambda_1\_\rho_1, ..., \lambda_k\_\rho_k$, where k is the *number of contexts*, the variable α stands for the pattern, and the variables $\lambda_1, ..., \lambda_k, \rho_1, ..., \rho_k$ constitute k contexts in pairs. Each variable is a recognizable subset

Proceedings of the 9th International Workshop on Finite State Methods and Natural Language Processing, pages 30–38, Blois (France), July 12-15, 2011. ©2011 Association for Computational Linguistics

of Σ^* and is usually given through a regular expression. We assume that every context (λ_ρ) is *total* i.e. it reaches the word boundaries although most implementations (e.g. FOMA) require word boundary markers (.#. λ_ρ .#.) in this case.

In the original use scenario – Two Level Morphology – CRs typically restrict allophonemes or allomorphophonemes to a relatively small number of contexts. More recently, CR has been used to express complete morphological lexicons in which case the total number of contexts can be in thousands (Yli-Jyrä, 2009).

CR constraints can also be applied to morphosyntax and surface syntax where the total number of conjunctive CR constraints can be significantly higher than in phonology. In an early manifestation of Finite State Intersection Grammar (FSIG) (Koskenniemi et al., 1992; Yli-Jyrä, 2003), both the patterns and the contexts were linguistically informed but quite complicated. More recent FSIG formalisms focus on local bracketed tree constraints (Yli-Jyrä, 2005) that are motivated by the well-known succinctness characteristics of packed forests.

Some of the decision problems for extended regular expressions and CRs in particular (Måns Hulden, pers.comm. 2010) are intractable and the state complexity of a compiled CR can be prohibitively large in the worst case scenarios. Therefore, the basic research on CR compilation algorithms increasingly tries to identify *islands of tractability* for the CR compilation problem so that larger systems could exploit CR and context-sensitive constraints without efficiency bottlenecks.

1.2 Prior Compilation Techniques

There are six important approaches (SF, GR, FO, IC, PF, WL) to the compilation of the CR constraints. Let us describe each of them in turn.

1. **SF: Star-Free Regular Expressions**

   The closure of the empty set $\emptyset$ and the singleton languages $\{w\}$ $(w \in \Sigma^*)$ under the operations of concatenation $(\cdot)$, intersection $(\cap)$ and complement $(^-)$ defines the *star-free* i.e. *counter-free* languages (McNaughton and Papert, 1971). Note that $\overline{\alpha \cap \beta} = \overline{\alpha} \cup \overline{\beta}$ (by De Morgan's laws) and $\overline{\emptyset} = \Sigma^*$. The star-free operators $(\cdot, \cap, \cup, ^-)$ give a compilation formula for CRs with $k = 1$ (Koskenniemi, 1983, 106):

   $$\overline{\overline{\lambda_1}\alpha\overline{\emptyset}} \cap \overline{\overline{\emptyset}\alpha\overline{\rho_1}} \tag{2}$$

   However, the length of the formula grows exponentially when k grows, being already high for two bilateral contexts (Yli-Jyrä, 2003):

   $$\overline{\overline{\lambda_2}\alpha\overline{\rho_1}} \cap \overline{\overline{\lambda_1}\alpha\overline{\rho_2}} \cap \overline{(\overline{\lambda_1} \cap \overline{\lambda_2})\alpha\overline{\emptyset}} \cap \overline{\overline{\emptyset}\alpha(\overline{\rho_1} \cap \overline{\rho_2})}. \tag{3}$$

2. **IC: Indexed Contexts**

   Karttunen et al. (1987) observe that when the pattern language α consists of atomic symbols, a multi context CR can be decomposed into simple CRs. This is done by indexing every atomic symbol in α by the context pairs $\lambda_i\_\rho_i$. The idea has two implementations:

   (a) In Karttunen et al. (1987) and Kaplan and Kay (1994), the atomic symbols are surrounded by indexed brackets. The method needs an extended alphabet such as $\Sigma \cup \{\langle_1, ..., \langle_k\} \cup \{\rangle_1, ..., \rangle_k\}$.

   (b) In Koskenniemi and Silfverberg (2010), the atomic symbols are themselves indexed. This method needs an extended alphabet such as $\Sigma \times \{1, ..., k\}$. Thus, each symbol in α is divided into k different variants, $\alpha_1, ..., \alpha_k$.

   In order to reflect the extended alphabet Σ', languages $\lambda_1, ..., \lambda_k, \rho_1, ..., \rho_k$ have to be replaced with the expanded ones $\lambda'_1, ..., \lambda'_k, \rho'_1, ..., \rho'_k$. The indexing is later cancelled by an appropriate homomorphism $g : \Sigma'^* \to \Sigma^*$ and the CR semantics is finally given by the formula

   $$g(\cap_{i=1}^{k} \alpha_i \Rightarrow \lambda'_i\_\rho'_i). \tag{4}$$

   The recognizer for the result is nondeterministic, but it is unclear if the result is ever smaller than a canonical automaton. Nevertheless, the extended alphabet has an undesirable effect on the number of transitions in various stages of the compilation process.

   The approach has been generalized beyond the atomic symbols to a slightly larger family of patterns languages: a modified IC formula applies to the case where, for all $w, w' \in \alpha$, the words w and w' are overlap-free or equivalent (Yli-Jyrä and Koskenniemi, 2004, formula 16 on page 18). The formula resembles an implementation of replace rules Kempe and Karttunen (1996) and is related to a former implementation of the CR operator in Xerox Finite State Tool (XFST) (Yli-Jyrä, 2003; Yli-Jyrä and Koskenniemi, 2004; Karttunen, 2004).

3. **GR: SF with a Restricted Homomorphism**

   The *generalized restriction (GR)* operation (Yli-Jyrä and Koskenniemi, 2004) increases the compactness of star-free expressions by using a marker alphabet Δ, such that $\Delta \cap \Sigma = \emptyset$, and an operation that removes a finite number of markers from words.

   Let $\Sigma_\Delta = \Sigma \cup \{\Delta\}$ and let $f : \Sigma_\Delta^* \to \Sigma^*$ be a string homomorphism defined by $h(a) = a$, $h(\diamond) = \epsilon$, $h(\epsilon) = \epsilon$, $h(x \cdot y) = h(x) \cdot h(y)$ for all $a \in \Sigma$, $\diamond \in \Delta$. Within the method, the homomorphism h can be replaced with its restriction $h_d = h_{|(\overline{\emptyset}(\Delta\overline{\emptyset})^d)}$ where $d \in \mathbb{N}$. Since star-free languages are closed under the restriction of h_d, it extends star-free regular expressions.

   For all $d \in \mathbb{N}$, the GR operation is syntactically represented by the operator $\overset{d\Delta}{\Longrightarrow}$ whose semantics is defined over d-marker languages $W, W' \subseteq \overline{\emptyset}(\Delta\overline{\emptyset})^d$ by

   $$W \overset{d\Delta}{\Longrightarrow} W' = \overline{h_d(W - W')}. \tag{5}$$

   We will call the left side, W, the *pattern (language)* and the opposite side, W', the *context (language)*. Let $\Delta = \{\diamond\}$. The semantics of a CR constraint is expressed by:

   $$(\overline{\emptyset}\diamond\alpha\diamond\overline{\emptyset}) \overset{2\Delta}{\Longrightarrow} \cup_{i=1}^{k}(\lambda_n\diamond\alpha\diamond\rho_n). \tag{6}$$

   Note that (5) requires a deterministic or codeterministic recognizer for W'.

4. **FO: A Fragment of Second-Order Logic**

   Various logical formalisms have been used for defining the semantics of the CR operation exactly (Koskenniemi, 1983; Yli-Jyrä and Koskenniemi, 2004; Vaillette, 2004; Hulden, 2008). Koskenniemi (1983, 36) defines a CR with $k = 1$ through a logical expression (7) but did not explicate any model-theoretic semantics of the logic itself.

   $$\begin{aligned}&\{w|(w = vxy \wedge x \in \alpha)\\ &\to (v \in \Sigma^*\lambda_1 \wedge y \in \rho_1\Sigma^*)\}.\end{aligned} \tag{7}$$

   In finite model theory, the semantics of the CR operation can be defined precisely through monadic second-order logic (MSO) or, if the operands are star-free, in its first-order (FO) fragment. In both cases, the formula is interpreted over finite words. The semantics of MSO relies on automata over an extended alphabet, reflecting the power set of the variables in the formula. For example, variables v and y would induce the extended alphabet $\Sigma' = \Sigma \times 2^{\{v,y\}}$.

   In Yli-Jyrä and Koskenniemi (2004) and Hulden (2008), the semantics of FO variables has been defined with markers. The markers are often cheaper than the set-based encoding of FO variables as they extend the alphabet only by one new symbol per variable.

   Customized predicate logics (Vaillette, 2004; Hulden, 2008) add syntactic sugar to the usual MSO logic through substring variables $x, y, z, \ldots$. In addition, regular expressions α, λ_1, ρ_1 etc. can be used in the predicates. With these extensions, the model theoretic semantics of CR can be expressed through such elegant formulas as

   $$(\forall x)(\mathit{matches}(x, \alpha) \to \mathit{btw}(x, \lambda_1, \rho_1)). \tag{8}$$

5. **PF: Prefix-Free Patterns**

   If we assume that that the pattern α (as a set of strings) does not contain proper prefixes (symmetrically: proper suffixes), one marker in the GR pattern language becomes redundant. This observation helps to reduce the 2-marker GR approach to a 1-marker GR approach whenever the assumption holds for the patttern α:

   $$(\overline{\emptyset}\diamond\alpha\overline{\emptyset}) \overset{1\Delta}{\Longrightarrow} \cup_{i=1}^{k}(\lambda_n\diamond\alpha\rho_n).$$

CRs with prefix-free patterns occur naturally inside the XFST-style replace rules (Yli-Jyrä, 2008b), bracketed FSIGs (Yli-Jyrä, 2008a), and partition-based grammars (Grimley-Evans et al., 1996). In these applications, each pattern match can be unambiguously marked with one marker only.

The assumption of prefix-freeness is trivially true when $\alpha \subseteq \Sigma$. This assumption was used in Yli-Jyrä (2009), where also an optimized compilation algorithm for the 1-marker GR was presented.

A variant of this approach is in place in Partition Based Two Level Morphology (Grimley-Evans et al., 1996) where multi character patterns form adjacent blocks into which the whole word is implicitly partitioned. As each of the block is bracketed, the blocks cannot be prefixes or suffixes of one another.

6. **WL: Weighted Logic**

The weighted MSO logic (Droste and Gastin, 2009) can be used to define the characteristic series $\mathbb{1}_L \in \mathbb{B}\langle\langle\Sigma^*\rangle\rangle$ of any recognizable language $L \in \Sigma^*$ and, in particular, of the language of the constraint $\alpha \Rightarrow \lambda_1 - \rho_1, ..., \lambda_k - \rho_k$. For any word $w \in c_1...c_n \in \Sigma^*$, assume that $\alpha'(v,y), \lambda'_1(v), ..., \lambda'_k(v), \rho'_1(y), ..., \rho'_k(y)$ are appropriate wMSO($\mathbb{B}, \Sigma$) formulas defining the membership tests $(c_v...c_y \in \alpha)$, $(c_1...c_{v-1} \in \lambda_1)$, ..., $(c_1...c_{v-1} \in \lambda_k)$, $(c_{y+1}...c_n \in \lambda_1)$, ..., $(c_{y+1}...c_n \in \lambda_k)$. Then the formula

$$\forall v.\forall y.(\alpha'(v,y) \rightarrow \vee_{i=1}^{k} \lambda'_i(v) \wedge \rho'_i(y))$$

defines the characteristic series $\mathbb{1}_L$ for the constraint $\alpha \Rightarrow \lambda_1 - \rho_1, ..., \lambda_k - \rho_k$.

Each universally quantified variable must be eliminated separately because each elimination asserts that the quantifier's scope is expressing a *recognizable step function* (Droste and Gastin, 2009). This is contrasted to the (unweighted) predicate logic of Hulden (2008) where the quantified variables are defined over position pairs. The elimination of the weighted universal quantifiers has been described in the proof of Lemma 5.4 in Droste and Gastin (2009)

In sum, the prior CR compilation methods can be characterized, on average, by the following properties:

1. a product alphabet (IC, (FO,) WL)
2. the pattern-context contrast (all)
3. substring quantification (all but PF, WL)
4. relies on deterministic automata (all)
5. uses De Morgan duals (nearly all)
6. unavoidable DFA result (SF, GR, FO, PF).

1.3 The Overview of the Unconventional Approach

The method presented in the following sections is nonconventional in many respects as it takes advantage of the following observations:

1. **O(1) Markers.** The GR method has demonstrated that adding $O(1)$ markers to the alphabet is enough. We will thus use markers instead of a heavily extended alphabet. This also means that we start our thinking from the GR operation.

2. **Patternless GR.** One of the operands of the GR operation can be eliminated as the pattern $W \subseteq \overline{\emptyset}\diamond\overline{\emptyset}$ can be moved to the right side of the GR without any effect on the semantics: $\left(W \stackrel{1\Delta}{\Longrightarrow} W'\right) = \left(\overline{\emptyset}\diamond\overline{\emptyset} \stackrel{1\Delta}{\Longrightarrow} (W' \cup \overline{W})\right)$. The resulting *patternless* GR can be viewed as a form of a universal quantifier:

$$\left(\overline{\emptyset}\diamond\overline{\emptyset} \stackrel{1\Delta}{\Longrightarrow} W''\right) = \{c_1...c_n \mid \forall i \in \{0,...,n\}.c_1...c_i\diamond c_{i+1}...c_n \in W''\}. \quad (9)$$

3. **One Position.** The quantified positions can be eliminated one by one. A patternless 2-marker GR where $\Delta = \{\diamond_1, \diamond_2\}$ and $W' \subseteq W = \overline{\emptyset}\diamond_1\overline{\emptyset}\diamond_2\overline{\emptyset}$ reduces to a pair of nested 1-marker GRs:

$$\left(W \stackrel{2\Delta}{\Longrightarrow} W'\right) = \left(\overline{\emptyset}\diamond\overline{\emptyset} \stackrel{1\{\diamond_1\}}{\Longrightarrow} \left(\overline{\emptyset}\diamond\overline{\emptyset} \stackrel{1\{\diamond_2\}}{\Longrightarrow} W'\right)\right). \quad (10)$$

The approach is comparable to weighted logic where one *cannot generally* remove two universally quantified variables at once because the resulting weighted automaton is not necessarily finite.

4. **Determinism and Co-determinism.** Combinations of left and right sequential transducers (Johnson, 1972; Skut et al., 2004; Peikov, 2006) have been applied in the compilation of context-dependent rewriting rules. Analogously, the recognizer for the context language W' can be determinized and co-determinized "inwards", towards the marker (Section 2.3).

5. **No Complementations.** The local structure of the "inward" deterministic recognizer for the pattern language W' can be used directly as if it were a readily compiled constraint (Section 3). Thus, the "double complementation" needed by many prior methods is avoided.

6. **NFA Result.** The compilation can result into a nondeterministic automaton (NFA). In applications, NFAs can be used as constraints since they are closed under the intersection operation.

The rest of the paper is committed to the realization of the new core operation: the patternless GR $(\bar{\emptyset}\diamond\bar{\emptyset} \overset{1\{\diamond_2\}}{\Longrightarrow} W')$. A patternless GR operation can express a CR or even a combination of CRs. This operation is described in Section 3.

Before the section, some prerequisites are given (Section 2), and after the section, the paper is concluded with complexity analysis and remarks (Section 4).

2 The Prerequisites

2.1 Automata

For overviews and the terminology of finite automata, the reader is referred to a text book such as Hopcroft et al. (2006).

A (nondeterministic) *finite automaton* (fa) is a 5-tuple $\mathcal{A}=(Q, I, F, \Sigma, \delta)$ with states Q, initial states I, final states F, input alphabet Σ and the transition relation $\delta \subseteq Q \times \Sigma \times Q$. For every state $q \in Q$ and letter $a \in \Sigma$, the set of states $\{r | (q, a, r) \in \delta\}$ reached by input a is denoted by qa. Extend the notation to a state set $P \subseteq Q$ and a word $w = a_1...a_n \in \Sigma^*$ in such a way that $Pa = \{q \mid p \in P, (p, a, q) \in \delta\}$ and $Pa_1...a_2 = (Pa_1)a_2...a_n$. The automaton recognizes the language $||\mathcal{A}|| = \{w \in \Sigma^* \mid Iw \cap P \neq \emptyset\}$.

Let $\mathcal{A} = (Q, I, F, \Sigma, \delta)$ be a fa. Denote its structural reversal $(Q, F, I, \Sigma, \delta')$ where $\delta' = \{(r, a, q) \mid (q, a, r) \in \delta\}$ by $\mathcal{A}^{\mathrm{R}}$. Denote by $\Sigma_\Delta = \Sigma \cup \Delta$ an alphabet such that $\Delta \cap \Sigma = \emptyset$.

2.2 Barrier Deterministic Automata

Definition 2.1. *Let* $\mathcal{A} = (Q, I, F, \Sigma_\Delta, \delta)$. *The fa* $\mathcal{A}$ *is* barrier deterministic with respect to the marker set Δ *if*

1. *there is at most one initial state, i.e.* $|I| \leq 1$
2. *the states* Q *can be divided into the sets of left and right states* Q_1 *and* Q_2 *in such a way that* $\delta \subseteq (Q_1 \times \Delta \times Q_2) \cup (Q_1 \times \Sigma \times Q_1) \cup (Q_2 \times \Sigma \times Q_2)$
3. *the left states are deterministic i.e.* $|qa| \leq 1$ *for every state* $q \in Q_1$ *and letter* $a \in \Sigma$.

Algorithm 1 BARRIERDET$(\mathcal{A}, \Delta)$: Determinization until Δ-barrier

Require: A fa $\mathcal{A} = (Q, I, F, \Sigma_\Delta, \delta)$

$done \leftarrow F' \leftarrow \delta' \leftarrow \emptyset$; $Q' \leftarrow \{(0, I)\}$
while $Q' \neq done$ **do**
  Pick a state (s, P) from $Q' - done$;
  Insert the state (s, P) to $done$
  for all $a \in \Sigma_\Delta$ with $Pa \neq \emptyset$ **do**
    if $s = 0$ and $a \in \Sigma$ **then**
      Insert the state $(0, Pa)$ to Q';
      Insert the triplet $((0, P), a, (0, Pa))$ to δ'
    else
      for all $r \in Pa$ **do**
        insert $((s, P), a, (1, \{r\}))$ to δ', and $(1, \{r\})$ to Q'
      end for
    end if
  end for
end while
return $\mathcal{A}'=(Q', \{(0, I)\}, Q' \cap (\{1\} \times F), \Sigma_\Delta, \delta')$

Ensure: (see the referrence in the text)

Let $\mathcal{A}=(Q, I, F, \Sigma_\Delta, \delta)$ be a fa. Algorithm 1 implements a function called BARRIERDET. BARRIERDET$(\mathcal{A}, \Delta)$ is a barrier deterministic automaton $\mathcal{A}' = (Q_1 \cup Q_2, I', F', \Sigma_\Delta, \delta')$ with

- $|I| \leq 1$, $Q_1 \cap Q_2 = \emptyset$, $\delta \subseteq (Q_1 \times \Delta \times Q_2) \cup (Q_1 \times \Sigma \times Q_1) \cup (Q_2 \times \Sigma \times Q_2)$, and $|qa| \leq 1$ for every state $q \in Q_1$ and letter $a \in \Sigma$.
- $Q_2 \subseteq \{1\} \times Q$ and $\delta' \cap (Q_2 \times \Sigma \times Q_2) = (\{1\} \times \delta) \cap (Q_2 \times \Sigma \times Q_2)$
- $||\mathcal{A}'|| = ||\mathcal{A}|| \cap \Sigma^*\Delta\Sigma^*$.

2.3 Inward Deterministic Automata

Definition 2.2. *Let $\mathcal{A} = (Q, I, F, \Sigma_\Delta, \delta)$. The automaton $\mathcal{A}$ is* inward deterministic *with respect to the marker set Δ if both $\mathcal{A}$ and $\mathcal{A}^{\mathrm{R}}$ are barrier deterministic with respect to the marker set Δ.*

An inward deterministic automaton $\mathcal{A}'' =$ INWARDDET$(\mathcal{A}, M)$ with $||\mathcal{A}''|| = ||\mathcal{A}|| \cap \Sigma^*\Delta\Sigma^*$ is given by

$$\text{INWARDDET}(\mathcal{A}, M) = \text{BARRIERDET}(\text{BARRIERDET}(\mathcal{A}, \Delta)^{\mathrm{R}}, \Delta)^{\mathrm{R}}. \quad (11)$$

Note that $\mathcal{A}''$ has at most one path for every $v\diamond y \in \Sigma^*\Delta\Sigma^*$ where $\diamond \in \Delta$. The definition is illustrated in Figure 1.

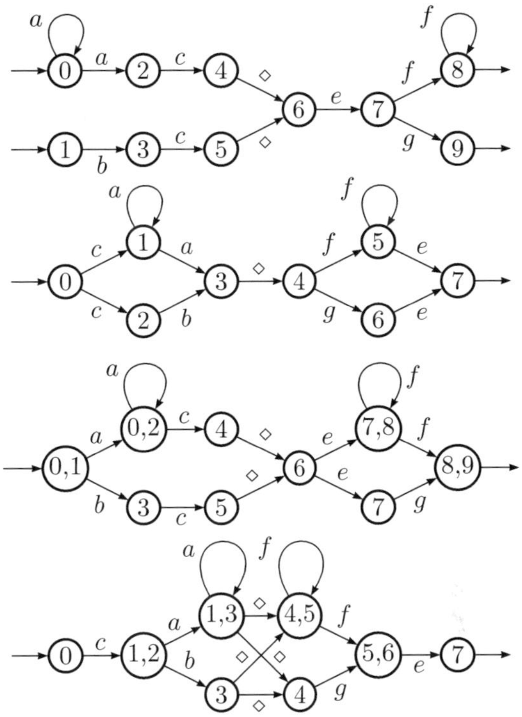

Figure 1: The lower two automata are inward deterministic (with $\Delta = \{\diamond\}$), while the upper two automata are not inward deterministic.

3 Compiling Patternless GR Constraints

Let $\mathcal{A} = (Q, I, F, \Sigma_{\{\diamond\}}, \delta)$ be an automaton that is inward deterministic with respect to $\{\diamond\}$. This section describes how a recognizer for the language $\Sigma^* - h_1(\Sigma^*\diamond\Sigma^* - ||\mathcal{A}||)$ of the patternless GR constraint $(\overline{\emptyset}\diamond\overline{\emptyset} \overset{1\{\diamond\}}{\Longrightarrow} W')$ with $W' = ||\mathcal{A}||$ is constructed.

The language $L = \Sigma^* - h_1(\Sigma^*\diamond\Sigma^* - W')$ is described either through a double complement or positively:

- Any word $w \in \Sigma^*$ such that $h_1^{-1}(w) \not\subseteq W'$ is "nogood" i.e. $w \notin L$
- Any word $w \in \Sigma^*$ such that $h_1^{-1}(w) \subseteq W'$ is "good" i.e. $w \in L$.

The positive description for L has an interpretation in an inward deterministic recognizer $\mathcal{A}$. Let $w = c_1 ... c_n \in \Sigma^*$. If $w \in L$ then $\mathcal{A}$ has two disjoint w-labeled (incomplete) paths:

1. An initial left context path $\pi_l = \langle l_0, l_1, ..., l_n \rangle$ that starts from the initial state $l_0 = i$ and ends at the state l_n.
2. A final right context path $\pi_r = \langle r_0, r_1, ..., r_n \rangle$ that starts from the final state $r_n = f$ and proceeds left-deterministically to the state r_0.

These two paths in the automaton $\mathcal{A}$ are connected with $n+1$ transitions on the $\diamond$-marker, and they thus form $n+1$ complete runs, one for each $n+1$ marked word in the language $h_1^{-1}(w)$. They constitute a ladder-shaped substructure as illustrated in Figure 2.

Let $Z \subseteq \Sigma^*\diamond\Sigma^*$ be a marked language. Then Z is *closed* under variant markings, if $Z = h_1^{-1}(h_1(Z))$. In this sense, the largest closed subset of $||\mathcal{A}||$ is LADDER$(||\mathcal{A}||) = \Sigma^*\diamond\Sigma^* - h_1^{-1}(h_1(\Sigma^*\diamond\Sigma^* - ||\mathcal{A}||))$. We now have the equivalence between the double complement description and the positive description for the language L:

$$\Sigma^* - h_1(\Sigma^*\diamond\Sigma^* - W') = h_1(\text{LADDER}(||\mathcal{A}||)).$$

SUPERPOSE$(\mathcal{A}, \diamond)$ (Algorithm 2) detects the sublanguage LADDER$(||\mathcal{A}||)$ from $\mathcal{A}$ and constructs

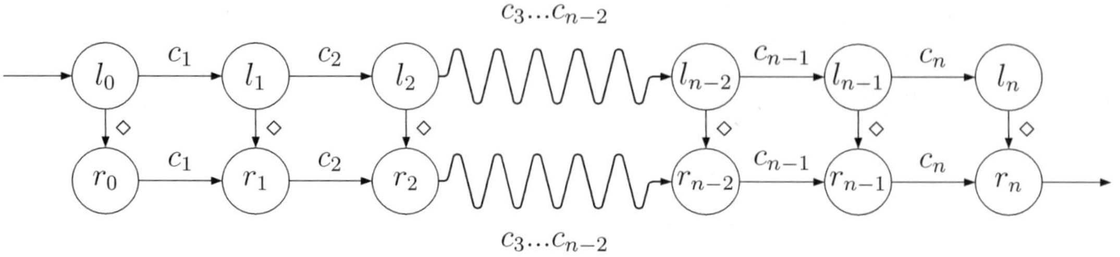

Figure 2: The ladder-shaped substructure of $\mathcal{A}$ corresponding to the word $c_1 \ldots c_n$.

a recognizer $\mathcal{A}''$ for its homomorphic image $h_1(\text{LADDER}(||\mathcal{A}||)$. The lines 3-6 optimize the algorithm by restricting its state set to the accessible part. In practice, this optimization can be easily incorporated to the main construction that is on lines 1 and 2.

Algorithm 2 SUPERPOSE($\mathcal{A}$,$\diamond$)

Require: Inward deterministic NFA
$\mathcal{A} = (Q, \{i\}, \{f\}, \delta)$ with $\mathcal{L}(\mathcal{A}) \subseteq \Sigma^* \diamond \Sigma^*$

1: $Q' \leftarrow \{(l, r) \mid (l, \diamond, r) \in \delta\}$;
$I' \leftarrow \{(l, r) \in Q' \mid l \in I\}$;
$F' \leftarrow \{(l, r) \in Q' \mid r \in F\}$

2: $\delta' \leftarrow \{((l, r), a, (l', r')) \mid$
$(l, r), (l', r') \in Q', l' \in la, r' \in ra\}$

3: $\mathcal{A}' = (Q', I', F', \Sigma, \delta')$; $P \leftarrow I'$

4: **while** $P\Sigma - P \neq \emptyset$ **do**

5: $P \leftarrow P \cup P\Sigma$

6: **end while**

7: **return** $\mathcal{A}''=(P, I', F' \cap P, \Sigma, \delta'(\cap P \times \Sigma \times P))$

Ensure: $||\mathcal{A}''|| = h_1(\text{LADDER}(||\mathcal{A}||))$

4 Evaluation

4.1 The Worst-Case Complexity Analysis

The complexity of INWARDDET (Algorithm 1) alone is similar to the general determinization algorithms: exponential to the size of the input. Let l and r be the size of the left-context component and the right-context component of the automaton that is an input to the inward determinization algorithm. Denote the left-context and right-context state sets of the result of INWARDDET, respectively, by Q and R. The respective sizes of the Q and R components of the inward deterministic result are then $O(2^l)$ and $O(2^r)$.

The SUPERPOSE algorithm (Algorithm 2) assumes a nondeterministic automaton that is inward deterministic with respect to the marker $\diamond$. Such an automaton contains $O(|Q||R|)$ marker transitions and $O((|Q| + |R|)|\Sigma|)$ normal transitions because the states have only one transition per a letter. The size of the projection of the inward deterministic automaton is polynomial to the size of the inward deterministic automaton. Namely, it contains $O(|Q||R|)$ states that corresponds to $\diamond$-transitions in the input. Since the result is nondeterministic, a state (q, r) can have, for every letter $a \in \Sigma$, a transition to any of the states $\{(q', r') | \delta(q, a) = \{q'\}, r' \in \delta(r, a)\}$. The total number of transitions is $O(|Q||R|^2|\Sigma|)$. Based on this, the time complexity of the SUPERPOSE is $O(|Q||R|^2|\Sigma|)$ if we assume that each of result transitions can be created in constant time.

The worst case nondeterministic state complexity of the output of the INWARDDET and SUPERPOSE methods is $O(2^l(2^r)^2|\Sigma|)$ i.e. $O(2^s)$ where $s = l + r$. Recall that this is applicable to patternless GRs only. The patternless GR is directly usable when the pattern language α of the CR constraint is prefix-free or suffix-free. In all other cases, the compilation of CRs requires more general, but less efficient methods that involve two markers (possibly through nested patternless GRs).

4.2 Updating the Best Practice

The comparative sizes of minimal deterministic, codeterministic and inward deterministic representations of the context language W' may differ significantly. For example, the deterministic or codeterministic automaton recognizing the language $\Sigma^n a \Sigma^* \diamond \Sigma^* a \Sigma^n$ (for any large enough $n \in \mathbb{N}$) is exponentially larger than the corresponding inward deterministic automaton. The comparative size difference means that using (INWARDDET+)SUPERPOSE to compile this patternless GR would be an es-

smallest representation		recommendation	
for λ	for ρ	for $\lambda\diamond\rho$	method
determ.	determ.	determ.	GR with DFAs
determ.	co-det.	inw.det.	SUPERPOSE
co-det.	co-det.	co-det.	GR with r-DFAs

Table 1: The choice for the compilation method when other known methods cause immediate blow-up in the representation of contexts.

sential improvement over the state-of-the-art methods where determinization (GR with DFAs) or co-determinization (GR with reverse DFAs) is the first step of the compilation. There are also opposite situations where (INWARDDET+)SUPERPOSE is less likely the most appropriate method (Table 1). Clearly, this kind of rules of thumb will be refined when we can evaluate the predictions with additional practical experiments.

The differences between the efficiency of the methods are often less dramatic in practice. The initial experiments with some 1100 CR constraints from a syntactic FSIG grammar (Voutilainen, 1997) indicate that the size of the inward deterministic automaton is typically very close (1.0 - 4.0 $\times$) to the corresponding minimal deterministic automaton. More careful implementation and experiments are needed in order to find significant differences in efficiency.

According to the author's experiences, it is complicated to add the barrier and inward determinization algorithms to the existing finite-state libraries and tools. Namely, many finite state tools, such as XFST, FOMA, and SFST, typically store the intermediate results as canonical automata. Therefore, the current work suggests that the tools should handle also nondeterministic and co-deterministic automata as full citizens of the finite-state calculus.

Perhaps the cleanest way to add the currently presented algorithms to finite state libraries is to encapsulate the barrier determinization, the reversal and the SUPERPOSE algorithm into one routine where they can store and optimize the nondeterministic automata as needed. However, this seems to be counterproductive from the perspective of reusability.

Perhaps the best practice for using the currently presented method is to use multiple methods and avoid expensive determinizations whenever possible.

4.3 Further Work

There are some possibilities for optimizations and extensions in the presented algorithms: (1) The inward determinization can be optimized by adding some filtering for states that cannot be used by the SUPERPOSE algorithm. (2) A notion of minimality can be adapted to inward deterministic automata and the minimized inward deterministic automata can help reduce the size of the compiled result. (3) The current method for CR compilation could be embedded in methods that compile replace rules or methods where the constraints or rules are compiled on "the fly". (4) a weighted variant of the current method should be compared against Droste and Gastin (2009).

Acknowledgments

This work was supported by the Academy of Finland grant number 128536 "Open and Language Independent Automata-Based Resource Production Methods for Common Language Research Infrastructure". I am also indebted to Måns Hulden, Andreas Maletti and Jacques Sakarovitch and the anonymous reviewers for their critical and constructive remarks.

References

Manfred Droste and Paul Gastin. 2009. Weighted automata and weighted logics. In Manfred Droste, Werner Kuich, and Heiko Vogler, editors, *Handbook of Weighted Automata*, Monographs in Theoretical Computer Science, chapter 5, pages 175–211. Springer-Verlag, Berlin Heidelberg.

Edmund Grimley-Evans, George Anton Kiraz, and Stephen G. Pulman. 1996. Compiling a partition-based two-level formalism. In *16th International Conference on Computational Linguistics (COLING 1996)*, volume 1, pages 454–459, Center for Sprogteknologi, Copenhagen, Denmark.

John E. Hopcroft, Rajeev Motwani, and Jeffrey D. Ullman. 2006. *Introduction to Automata Theory, Languages, and Computation (3rd Edition)*. Addison-Wesley Longman Publishing Co., Inc., Boston, MA, USA.

Måns Hulden. 2008. Regular expressions and predicate logic in finite-state processing. In Jakub Piskorski,

Bruce Watson, and Anssi Yli-Jyrä, editors, *Finite-state methods and natural language processing*. IOS Press, Amsterdam, The Netherlands.

C. Douglas Johnson. 1972. *Formal Aspects of Phonological Description*. Number 3 in Monographs on linguistic analysis. Mouton, The Hague.

Ronald M. Kaplan and Martin Kay. 1994. Regular models of phonological rule systems. *Computational Linguistics*, 20(3):331–378.

Lauri Karttunen, Kimmo Koskenniemi, and Ronald M. Kaplan. 1987. A compiler for two-level phonological rules. Report CSLI-87-108, Center for Study of Language and Information, Stanford University, CA.

Lauri Karttunen. 2004. Restriction operator error: Technical note. Web page `http://www.stanford.edu/~laurik/fsmbook/errata/restriction-operator.html` read on Oct 7, 2011.

André Kempe and Lauri Karttunen. 1996. Parallel replacement in finite state calculus. In *16th International Conference on Computational Linguistics (COLING 1996)*, volume 2, pages 622–627, Center for Sprogteknologi, Copenhagen, Denmark.

Kimmo Koskenniemi and Miikka Silfverberg. 2010. A method for compiling two-level rules with multiple contexts. In *Proceedings of the 11th Meeting of the ACL Special Interest Group on Computational Morphology and Phonology*, SIGMORPHON '10, pages 38–45, Stroudsburg, PA, USA. Association for Computational Linguistics.

Kimmo Koskenniemi, Pasi Tapanainen, and Atro Voutilainen. 1992. Compiling and using finite-state syntactic rules. In *Proceedings of the 15th International Conference on Computational Linguistics, COLING'92*, volume 1, pages 156–162. International Committee on Computational Linguistics, Nantes, France.

Kimmo Koskenniemi. 1983. *Two-level morphology: a general computational model for word-form recognition and production*. Number 11 in Publications. Department of General Linguistics, University of Helsinki, Helsinki.

Robert McNaughton and Seymour Papert. 1971. *Counter-Free Automata*. Number 65 in Research Monograph. MIT Press, Cambridge, Massachusetts.

Ivan Petrov Peikov. 2006. Direct construction of a bimachine for context-sensitive rewrite rule. Master's thesis, Sofia University St. Kliment Ohridski, Faculty of Mathematics and Computer Science, Department of Mathematical Logic and Applications, Sofia, Bulgaria.

Wojciech Skut, Stefan Ulrich, and Kathrine Hammervold. 2004. A bimachine compiler for ranked tagging rules. In *Proceedings of the 20th International Conference on Computational Linguistics*, COLING '04, Stroudsburg, PA, USA.

Nathan Vaillette. 2004. *Logical Specification of Finite-State Transductions for Natural Language Processing*. Ph.D. thesis, Department of Linguistics, Ohio State University.

Atro Voutilainen. 1997. Designing a (finite-state) parsing grammar. In Emmanuel Roche and Yves Schabes, editors, *Finite-State Language Processing*, chapter 9, pages 283–310. A Bradford Book, the MIT Press, Cambridge, MA, USA.

Anssi Yli-Jyrä and Kimmo Koskenniemi. 2004. Compiling contextual restrictions on strings into finite-state automata. In *The Eindhoven FASTAR Days, Proceedings*, number 04/40 in Computer Science Reports, The Netherlands. Technische Universiteit Eindhoven.

Anssi Yli-Jyrä. 2003. Describing syntax with star-free regular expressions. In *Proceedings of the tenth conference on European chapter of the Association for Computational Linguistics - Volume 1*, EACL '03, pages 379–386, Stroudsburg, PA, USA. Association for Computational Linguistics.

Anssi Yli-Jyrä. 2005. *Contributions to the Theory of Finite-State Based Grammars*. Number 38 in Publications. Department of General Linguistics, University of Helsinki.

Anssi Yli-Jyrä. 2008a. Applications of diamonded double negation. In Thomas Hanneforth and Kay-Michael Würzner, editors, *Finite-State Methods and Natural Language Proceedings. 6th International Workshop, FSMNLP 2007, Potsdam, Germany, September 14-16. Revised Papers*, pages 6–30. Potsdam University Press, Potsdam, Germany.

Anssi Yli-Jyrä. 2008b. Transducers from parallel replacement rules and modes with generalized lenient composition. In Thomas Hanneforth and Kay-Michael Würzner, editors, *Finite-State Methods and Natural Language Proceedings. 6th International Workshop, FSMNLP 2007, Potsdam, Germany, September 14-16. Revised Papers*, pages 196–212. Potsdam University Press, Potsdam, Germany.

Anssi Yli-Jyrä. 2009. An efficient double complementation algorithm for superposition-based finite-state morphology. In Kristiina Jokinen and Eckhard Bick, editors, *Proceedings of the 17th Nordic Conference of Computational Linguistics, NODALIDA 2009, May 14-16, 2009*, volume 4 of *NEALT Proceedings Series*, Odense, Danmark. Northern European Association for Language Technology.

Constraint Grammar parsing with left and right sequential finite transducers

Mans Hulden
University of Helsinki
mans.hulden@helsinki.fi

Abstract

We propose an approach to parsing Constraint Grammars using finite-state transducers and report on a compiler that converts Constraint Grammar rules into transducer representations. The resulting transducers are further optimized by conversion to left and right sequential transducers. Using the method, we show that we can improve on the worst-case asymptotic bound of Constraint Grammar parsing from cubic to quadratic in the length of input sentences.

1 Introduction

The Constraint Grammar (CG) paradigm (Karlsson, 1990) is a popular formalism for performing part-of-speech disambiguation, surface syntactic tagging, and certain forms of dependency analysis. A CG is a collection of hand-written disambiguation rules for part-of-speech or syntactic functions. The popularity of CGs is explained by a few factors. They typically achieve quite high F-measures on unrestricted text, especially for free word-order languages (Chanod and Tapanainen, 1995; Samuelsson and Voutilainen, 1997). Constraint Grammars can also be developed by linguists rather quickly, even for languages that have only meager resources available as regards tagged or parsed corpora, although it is hard to come by exact measures of how much effort development requires. One drawback to using CG, however, is that applying one to disambiguate input text tends to be very slow: for example, the Apertium project (Forcada et al., 2009), which offers the option of using both n-gram models and CG (by way of the *vislcg3* compiler (Bick, 2000)), reports that using n-gram models currently results in ten times faster operation, although at the cost of a loss in accuracy.

In this paper, we describe a process of compiling individual CG rules into finite-state transducers (FSTs) that perform the corresponding disambiguation task on an ambiguous input sentence. Using this approach, we can improve the worst-case running time of a CG parser to quadratic in the length of a sentence, down from the cubic time requirement reported earlier (Tapanainen, 1999). The method presented here implements faithfully all the operations allowed in the CG-2 system documented in Tapanainen (1996). The same approach can be used for various extensions and variants of the Constraint Grammar paradigm.

The idea of representing CG rules as FSTs has been suggested before (Karttunen, 1998), but to our knowledge this implementation represents the first time the idea has been tried in practice.[1] We also show that after compiling a collection of CG rules into their equivalent FSTs, the individual transducers can further be converted into left and right sequential transducers which greatly improves the speed of application of a rule.

In the following, we give a brief overview of the CG formalism, discuss previous work and CG parsers, provide an account of our method, and finally report on some practical experiments in compiling large-scale grammars into FSTs with our CG-rule-to-transducer compiler.

2 Constraint Grammar parsers

A Constraint Grammar parser occupies the central role of a system in the CG framework. A CG system

[1] However, Peltonen (2011) has recently implemented a subset of CG-2 as FSTs using a different method.

Proceedings of the 9th International Workshop on Finite State Methods and Natural Language Processing, pages 39–47,
Blois (France), July 12-15, 2011.

is usually intended to produce part-of-speech tagging and surface syntactic tagging from unrestricted text. Generally, the text to be processed is first tokenized and subjected to morphological analysis, possibly by external tools, producing an output where words are marked with ambiguous, alternative readings. This output is then passed as input to a CG parser component. Figure 1 (left) shows an example of intended input to a CG parser where each indented line following a lemma represents an alternative morphological and surface syntactic reading of that lemma; an entire group of alternative readings, such as the five readings for the word *people* in the figure is called a *cohort*. Figure 1 (right) shows the desired output of a CG disambiguator: each cohort has been reduced to contain only one reading.

2.1 Constraint grammar rules

A CG parser operates by removing readings, or by selecting readings (removing the others) according to a set of CG rules. In its standard form there exists only these two types of rules (`SELECT` and `REMOVE`). How the rules operate is further conditioned by constraints that dictate in which environment a rule is triggered. A simple CG rule such as:

```
REMOVE (V) IF (NOT *-1 sub-cl-mark)
              (1C (VFIN)) ;
```

would remove all readings that contain the tag `V`, if there (a) is no subordinate clause mark anywhere to the left (indicated by the rule scope (NOT $*-1$), *and* (b) the next cohort to the right contains the tag VFIN in *all* its readings (signaled by 1C (VFIN)). Such a rule would, for instance, disambiguate the word *people* in the example sentence in Figure 1, removing all other readings except the noun reading. Rules can also refer to the word-forms or the lemmas in their environments. Traditionally, the word-forms are quoted while the lemmas are enclosed in brackets and quotation marks (as in ``` ``<counselors>'' ``` vs. ``` ``counselor'' ``` in fig. 1).

In the example above, only morphological tags are being used, but the same formalism of constraints is often used to disambiguate additional, syntactically motivated tags as well, including tags that mark phrases and dependencies (Tapanainen, 1999; Bick, 2000). Additional features in the rule formalism include `LINK` contexts, Boolean operations, and `BARRIER` specifications. For example, a more complete rule such as:

```
"<word>" REMOVE (X) IF
(*1 A BARRIER C LINK *1 B BARRIER C);
```

would remove the tag `X` for the word-form `word` if the first tag `A` were followed by a `B` somewhere to the right, and there was no `C` before the `B`, except if the first `A`-tagged reading also contained `C`.

It is also possible to add and modify tags to cohorts using `ADD` and `MAP` operations, which work exactly as the `SELECT` and `REMOVE` operations as regards the contextual target specification.

2.2 Parser operation

Given a collection of CG rules, the job of the parser is to apply each rule to the set of input cohorts representing an ambiguous sentence as in Figure 1, and remove or select readings as the rule dictates. The formalism specifies no particular rule ordering per se, and different implementations of the CG formalism apply rules in varying orders (Bick, 2000). In this respect, it is up to the grammar writer to design the rules so that they operate correctly no matter in what order they are called upon. The parser iterates rule application and removes readings until no rule can perform any further disambiguation, or until each cohort contains only one reading. Naturally, since no rule order is explicit, most parser implementations (Tapanainen, 1996; Bick, 2000) tend to use complex techniques to predict if a certain rule can apply at all to avoid the costly process of checking each reading and its respective contexts in an input sentence against a rule for possible removal or selection.

2.3 Computational complexity

Tapanainen (1999) gives the following complexity analysis for his CG-2 parsing system. Assume that a sentence of length n contains maximally k different readings of a token, and is to be disambiguated by a grammar consisting of G rules. Then, testing whether to keep or discard a reading with respect to a single rule can be done in $O(nk)$, with respect to all rules, in $O(Gnk)$, and with respect to all rules and all tokens in $O(n^2Gk)$. Now, in the worst case, applying all rules to all alternative readings only results in the discarding of a single reading. Hence, the process must in some cases be repeated $n(k-1)$ times,

```
"<Business>"
        "business" <*> N NOM SG
"<people>"
        "people" N NOM SG/PL
        "people" V PRES -SG3 VFIN
        "people" V IMP VFIN
        "people" V SUBJUNCTIVE VFIN
        "people" V INF
"<can>"
        "can" V AUXMOD Pres VFIN

"<play>"
        "play" N NOM SG
        "play" V PRES -SG3 VFIN
        "play" V IMP VFIN
        "play" V SUBJUNCTIVE VFIN
        "play" V INF
"<a>"
        "a" <Indef> DET CENTRAL ART SG
"<role>"
        "role" <Count> N NOM SG
"<as>"
        "as" ADV AD-A>
        "as" <**CLB> CS
        "as" PREP
"<counselors>"
        "counselor" <DER:or> <Count> N NOM PL
"<and>"
        "and" CC
"<teachers>"
        "teacher" <DER:er> <Count> N NOM PL
"<.>"
        "." PUNCT Pun
```

```
"<Business>"
        "business" <*>  N NOM SG
"<people>"
        "people" N NOM SG/PL
"<can>"
        "can" V AUXMOD Pres VFIN
"<play>"
        "play" V INF
"<a>"
        "a" <Indef> DET CENTRAL ART SG
"<role>"
        "role" <Count> N NOM SG
"<as>"
        "as" PREP
"<counselors>"
        "counselor" <DER:or> <Count> N NOM PL
"<and>"
        "and" CC
"<teachers>"
        "teacher" <DER:er> <Count> N NOM PL
"<.>"
        "." PUNCT Pun
```

Figure 1: Example input (left) and output (right) from a Constraint Grammar disambiguator.

yielding a total complexity of $O(n^3Gk^2)$. As mentioned above there are various heuristics one can use to avoid blindly testing rules against readings where they cannot apply, but none that guarantee a lower complexity.

3 Related work

Many constraint-based tagging systems can be speeded up by appropriate use of finite-state transducers. For example, Roche and Schabes (1995) show that a Brill tagger (Brill, 1995) can be applied in linear time by constructing a sequential (input-deterministic) transducer that performs the same task as applying a set of transformation-based learning (TBL) rules that change tags according to contextual specifications. This method does not, however, transfer to the problem of CG implementations: for one, TBL rules are vastly simpler in their expressive power, limited only to a few simple templatic statements of tag replacement, while the CG formalism allows for an unlimited number of Boolean and linking constraints; secondly, TBL rules target tags, not words, while CG allows for rules to target any mix of both; thirdly, TBL rules only replace single tags with other single tags and do not remove tags from sets of alternative tags.[2]

Additionally, Koskenniemi (1990); Koskenniemi et al. (1992) have proposed a constraint-based method for surface-syntactic tagging that can be directly implemented—at least in theory—as the intersection of constraints encoded by finite automata. This formalism has been called alternatively by the name *finite-state intersection grammar* and *parallel constraint grammar*, and has later been pursued

[2] This last circumstance is actually only a theoretical inequivalence: a set of CG tags could conceivably be encoded as a single symbol, and the problem of removing tags from a set of tags could be reduced to changing set-representing tags into other such tags, bringing TBL closer to the CG formalism. However, then each possible word targeted (since in CG, words are considered tags as well) would have to be a member of this powerset of tags, causing an exponential explosion in the tag alphabet size.

by Tapanainen (1997) and Yli-Jyrä (2005), among others. While a finite-state implementation of this formalism in theory also offers linear-time performance, it remains unclear whether the massive constants stemming from an explosion in the size of the automata that encode intermediate results can be avoided and a practical parsing method produced (Yli-Jyrä, 2005).

4 Overview of method

Previous CG compilers operate by choosing a rule and a reading and scanning the context to the left and the right to decide if the reading should be removed, possibly using additional information in the form of bookkeeping of where and which rules can potentially apply in a given sentence. In contrast, the approach taken here is to construct a FST from each rule. This transducer is designed so that it acts upon a complete input string representing a sentence and ambiguous cohorts. In one go, it applies the rule to all the readings of the sentence, removing the readings the rule dictates and retaining all others.

For reasons of simplicity, instead of directly operating on the types of inputs given in Figure 1, we assume that the transducer will act upon a slightly modified, more compact string representation of an ambiguous sentence. Here, an entire sentence is represented as a single-line string, with certain delimiter marks for separating cohorts and lemmas. The changes can be illustrated in the following snippet: the cohort

```
"<as>"
        "as" ADV
        "as" PREP
```

is represented as a string in the format

```
$0$ "<as>" #BOC# |
#0# "as" ADV     |
#0# "as" PREP    | #EOC#
```

That is, we have symbols for representing beginnings and endings of cohorts (`#BOC#`, `#EOC#`), and delimiters between every reading (|). Additionally, the symbol `#X#` is used to mark readings that have been removed, and the symbol `#0#` readings that are still possible. The choice of symbols is arbitrary; their role is only to make the data representation compact and suitable for targeting by regular language/FSTs.

The task of each constructed rule transducer, then, is actually only to change `#0#`-symbols into `#X#`-symbols for those readings that should be removed by the rule, of course making sure we never remove the last remaining reading as per CG requirements.

For example, removal of the `ADV`-reading for the word *as* in the above cohort would result in the output string:

```
$0$ "<as>" #BOC#   |
#X# "as"   ADV     |
#0# "as"   PREP    | #EOC#
```

5 Left/right sequential transducers

The output of the compilation process is a transducer that removes readings as the corresponding rule requires—in practice only changing `#0#` symbols into `#X#` symbols wherever warranted. However, if the rule contexts are complicated, this transducer may contain many alternative paths with `#0#:#0#` or `#0#:#X#` labels going out from the same state, only one of which contains a path to a final state with any input string: i.e. the transducer is not sequential. This is because more context to the right needs to be seen by the transducer to decide whether to retain or remove a reading. In the case of large rules, this may involve substantial backtracking when applying a transducer against an input string. The time taken to apply a rule transducer is still linear in the length of the string, but may hide a large constant, which is in effect the size of the transducer.

However, we a priori know that each rule transducer is *functional*, i.e. that each input string maps to maximally one output string (rules are never ambiguous in their action). Such transducers T can be broken up by a process called bimachine factorization into two unambiguous transducers: a left sequential T_l and a right sequential one T_r, such that the effect of the original transducer is produced by first applying the input word to T_l, and then applying T_r to the reverse of T_l's output (Schützenberger, 1961; Reutenauer and Schützenberger, 1991; Roche, 1995; Kempe, 2001). In other words, the two separate transducers fulfill the condition that:

$$T = T_l \circ \mathit{Reverse}(T_r) \tag{1}$$

Performing this factorization of the rule transducers then allows further efficiency gains. For instance, as table 1 shows, some rules with long contexts produce transducers with thousands of states. Converting these rules to the equivalent left and right sequential ones removes a large time constant from the cost of applying a rule. It could be noted that the rule transducers are also directly *sequentiable* into a single sequential transducer (Schützenberger, 1977), and we could apply such a sequentialization algorithm (Mohri, 1997) on them as well. Sequentializing an FST in effect postpones ambiguous output along transducer paths until the ambiguity is resolved, emitting zeroes during that time. Performing this type of sequentialization on rule FSTs is in practice impossible, however. As each ambiguity may last several cohorts ahead, the equivalent sequential transducer must "remember" arbitrary non-outputted strings for a long time, and will be exponential in size to the original one. By contrast, the resulting left and right sequential rule FSTs are actually smaller than the original rule FSTs.

6 Construction

Since each rule can operate in complex ways, we break down the process of compiling a rule into several smaller transducers which are joined by composition ($\circ$). This is similar to techniques used for compiling phonological rewrite rules into FSTs (Kaplan and Kay, 1994; Kempe and Karttunen, 1996). The entire construction process can be encapsulated in the composition of a few auxiliary transducers. Compilation of a basic rule of the format

```
SELECT/REMOVE (X) IF
(SCOPE#1 COND#1) ... (SCOPE#n COND#n)
```

can be expressed with the general construction

$$\begin{array}{c}\texttt{MarkFormTarget} \circ \\ \texttt{Constrain} \circ \\ \texttt{Cond}_1 \circ \ldots \circ \texttt{Cond}_n\end{array} \quad (2)$$

These operate as follows:

- `MarkFormTarget` is a transducer that changes `#0#`-symbols temporarily to `#1#`-symbols (signaling pending removal) for those cohorts that contain the target reading (if the rule is a REMOVE rule), or for retention (if it is a SELECT rule).
- `Constrain` changes `#1#`-symbols back into `#0#` symbols whenever the last reading would be removed.
- $\texttt{Condition}_k$ changes the corresponding temporary symbols into `#X#`-symbols whenever all the conditions are met for removal, otherwise changing them back to `#0#`-symbols.

The actual conditions expressed in the `Cond` transducer are fairly straightforward to express as Boolean combinations of regular languages since we have explicit symbols marking the beginnings and endings of cohorts as well as readings. Each condition for a rule firing—e.g. something occurring n cohorts (or more) to the left/right—can then be expressed in terms of the auxiliary symbols that separate cohorts and readings.

6.1 Detailed example

Figure 2 contains a working example of the rule compilation strategy in the form of a script in the Xerox formalism compilable with either the *xfst* (Beesley and Karttunen, 2003) or *foma* (Hulden, 2009) FST toolkits. The majority of the example consists of function and transducer definitions common for compiling any CG-rule, and the last few lines exemplify the actual compilation of the rules. Briefly, compiling a rule with the example code, entails as a preliminary the composition of the following transducers:

- `InitialFilter` disallows, for efficiency reasons, all input that is not correctly formatted.
- `MarkFormTarget(Wordform,Target)` is a function that performs the provisional marking of all target readings and cohorts that could be affected by the rule, given the wordform and the target tag.
- `ConstrainS` for `SELECT`-rules (and `ConstrainR` for `REMOVE`-rules), is a transducer that checks that we would not remove the last reading from any cohort, should the rule be successful and reverts auxiliaries `#1#` to `#0#` in this case. Also, each potentially affected cohort which is by default headed by `$0$`, is mapped ambiguously to `$A$` or

R. These symbols serve to denote whether a change in that cohort is to be later accepted or rejected, based on the rule contexts.

These three transducers are again composed with a transducer that restricts the occurrence of the A-symbol to those cohorts where the rule contexts are in place. This is followed by the composition with a Cleanup-transducer that restores all auxiliaries, leaving all readings to only be marked #0# (current) or #X# (removed), and all heads marked 0.

The actual implementation is a stand-alone compiler written in C using *flex* and the *foma* API for the transducer construction functions. It handles additional chained LINK contexts, supports set definitions as is the case in the standard CG variants. These additions require dynamic insertions of auxiliary symbols based on the number of linked contexts and defined sets and cannot be captured in static scripts. However, the compilation method and the use of auxiliary symbols is identical in the example script in figure 2. The outputs of the example script are non-sequential transducers that model CG rules that can later be converted to left and right sequential ones for faster application speed.

7 Analysis

Assuming a grammar with G rules and a maximum of k possible readings per word, applying one rule transducer to an entire sentence of n possibly k-way ambiguous words takes time $O(nk)$: we apply the transducer (or the left-sequential and right-sequential transducers) to the string representing the sentence whose string representation length is maximally nk in linear time. Now, applying an entire set of G rules in some order can be done in $O(Gnk)$ time. Making no assumptions about the structure of the input, in the worst case one such round of disambiguation only removes a single reading from a single cohort. Applying the entire set of disambiguation rules must then be done (in the worst case) $n(k-1)$ times. Hence, the total time required to be guaranteed of disambiguation of a sentence is of the order $O(Gn^2k^2)$.

The improvement over the prior parsers that operate in $O(Gn^3k^2)$ as analyzed in Tapanainen (1999) comes precisely from the ability to compile a constraint rule into a FST. In that earlier analysis, it was assumed that it takes $O(nk)$ time to resolve whether to keep or discard some chosen alternative reading in a cohort. That is, the underlying idea was to test each *reading* for possible removal separately. The improvement—that we can apply one rule to *all* the cohorts and readings in a sentence in time $O(nk)$—is due to the transducer representation of the rule action.

SC	n		$-n$		$*n$		$*-n$	
	$\|T\|$	$\|B\|$	$\|T\|$	$\|B\|$	$\|T\|$	$\|B\|$	$\|T\|$	$\|B\|$
1	72	44	39	37	47	32	27	31
2	214	77	77	61	74	38	33	37
3	640	143	153	109	108	44	39	43
4	1918	275	305	205	148	50	45	49
5	5752	539	609	397	194	56	51	55
6	17254	1067	1217	781	246	62	57	61
7	51760	2123	2433	1549	304	68	63	67

Table 1: Example sizes (number of states) of single rules of varying left and right scope represented as transducers, both individually and as separate left-sequential and right-sequential transducers. The $|T|$ represents the size of the single transducer, and the $|B|$-columns the sums of the sizes of the LR-sequential ones.

Additionally, the constant G can in theory be eliminated. Given a set of rules represented as transducers, $R_1 \ldots R_n$, these rules can be combined into a larger transducer R by composition:

$$R_1 \circ \ldots \circ R_n \tag{3}$$

Subsequently, this transducer R can be converted into a left and a right sequential transducer as above, yielding $O(n^2k^2)$. In practice, such a construction is not feasible, however, because the composed transducer invariably becomes too large in any actual grammar. The approach is still partially useful as our practical experiments show that rules that target the same tags can be composed without undue growth in the composite transducer. In actual grammars, it is often the case that a large number of different rules operate on removal or selection of the same tag, and in such a case, the individual rule transducers can further be grouped and combined to a certain extent.

```
##############################################################
# Auxiliary definitions                                      #
##############################################################
# $0$ = heads all cohorts                                    #
# $1$ = temporary auxiliary for marking cohort               #
# $A$ = temporary auxiliary for marking "acceptance" of rule #
# $R$ = temporary auxiliary for marking "rejection" of rule  #
# #0# = marks all readings that are alive                    #
# #X# = marks all dead readings                              #
# #1# = temporary auxiliary: marks readings that are about to #
#       be retained                                          #
# #2# = temporary auxiliary: marks readings that are about to #
#       be removed                                           #
# #BOC# = marks a beginning of each cohort                   #
# #EOC# = marks the end of each cohort                       #
##############################################################

define DEL "| " ;
define ALIVE ["#0# "|"#1# "|"#2# "] ;
define AUX "$0$ "|"$1$ "|"$A$ "|"$R$ "|
           "#0# "|"#1# "|"#X# "|"#2# "| DEL |"#BOC# "|"#EOC# ";

define InitialFilter  ~$AUX ["$0$ " ~$AUX "#BOC# "
       ([DEL ["#0# "|"#X# "] ~$AUX]+ DEL) "#EOC# "]* ;

define NoMarkedReading ~$["#1# "|"#EOC# "] "#EOC# " ;
define NoLiveReading   ~$["#0# "|"#EOC# "] "#EOC# " ;
define NoMarkedHead    "$0$ " ~$["#EOC# "] ;
define MarkedHead      "$1$ " ~$["#EOC# "] ;

define ConstrainS      "$1$ " -> "$0$ " || _ NoMarkedReading |
                                            NoLiveReading .o.
        "#1# " -> "#0# " || NoMarkedHead _                .o.
        "#0# " -> "#1# ","#1# " -> "#0# " || MarkedHead _  .o.
        "$1$ " -> ["$A$ "|"$R$ "]                         .o.
        "#1# " -> "#2# " || "$A$ " \"#EOC# "* _ ;

define ConstrainR    "$1$ " -> "$0$ " || _ NoMarkedReading  .o.
                     "#1# " -> "#0# " || NoMarkedHead _     .o.
                     "$1$ " -> "$0$ " || _ NoMarkedReading  .o.
                     "$1$ " -> "$0$ " || _ NoLiveReading    .o.
                     "#1# " -> "#0# " || NoMarkedHead _     .o.
                     "$1$ " -> ["$A$ "|"$R$ "]              .o.
                     "#1# " -> "#2# " || "$A$ " \"#EOC# "* _ ;

define Cleanup  "#1# " -> "#0# " .o. "#2# " -> "#X# " .o.
                "$A$ "|"$R$ " -> "$0$ ";

define MarkFormTarget(WORDFORM,TARGET)
                         "$0$ " -> "$1$ " || _ WORDFORM .o.
                         "#0# " -> "#1# " || _ TARGET ;
define InvCR [[?* ["$A$ ":"$R$ "] [?|["$A$ ":"$R$ "]]*]]   .o.
             "#2# "->"#1# " || "$R$ " \"#EOC# "* _ ;
define CompileRule(X) X .o. ~[X .o. InvCR].l  .o. Cleanup;
define MATCHCOHORT(X) [\"#BOC# "* "#BOC# " \"#EOC# "* DEL ALIVE
                      \DEL* X \"#EOC# "* "#EOC# " ~$"#BOC# "];
define MATCHCOHORTC(X) [\"#BOC# "* "#BOC# " [[DEL DEAD \DEL*]*
                 [DEL ALIVE \DEL* X \DEL*] [DEL DEAD \DEL*]*]+
                  DEL "#EOC# " ~$"#BOC# "];
define ANYCOHORT [\"#BOC# "* "#BOC# "
                  \"#EOC# "* "#EOC# " ~$"#BOC# "];

######################################################
# Actual compilation of an example rule using the above #
# auxiliary functions and definitions                #
######################################################

# Rule 1: SELECT (V) IF (1 (ADJ));
define Rule1Pre InitialFilter .o.
                MarkFormTarget(?*, \DEL* "V " \DEL*) .o.
                ConstrainS .o.
        "$A$ " => _ ANYCOHORT MATCHCOHORT(\DEL* "ADJ " \DEL*);
regex  CompileRule(Rule1Pre);

# Rule 2: SELECT (X) IF (*-1C (A) BARRIER (B)) (1 (C));
define Rule21Pre InitialFilter                    .o.
        MarkFormTarget(?*,\DEL* "X " \DEL*)      .o.
        ConstrainS                               .o.
        "$A$ " => MATCHCOHORTC(\DEL* "A " \DEL*)
        [ANYCOHORT - MATCHCOHORT(\DEL* "B " \DEL*)]* _ ;

define Rule22Pre InitialFilter                 .o.
        MarkFormTarget(?*,\DEL* "X " \DEL*) .o.
        ConstrainS                          .o.
        "$A$ " => _ ANYCOHORT MATCHCOHORT(\DEL* "C " \DEL*);

# Rule is split into two parts that are intersected
regex CompileRule(Rule21Pre & Rule22Pre);
```

Figure 2: Complete *foma* code example that compiles two different CG rules with the method.

8 Some practical experiments

8.1 Grammar compilation

We have built a CG-to-transducer compiler that converts rules in the CG-2 format (Tapanainen, 1996) into the type of FSTs discussed above. The compiler itself relies on low-level finite-state machine construction functions available in the *foma* FST library (Hulden, 2009). To test the compiler against large-scale grammars, we have run it on Constraint Grammars of Finnish (Karlsson, 1990),[3] and Basque (Aduriz et al., 1997). Both grammars are quite large: the Finnish grammar consists of 1,019 rules, and the Basque of 1,760 rules. Table 2 shows the results of compiling all rules into individual transducers. In the table, what is given is the sum total of states and transitions of all transducers ($\Sigma|T|$), and the sum total of states and transitions for the left and right sequential transducers ($\Sigma|B|$). As can be seen, the sequentialized transducers together are substantially smaller than the non-sequentialized transducers. Compilation time for the respective grammars is currently 2 min 59 sec. (Basque) and 1 min 09 sec. (Finnish).[4]

8.2 Rule transducer size growth

Naturally, there is a limit to the complexity of rules that can be compiled into FSTs. Rules that depend on long-distance left and right contexts will grow quickly in size when represented as FSTs. Table 1 shows the sizes of different transducers compiled from a single rule type

$$\texttt{SELECT (X) IF (SCOPE (Y))} \qquad (4)$$

where SCOPE represents various rule scopes. For instance, the scope $*-3$ (condition holds three or more words to the left) results in a transducer of 39 states, and a left and right sequential transducer whose sum total of states are 43. Complex rules with

[3] Converted from the original to the more modern notation by Trond Trosterud at the University of Tromsø in 2010.

[4] on a 2.8GHz Intel Core 2 Duo.

	Basque	Finnish
Rules	1,760	1,019
$\Sigma\|T\|$	469,938 states	231,786 states
	11,229,332 trans.	2,741,165 trans.
$\Sigma\|B\|$	213,445 states	102,913 states
	4,812,185 trans.	1,230,118 trans.

Table 2: Sums of sizes of resulting transducers with two large-scale grammars.

multiple conditions may grow larger than the simple, single-context rules in the table, but nevertheless, the results indicate that most grammars should be representable as FSTs in practice. In our test grammars, the longest scope ever used for a condition was 6 cohorts to the right (in Basque)—although e.g. Voutilainen (1999) reports on sometimes needing slightly longer contexts than this for a grammar of English (max. 9).

Since the bimachine factorization used in constructing the left and right sequential transducers introduces unique auxiliary symbols to signal pending ambiguity during the left-to-right pass, which is later resolved, there is some slight growth of the alphabet in these transducers. However, this growth is fairly small: the sequentialization of all the rules in the two grammars tested could be performed with a maximum of 8 auxiliary symbols, usually only one or two for the majority of the rules.

8.3 Grammar analysis

The fact that we can compile each rule in a Constraint Grammar into a finite state transducer also yields other benefits apart from rule application speed. Grammars can be analyzed with respect to errors in detailed fashion with methods that go beyond existing debugging capabilities in CG parsers. For example, the formalism allows for vacuous rules, i.e. rules that never act on any input. Consider, for example: `SELECT (X) IF (NOT 0 (X))`.

Such rules are quite a common redundancy in actual CG grammars and tend to go undetected. While the above rule is easily seen at first glance to be vacuous, more complex rules are more demanding to analyze in this respect. For example, the rule

```
SELECT (ADB) IF (0C ADJ-ADB)
(-1 KASEZGRAM OR ERG OR PAR);
```

was encountered in an actual grammar. It is indeed vacuous, but to detect this, we need to analyze the sets `ADJ-ADB`, `KASEZGRAM`, `ERG`, and `PAR`, as well as the logic of the rule.

Using finite-state techniques, we can calculate, for a rule transducer `R` its intersection with the set of all transducers that change `#0#` symbols into `#X#`-symbols.

$$R \cap (\texttt{?:?}^* \ \texttt{\#0\#:\#X\#} \ \texttt{?:?}^*) \quad (5)$$

yielding a transducer whose domain contains all the inputs that are affected by the rule `R`, and allowing us to answer the question whether the rule is vacuous. Similar techniques can be used to analyze rule redundancy (are two superficially distinct rules equivalent), and rule subsumption; does R_1 subsume R_2, making it redundant, or do rules R_1 and R_2 together act identically to R_3 alone, and so forth.

9 Conclusion & future work

We have presented a method for compiling individual Constraint Grammar rules into finite-state transducers. This reduces the worst-case time requirements for CG parsing from cubic to quadratic. The possibility of further conversion of rule transducers into left and right sequential ones cuts down on the time constants involved in rule disambiguation. Testing an implementation against wide-coverage grammars seems to indicate that the method is practical even for large grammars. Integrating the approach proposed here with earlier strategies to CG-parsing—most important being efficient tracking of which rules can potentially apply to an input at any given stage to avoid applying transducers unnecessarily—remains an important next practical step.

Acknowledgements

I am grateful to Atro Voutilainen for sharing his insights and providing me with relevant examples and sources, and also to the IXA group at the University of the Basque Country for providing grammars and resources. This research has received funding from the European Commission's 7th Framework Program under grant agreement no. 238405 (CLARA).

References

Aduriz, I., Arriola, J. M., Artola, X., de Ilarraza, A. D., K., G., and M., M. (1997). Morphosyntactic disambiguation for Basque based on the Constraint Grammar Formalism. In *Proceedings of Recent Advances in NLP (RANLP97)*.

Beesley, K. R. and Karttunen, L. (2003). *Finite State Morphology*. CSLI Publications, Stanford, CA.

Bick, E. (2000). *The Parsing System "Palavras": Automatic Grammatical Analysis of Portuguese in a Constraint Grammar Framework*. Aarhus University Press.

Brill, E. (1995). Transformation-based error-driven learning and natural language processing: A case study in part-of-speech tagging. *Computational Linguistics*, 21(4):543–565.

Chanod, J. P. and Tapanainen, P. (1995). Tagging French: comparing a statistical and a constraint-based method. In *Proceedings of the 7th EACL*, pages 149–156.

Forcada, M. L., Tyers, F. M., and Ramírez-Sánchez, G. (2009). The free/open-source machine translation platform Apertium: Five years on. In *Proceedings of FreeRBMT'09*, pages 3–10.

Hulden, M. (2009). Foma: a finite-state compiler and library. In *Proceedings of the 12th EACL*, pages 29–32.

Kaplan, R. M. and Kay, M. (1994). Regular models of phonological rule systems. *Computational Linguistics*, 20(3):331–378.

Karlsson, F. (1990). Constraint grammar as a framework for parsing running text. In *COLING '90*, volume 3, pages 168–173, Helsinki, Finland.

Karttunen, L. (1998). The proper treatment of optimality theory in computational phonology. In *Proceedings of FSMNLP*.

Kempe, A. (2001). Factorization of ambiguous finite-state transducers. *Lecture Notes in Computer Science*, 2088:170–181.

Kempe, A. and Karttunen, L. (1996). Parallel replacement in finite state calculus. In *Proceedings of the 34th ACL*.

Koskenniemi, K. (1990). Finite-state parsing and disambiguation. In *COLING '90*, pages 229–232.

Koskenniemi, K., Tapanainen, P., and Voutilainen, A. (1992). Compiling and using finite-state syntactic rules. In *COLING '92*, pages 156–162.

Mohri, M. (1997). On the use of sequential transducers in natural language processing. In Roche, E. and Schabes, Y., editors, *Finite-State Language Processing*, pages 355–382. MIT Press.

Peltonen, J. (2011). *Rajoitekielioppien toteutuksesta äärellistilaisin menetelmin [On the Implementation of Constraint Grammars Using Finite State Methods]*. MA Thesis, University of Helsinki.

Reutenauer, C. and Schützenberger, M.-P. (1991). Minimization of rational word functions. *SIAM Journal of Computing*, 20(4):669–685.

Roche, E. (1995). Factorization of Finite-State Transducers. *Mitsubishi Electric Research Laboratories*, pages 1–13.

Roche, E. and Schabes, Y. (1995). Deterministic part-of-speech tagging with finite-state transducers. *Computational Linguistics*, 21(2):227–253.

Samuelsson, C. and Voutilainen, A. (1997). Comparing a linguistic and a stochastic tagger. In *Proceedings of the 8th EACL*, pages 246–253.

Schützenberger, M.-P. (1961). A remark on finite transducers. *Information and Control*, 4:185–196.

Schützenberger, M.-P. (1977). Sur une variante des fonctions séquentielles. *Theoretical Computer Science*, 4:47–57.

Tapanainen, P. (1996). *The Constraint Grammar Parser CG-2*. Publications 27, Department of General Linguistics. University of Helsinki.

Tapanainen, P. (1997). Applying a finite-state intersection grammar. In Roche, E. and Schabes, Y., editors, *Finite-State Language Processing*, pages 311–327. MIT Press.

Tapanainen, P. (1999). *Parsing in two frameworks: finite-state and functional dependency grammar*. PhD Thesis, University of Helsinki.

Voutilainen, A. (1999). Hand-crafted rules. In Van Halteren, H., editor, *Syntactic Wordclass Tagging*, pages 217–246. Springer.

Yli-Jyrä, A. (2005). *Contributions to the Theory of Finite-State Based Linguistic Grammars*. PhD Thesis, University of Helsinki.

E-Dictionaries and Finite-State Automata for the Recognition of Named Entities

Cvetana Krstev
Faculty of Philology,
University of Belgrade

Duško Vitas
Faculty of Mathematics,
University of Belgrade

Ivan Obradović
Faculty of Mining and Geology,
University of Belgrade

Miloš Utvić
Faculty of Philology,
University of Belgrade

Abstract

In this paper we present a system for named entity recognition and tagging in Serbian that relies on large-scale lexical resources and finite-state transducers. Our system recognizes several types of name, temporal and numerical expressions. Finite-state automata are used to describe the context of named entities, thus improving the precision of recognition. The widest context was used for personal names and it included the recognition of nominal phrases describing a person's position. For the evaluation of the named entity recognition system we used a corpus of 2,300 short agency news. Through manual evaluation we precisely identified all omissions and incorrect recognitions which enabled the computation of recall and precision. The overall recall $R = 0.84$ for types and $R = 0.93$ for tokens, and overall precision $P = 0.95$ for types and $P = 0.98$ for tokens show that our system gives priority to precision.

1 Introduction

Recognition of named entities (NER) has been a hot topic in Natural Language Processing community for more than fifteen years. Ever since their introduction in the scope of the Sixth Message Understanding Conference (Grishman and Sundheim, 1996) they have not ceased to arouse interest of developers of various NLP applications. The nature of proper names, as a sub-class of named entities, for Serbian was analyzed in (Vitas et al., 2007) especially in connection with its inflectional and derivational richness. However, to the best of our knowledge, beside some small-scale experiments, no effective NER system was yet produced for Serbian. In this paper we present a working system for recognition of various named entities in Serbian newspaper texts, as well as results of the evaluation of this system on a corpus of short agency news.

2 General Resources

The primary resources that we have used for the NER task are Serbian morphological e-dictionaries. The development of our e-dictionaries follows the methodology and format known as DELA presented for French in (Courtois and Silberztein, 1990). The system of Serbian e-dictionaries covers both general lexica and proper names, as simple words and compounds, and their level of development is presented in Table 1. It is obvious from the given data that dictionaries of compounds are still of a modest size and need to be further developed. On the other hand, they comprise not only entries collected from traditional sources, like dictionaries, but also entries extracted from processed texts, which enhances their usability.

Our e-dictionaries provide for a word form with possible values of grammatical categories (case, number, gender, etc.), as well as its lemma (or regular form) together with various additional markers that specify the derivational, syntactic, semantic or usage features of the lemma. The example *Grka,Grk.N+NProp+Hum+Inh+GR:ms2v* illustrates this approach: *Grka* 'a native or inhabitant of Greece' is a form of a noun (N) *Grk*, which is a proper name (+NProp), used for humans (+Hum) inhabiting a certain place (+Inh) in Greece (+GR)

Proceedings of the 9th International Workshop on Finite State Methods and Natural Language Processing, pages 48–56,
Blois (France), July 12-15, 2011.

	Simple words		Compounds	
	lemmas	forms	lemmas	forms
General lexica	89,965	3,843,261	4,531	99,682
Geopolitical proper names	7,873	212,809	720	7,049
Serbian personal names	20,758	275,088		
Foreign proper names	6,673	47,087		
Total	125,269	4,378,245	5,251	106,731

Table 1: The system of Serbian e-dictionaries

Values of grammatical categories further state that it is a masculine gender (m) animate noun (v) in the singular from (s) in the genitive case (2).

The rich set of semantic markers is particularly useful in the NER tasks. We will discuss these markers in more detail in section 3. A full list of grammatical categories used in Serbian e-dictionaries and their values as well as an extensive but not exhaustive list of markers is given in chapter 1 of (Krstev, 2008). For proper names, the system of markers relies on (Grass et al., 2002).

Among general resources used are also dictionary graphs in the form of FSTs that recognize and grammatically tag certain classes of simple words and compounds that are generally not to be found in dictionaries because it is not possible to produce a finite list of their canonic forms. They cover simple words such as Roman numerals, interjections with repetition of one or more graphemes (e.g. *jaooo* 'ouuuuch') and acronyms which are not generally known and regularly used. Dictionary graphs are also used to correctly tag numerals written with several digits, words or their combination (e.g. *18 milijardi i 800 miliona* '18 billions and 800 millions'), compound nouns or adjectives starting with digits (e.g. *21-godišnji* '21 years old'), and 'inflected' forms of acronyms (e.g. *MOK-a* 'the genitive case of MOK — International Olympics Committee') as well as their 'derivational' forms (e.g. *DSS-ovac* 'a member of DSS (political party)'). The core set of dictionary graphs for Serbian is described in chapter 7 of (Krstev, 2008).

3 The Selection of Named Entities

The number of named entity types targeted in a NER task can vary from just a few to quite a number of them. For instance, in the MUC-6 task only three tags were introduced: ENAMEX, TIMEX, NUMEX, each with just a few attributes for further refinement (Chinchor, 1995). On the other hand, Sekine and Nobata (Sekine and Nobata, 2004) proposed a named entity hierarchy which included as many as 200 different categories and which refined 'standard' categories by introducing subcategories, as for example MEASUREMENT for NUMEX, but also introduced many new categories, such as PRODUCT, FACILITY, EVENT, etc. A detailed multilevel taxonomy is incorporated in the Prolex multilingual database (Maurel, 2008). Detailed guidelines about how to tag named entities in texts are given in chapter 13 of TEI Guidelines P5 (Burnard and Bauman, 2008). The guidelines provide tags and attributes for names, dates, people and places that enable a very refined description of these basic classes of named entities; no indications are given, however, as to how the named entity tagging is to be preformed. A more detailed discussion on named entities is given in (Nadeau and Sekine, 2009).

In (Savary et al., 2010) the authors describe the tools and methods used to produce a linguistic resource, within the National Corpus of Polish, in which named entities are tagged in full detail and with high accuracy. However, our main objective was not to build a similar resource, minutely tagged with named entities in Serbian, that could be used as a kind of a gold standard in the future, but rather to develop a comprehensive, working and useful tool for NER in Serbian newspaper texts. Thus, we chose to tag entities that are considered as basic and hence included in most NER systems. In selecting the set of named entities to be recognized and tagged we also considered the lexical coverage of our electronic dictionaries, as well as the set of semantic markers used.

3.1 Numerical expressions

We considered two types of numerical expressions: money expressions and measurement expressions. By a money or measurement expressions we consider an expression consisting of a numeral (written using digits, words or their combination) followed by a currency or a measurement unit. The majority of currencies in use today are in our dictionary (marked with +Cur), as well as major measurement units (marked with +Mes). Besides their full names, currencies and measurement units in numerical expressions can be expressed by acronyms (e.g. USD), abbreviations (e.g. kg) and special symbols (e.g. €).

3.2 Temporal expressions

Two types of temporal expressions were considered: dates and times. In both cases, we distinguished expressions that represent a moment (however vaguely expressed) from those that represent a period (*od 1968. godine do danas* 'from the year 1968 until today', *od 11 do 13 sati* 'from 11 to 13'). As for dates, we were not looking only for precisely determined dates as in *13. decembra 2005.* 'on December 13th, 2005' but also for less formal expressions in which the year is omitted and the current year is presumed (*23. novembra* 'on November 23rd'), or the year can be inferred (*15. avgusta prošle godine* 'last year on August 15th'). We were also looking for expressions in which an exact day is not mentioned but the year is explicitly given (*u martu 1999. g.* 'in March 1999'), the year can be inferred (*u aprilu sledeće godine* 'in April next year'), or the current year is presumed (*za početak novembra* 'for the beginning of November'). Finally, we were looking also for expressions in which only the year is mentioned; however, in that case the word *godina* 'year' must also appear in full or abbreviated form (*za 2004. godinu* 'for the year 2004'). The names of days were recognized if they were related to a date (*u ponedeljak 2. januara* 'on Monday, January 2nd'), but not if they appeared on their own. Formal expressions of date and time were also recognized, such as *17. IV 2006* or *10:01h*.

3.3 Name expressions

We considered two types of name expressions: geopolitical names and personal names. In recognizing geopolitical names we distinguished four types: names of settlements (*Njujork* 'New York'), names of states (*Nemačka* 'Germany'), hydronyms (*Dunav* 'Danube', *Atlantski okean* 'Atlantic'), and oronyms (*Alpi* 'Alpes'). In recognizing names of states we were looking for both formal names (*Narodna republika Kina* 'Peoples Republic of China') and names in daily use (*Kina* 'China'). Some frequently used acronyms of states were also recognized (*SAD* 'USA'). Recognition of these geopolitical names was based on semantic markers in our e-dictionaries: besides the +Top marker, given to all geopolitical names, additional markers are assigned to settlements +Gr, states +Dr, bodies of water +Hyd, and elevations +Oro.

Recognition of personal names was also based on semantic markers in our e-dictionaries: namely, the markers +First, +Last, and +Nick are assigned to first names, surnames, and nicknames respectively. In order to avoid the ambiguity related to personal names in Serbian we recognized only full names, that is, names consisting of a first name and at least one surname. We do not see that as a serious drawback because in newspaper texts all persons, apart from those very prominent — like *Tito* and *Milošević* at their time — are referred to at least once by their full name. Various titles were also recognized when related to a person's full name (*prof. dr Kata Lazović*). Although a person's function, profession or role in the society is usually not considered as a named entity, we nevertheless recognized them when they directly preceded or followed a personal name, thus forming a nominal phrase: *prof. dr Slavica Đukić-Dejanović, direktor Kliničko-bolničkog centra* 'Prof. Dr. Slavica Đukić-Dejanović, director of the Hospital Medical Center' and *Predsednik Odbora za poljoprivredu u Vladi Republike Srbije Jela Veselić* 'the president of the Agricultural Committee in the Government of the Republic of Serbia Jela Veselić'. We think that this adds a significant value to the already recognized personal name.

4 Development of Local Grammars

Although our NER system strongly relies on e-dictionaries of simple words and compounds, the usage of dictionaries without additional resources can not result in a successful system due to a high level of ambiguity of both word forms and lemmas. There is an example that illustrates well the nature of this problem. In Serbian, *po* is a very frequently used preposition. The same string with the upper-case initial, *Po*, can represent four different proper names: the Italian river *Po*, the French commune *Pau* (on the northern edge of the Pyrenees), part of a personal name as in *Edgar Allan Poe*, and finally the chemical symbol for *Polonium*[1]. This and many other similar examples suggest that agreement and contextual constraints have to be taken into consideration if we want to obtain results with high recall and precision.

4.1 Personal Names

Due to the complexity and ambiguity of personal names in Serbian a simple lexical pattern consisting of a first name and surname, written in Unitex formalism (Paumier, 2008) as *<N+Hum+First>* *<N+Hum+Last>* would recognize full personal names with a very low precision (this is explained in full detail in chapter 6 of (Krstev, 2008)). However, precision can be significantly improved without any adverse effect on recall if case-number-gender agreement conditions are taken into account. Thus, for example, the pattern *<N+Hum+First:ms2>* *<N+Hum+Last:ms2>* recognizes masculine names (*m*) in the genitive case (*2*) while the pattern *<N+Hum+First:fs2>* *<N+Hum+Last:s1>* recognizes feminine names (*f*) in the genitive case. Note that the patterns for masculine and feminine names differ since surname parts in Serbian feminine full names do not inflect. However, Unitex FSTs that we used for recognition of personal names are more complex than these simple patterns since they take into account additional features of personal names, such as the optional use of titles, nicknames, an additional surname for women, middle name or initial, as well as the order in which the first name and the surname appear, etc.

Special graphs were produced for recognizing a person's position in the society that precedes or follows a personal name forming thus a nominal phrase (Figure 1). Such graphs recognize following basic forms of phrases:

1. *generalni sekretar (udruženja pravnika Srbije)*gen.phrase — Secretary General of the Lawyers Association of Serbia;
2. *šef službe (za mala i srednja preduzeća)*FOR-prep-phrase — Head of service for small and medium enterprises;
3. *direktor (i većinski vlasnik)*AND-conj-phrase — Director and majority shareholder;
4. *ministar (omladine (i sporta)*AND-conj-phrase)gen.phrase — Minister of Youth and Sports;
5. *ministar prosvete (u vladi Republike Srbije)*IN-prep-phrase — Minister of Education in the government of the Republic of Serbia;
6. *izvršni direktor (Beogradske banke AD*abb)gen.phrase — Executive Director of Belgrade Bank AD.

These basic structures can be combined in various ways to recognize more complex phrases as demonstrated by the example *Mirjana Dragaš, predsednik Upravnog odbora Republičkog zavoda za tržište rada i zamenik saveznog ministra za rad i socijalna pitanja* 'Mirjana Dragaš, Chairman of the Steering Committee of the Republic Institute for Labour Market and Deputy Federal Minister of Labour and Social Affairs'.

We already explained how we used graphs in order to improve precision in recognition of personal names. These graphs perform well on names that are in our e-dictionaries, but fail to recognize a full name if one or more of its constituents are unknown. Our e-dictionaries of personal names cover Serbian and English names and only a small number of other foreign names transcribed into Serbian. Consequently, if our graphs relied on e-dictionaries only, they would fail to recognize most foreign names in Serbian texts, except common English names. For that reason we developed additional graphs that improve recall of recognition of personal names. These graphs rely on already developed graphs that recognize a person's position in the society. Basically they function like this: if a phrase recognized as a (potential) person's position is preceded or followed by two unknown words both with upper-case initial

[1] It should be noted that all foreign names in Serbian texts are transcribed, regardless of whether they are written in Latin or Cyrillic alphabet.

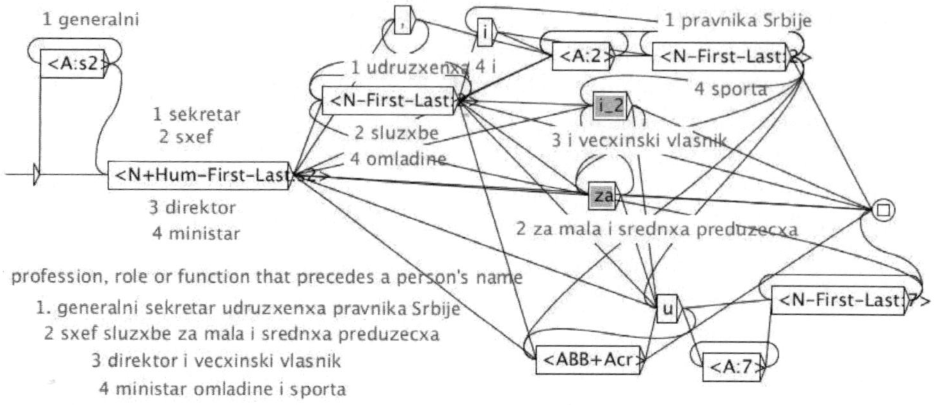

Figure 1: The graph recognizing functions, professions and roles preceding or following a personal name in the genitive case

or one personal name and one unknown word with upper-case initial then these two words are considered to form a full personal name (Figure 2).

Two examples of the recognition of personal names that were not in our e-dictionaries are: *Ministar odbrane Rumunije Teodor Atanasiu* 'Romanian Defence Minister Teodor Atanasiu' (only surname unknown) and *Gerasimov Ivanovič, član kolegijuma saveta međunarodnog saveza pravnika* 'Gerasimov Ivanovich, a member of the Collegium of the Council of the International Lawyers Association' (both first name and surname unknown). We developed 148 graphs that recognize personal names and their positions.

4.2 Geopolitical Names

Geopolitical names are ambiguous by themselves, namely, the same name can represent two or more different entities: a city and a state (e.g. *Luksemburg* 'Luxembourg'), mountain and a region (e.g. *Balkan*), etc., but they can also be ambiguous with other proper names or even common words. Thus, as in the case of personal names, tagging of geopolitical names cannot rely on e-dictionaries only. An additional problem in Serbian arises from the fact that the names of a number of countries coincide with the feminine gender relational adjectives derived from these names: e.g. *Francuska* 'France' can also mean 'French'. Thus, various constraints have to be used in order to keep the precision high.

Graphs for geopolitical names make intensive use of positive and negative right and left contexts implemented in Unitex (section 6.3 (Paumier, 2008)). We will illustrate how these graphs function on the example of the set of graphs recognizing names of states, which consists of four sub-graphs:

1. The basic graph recognizes all compound state names, all abbreviated states names, but only those simple word state names that are not ambiguous with any other proper or common name. To that end we use negative right context (Figure 3).

2. For ambiguous simple word state names that appear in a text in the genitive case we use a graph that recognizes such a name if some trigger noun appears before it, e.g. *predsednik* 'president', *skupština* 'parliament', etc. To that end we use the left context (the second part of Figure 3).

3. For simple word state names that are ambiguous with relational adjectives we use a graph that recognizes such a name if it is not followed by a common noun (thus preventing false recognitions in noun phrases like *Francuska banka* 'French bank') or if it is followed by an auxiliary verb (thus allowing correct recognitions in phrases like *Francuska je odlučila* 'France has decided'). To that end we use both positive and negative right contexts (third part of Figure 3).

4. Finally, we recognize as a state name every ambiguous simple word state name that appears in

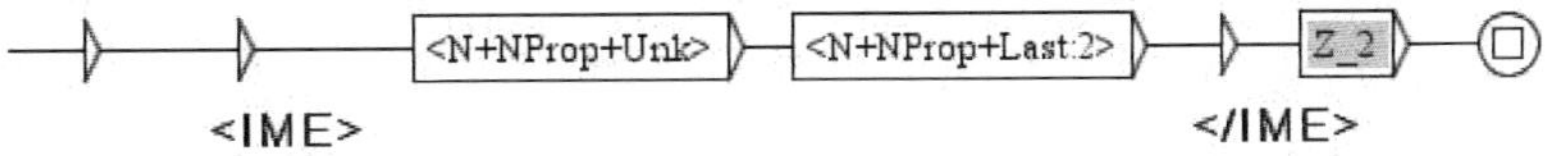

Figure 2: The graph that recognizes and tags a partially unknown personal name in the genitive case if followed by a person's position also in the genitive case

some kind of a list with other state names, provided that this list contains at least one unambiguous state name. At the bottom of Figure 3 is represented the path in a graph that matches a list of names in which the first state name is unambiguous, which is established by a basic graph described in item 1. This path will recognize two state names in *Srbija i Hrvatska* 'Serbia and Croatia', because the first name is unambiguous.

A similar approach is implemented for other types of geographic names. We developed 23 graphs for recognition of geopolitical names.

4.3 Other Named Entities

Recognition of money and measurement expressions also requires intensive use of graphs, particularly for the recognition of the numerical part of the expressions. For that, however, no special graphs were produced, since 40 dictionary graphs for recognition of multi-word numerals were already available and are in regular use for text processing, as described in section 2. Graphs for numerical expressions rely on information from e-dictionaries, and syntactic structures they have to cover are rather simple. We developed 12 graphs for recognition of measurement expressions and 10 for recognition of money expressions.

A collection of graphs was also produced for recognition of temporal expressions. These graphs, similar to the graphs for numerical expressions, use available dictionary graphs for multi-word numerals. As opposed to graphs for all other named entities, they use information from e-dictionaries to a much lesser degree. However, the expressions they have to recognize come in various different syntactic forms, which makes these graphs rather complex. We developed 29 graphs for recognition of date expressions and 14 for recognition of time expressions.

5 The Experiment and Evaluation

To evaluate the results produced by our graphs we used a collection of 2,300 short agency news dated from May 2005 to December 2006. The size of this corpus is approximately 117,000 simple word forms, and 4,273 sentences. Thus, an average news item consists of a little less than 2 sentences (1.86), and 51 simple word forms. This collection of news pertains to Serbian politics, both internal and external.

The graphs were applied to the corpus in the following order: measurement expressions, money expressions, dates, personal names and roles, time of day, geopolitical names. This order is the simple consequence of the fact that the graphs were applied in the order in which they were actually produced. The tagged texts where then handed to students who read them carefully and checked all the inserted tags[2]. The students also inserted a new attribute (PROVERA, 'check') into every tag with the value 'OK' if the named entity was correctly recognized and tagged, or 'NOK' if this was not the case or if it was only partially recognized. If the named entity was totally missed, the students inserted the appropriate tag with the value 'MISS' in the check attribute. One such example is: ...*od* <RS PROVERA='MISS'>*generalnog sekretara NATO* <IME PROVERA='MISS'>*Jap de Hop Shefera* </IME></RS>... 'by NATO Secretary General Jaap de Hoop Scheffer...'.[3]

It was not always easy to decide which value for the check attribute PROVERA is the most appropriate. We at present neglected the fuzzy nature of some named entities and always treated as correct, for instance, geographic place tags, although

[2]This task was accomplished by students of Library and Information Sciences at the Faculty of Philology, University Belgrade within the scope of the course 'Information Retrieval' during academic years 2009/2010 and 2010/2011.

[3]The tag IME (name) is embedded in the tag RS (reference string) which is used for tagging a position in the society.

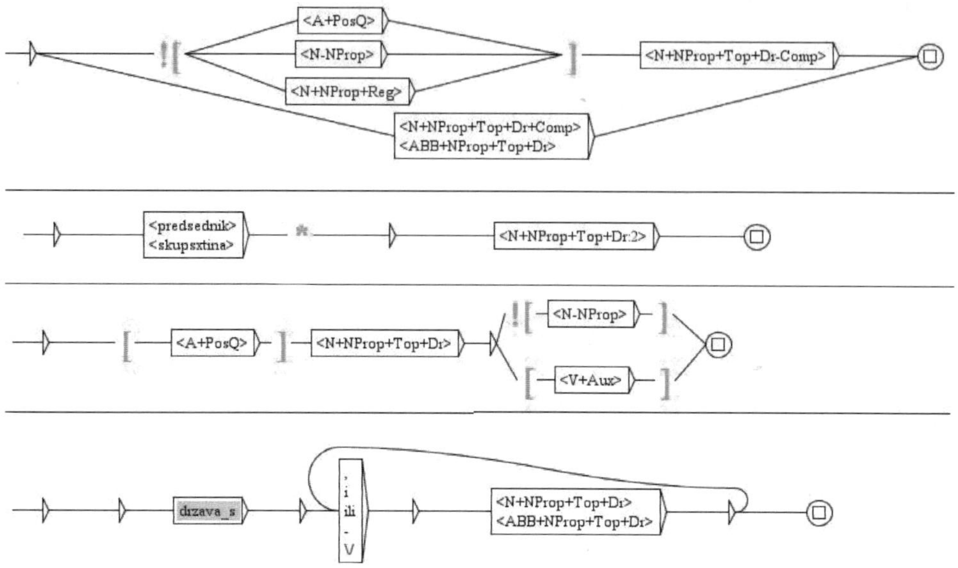

Figure 3: Simplified sub-graphs for recognition of state names

their actual usage could belong to another category, like organization. Also, it is clear that in *razgovori Beograda i Prištine* 'talks between Belgrade and Priština', Belgrade and Priština represent government institutions rather than locations. The authors in (Martineau et al., 2007) describe the NER approach for French which use the wider context to resolve such ambiguities. Their approach relies on a thorough description of phrasal verbs that does not yet exist for Serbian.

The results of our experiment are summarized in Table 2. The sample we used contained 9,677 NE tokens and 2,844 NE types, hence 3.4 tokens per type. At the top of the list of most frequent tokens are names of countries (TOP-C) followed by personal names (NAME), 3,115 and 3,056, respectively, accounting for 32.2% and 31.6% of the total number of tokens. Names of settlement (TOP-S) follow closely with 28.9%, and these three categories account for 92.7% of the total number of NE tokens. As for NE types, half of them represent personal names, another 20.5% are settlements followed by 10.9% for countries, reaching all together 81.4% of total NE types. The highest token/type ratio is 10.0 for names of countries and the lowest, one token per type, for temporal expressions representing date periods (DATE-P), which does not come as a surprise.

If we look at NE tokens only, the precision of our NER system is 0.98 whereas its recall is 0.93, yielding an overall F-measure of 0.95. The highest precision of 1.0 was reached for date periods, followed by names of countries, and names of settlements, both with a precision of 0.99. On the other hand, the lowest precision of 0.76 was achieved for names of water bodies (TOP-W), followed by 0.83 for temporal expressions representing time periods (TIME-P). However, names of water bodies have a recall of 1.0, hence an overall F-measure of 0.87. The lowest recall of only 0.56 for NE representing measures can be explained by an oversight in the construction of relevant graphs. Namely, we failed to include the units for time in the graphs, and since these units appear quite often in newspaper texts the graphs consequently failed to recognize them. This flaw will, of course, be removed in the future. Named entities representing measures have also the lowest F-measure of 0.71 followed by time periods with 0.77. On the other end are names of countries, which have an F-measure of as much as 0.99.

If we look at NE types, the results do not differ very much. The overall precision is 0.95, the recall 0.84, and the F-measure 0.89. The highest possible precision of 1.0 goes once again to date periods, but this time closely followed by currencies (CURR)

	OK		NOK		MISS		Token/	Precision		Recall		F-measure	
	Token	Type	Token	Type	Token	Type	Type	Token	Type	Token	Type	Token	Type
TOP-C	3,088	292	32	13	27	18	10.0	0.99	0.96	0.99	0.94	0.99	0.95
TOP-S	2,675	497	30	18	125	87	4.8	0.99	0.97	0.96	0.85	0.97	0.90
CURR	184	138	5	4	14	11	1.3	0.97	0.97	0.93	0.93	0.95	0.95
DATE-M	348	247	31	26	20	18	1.4	0.92	0.90	0.95	0.93	0.93	0.92
NAME	2,558	1,135	85	58	498	287	2.1	0.97	0.95	0.84	0.80	0.90	0.87
TIME-M	29	27	3	3	6	3	1.2	0.91	0.90	0.83	0.90	0.87	0.90
TOP-W	13	9	4	4	0	0	1.4	0.76	0.69	1.00	1.00	0.87	0.82
TOP-H	19	10	1	1	5	3	1.8	0.95	0.91	0.79	0.77	0.86	0.83
DATE-P	12	12	0	0	6	6	1.0	1.00	1.00	0.67	0.67	0.80	0.80
TIME-P	5	4	1	1	2	2	1.2	0.83	0.80	0.71	0.67	0.77	0.73
MEASURE	24	21	1	1	19	17	1.1	0.96	0.95	0.56	0.55	0.71	0.70
TOTAL	8,955	2,392	193	129	722	452	3.4	0.98	0.95	0.93	0.84	0.95	0.89

Table 2: Results of the experiment

and settlements, both at 0.97. Water bodies are once again at the bottom of the precision list with a score of 0.69, but due to a recall of 1.0, their F-measure is 0.82. Named entities representing measures have the lowest recall of 0.55 as well as the lowest F-measure of 0.70. The top of the F-measure list is a tie between names of countries and currencies, both with 0.95.

Finally, we would like to mention also the success rate of the recognition of a person's position in the society (RS). As these are not usually considered as NEs, we did not include them in the general overview table. However, for 2,991 tokens and 1,129 types related to such expressions, the precision was 0.88 and 0.94 respectively, with a recall of 0.84 for tokens and 0.78 for types, thus making their F-measure almost equal (0.86 vs. 0.85). Given the complexity and variety of such expressions this can be perceived as a very successful outcome.

The analysis of the obtained results showed that the causes of omissions and incorrect tagging were various and can be classified as follows:

- Typographic errors in the source text;
- Absence of a name in e-dictionaries;
- Oversights and minor deficiencies in the construction of graphs;
- Failure of a graph to cover all syntactic constructions.

Not much can be done in case of the first cause but our experiment proved very useful in detecting omissions and deficiencies in our e-dictionaries and graphs. Reducing the errors and omissions resulting from the fourth cause listed is most demanding in the case of graphs that recognize a person's positions, and it will ask for either production of additional graphs or substantial reconstruction of some of the existing ones. We will here only mention the most frequent cases.

- *...predsednik makedonske Komisije za odnose sa verskim zajednicama Cane Mojanovski...* '...President of the Macedonian Commission for Relations with Religious Communities Cane Mojanovski...' — the graph describing the position of a person (Figure 1) does not allow the preposition phrase *sa* 'with' within the preposition phrase *za* 'for'. The question is how much would be lost in precision by enhancing this graph to encompass such structures.
- Our graphs failed in many cases when the text contained a list of personal names with their positions, due to a lack of a straightforward link between the name and the position. One example is: *Predsednici Bugarske i Srbije Georgi Parvanov i Boris Tadić* 'Presidents of Bulgaria and Serbia Georgi Parvanov and Boris Tadić'.
- Our graphs failed in cases of nested structures as such cases were not envisaged, e.g. *portparol glavnog tužioca Haškog tribunala Karle del Ponte Florans Artman* 'spokesman for Chief

Prosecutor of Hague Tribunal Carla del Ponte, Florence Hartmann'.

6 Future Work

Although we see the evaluation results of our NER system as promising, there is still much to be done. Besides improving the existing system on the basis of the evaluation results, our future work will concentrate on enhancing NER system to recognize more NE categories. The classical entity-type still missing is organization, but in addition to that, existing e-dictionaries of Serbian support recognition of many other categories, such as inhabitants, events, urban proper names etc. We also plan to improve the performance of the NER system by organizing graphs in cascades, as suggested for French in (Friburger and Maurel, 2004) and by recognizing nested NE, especially recursive embedding of nominal phrases (see (Finkel and Manning, 2009)). After achieving these tasks we will move from NE recognition to information extraction by tackling the problem of normalizing the recognized NEs.

Acknowledgments

We would like to thank MSc and PhD students at the Faculty of Philology, University of Belgrade for their help in producing some of the graphs used in the NER system for Serbian: Sandra Gucul Milojević, Vanja Radulović and Jelena Jaćimović.

This research was supported by the Serbian Ministry of Education and Science under the grant #III 47003.

References

Lou Burnard and Syd Bauman. 2008. TEI P5: Guidelines for Electronic Text Encoding and Interchange.

Nancy Chinchor. 1995. MUC-6 Named Entity Task Definition (Version 2.1).

B. Courtois and M. Silberztein. 1990. *Dictionnaires électroniques du français*. Larousse, Paris.

Jenny Rose Finkel and Christopher D. Manning. 2009. Nested Named Entity Recognition. In *EMNLP*, pages 141–150. ACL.

Nathalie Friburger and Denis Maurel. 2004. Finite-state Transducer Cascades to Extract Named Entities in Texts. *Theor. Comput. Sci.*, 313(1):93–104.

Thierry Grass, Denis Maurel, and Odile Piton. 2002. Description of a multilingual database of proper names. In Elisabete Ranchod and Nuno J. Mamede, editors, *PorTAL*, volume 2389 of *Lecture Notes in Computer Science*, pages 137–140. Springer.

Ralph Grishman and Beth Sundheim. 1996. Message Understanding Conference-6: A Brief History. In *COLING*, volume 1, pages 466–471, Stroudsburg, PA, USA. Association for Computational Linguistics.

Cvetana Krstev. 2008. *Processing of Serbian - Automata, Texts and Electronic Dictionaries*. Faculty of Philology, University of Belgrade, Belgrade.

Claude Martineau, Elsa Tolone, and Stavroula Voyatzi. 2007. Les Entités Nommées : usage et degrés de précision et de désambiguïsation. In Catherine Camugli Gallardo, Matthieu Constant, and Anne Dister, editors, *Actes du 26ème Colloque international sur le Lexique et la Grammaire (LGC'07)*, pages 105–112, Bonifacio, France, October.

Denis Maurel. 2008. Prolexbase: a Multilingual Relational Lexical Database of Proper Names. In *LREC*. European Language Resources Association.

David Nadeau and Satoshi Sekine. 2009. A Survey of Named Entity Recognition and Classification. In Satoshi Sekine and Elisabete Ranchhod, editors, *Named Entities: Recognition, Classification and Use*, pages 3–28. John Benjamins Pub. Co., Amsterdam/Philadelphia.

Sébastien Paumier, 2008. *Unitex 2.1 User Manual*. http://www-igm.univ-mlv.fr/unitex/UnitexManual2.1.pdf.

Agata Savary, Jakub Waszczuk, and Adam Przepiórkowski. 2010. Towards the Annotation of Named Entities in the National Corpus of Polish. In Nicoletta Calzolari, Khalid Choukri, Bente Maegaard, Joseph Mariani, Jan Odijk, Stelios Piperidis, Mike Rosner, and Daniel Tapias, editors, *LREC*. European Language Resources Association.

S. Sekine and C. Nobata. 2004. Definition, Dictionaries and Tagger for Extended Named Entity Hierarchy. In *LREC*, Lisbon, Portugal.

Duško Vitas, Cvetana Krstev, and Denis Maurel. 2007. A Note on the Semantic and Morphological Properties of Proper Names in the Prolex Project. *Linguisticae Investigationes*, 30(1):115–133, January.

A Practical Algorithm for Intersecting Weighted Context-free Grammars with Finite-State Automata

Thomas Hanneforth
Linguistics Dept.
University of Potsdam, Germany
Thomas.Hanneforth@uni-potsdam.de

Abstract

It is well known that context-free parsing can be seen as the intersection of a context-free language with a regular language (or, equivalently, the intersection of a context-free grammar with a finite-state automaton). The present article provides a practical efficient way to compute this intersection by converting the grammar into a special finite-state automaton (the GLR(0)-automaton) which is subsequently intersected with the given finite-state automaton. As a byproduct, we present a generalisation of Tomita's algorithm to recognize several inputs simultaneously.

1 Introduction

At the least since the paper of Billot and Lang (1989) which defined parsing as the intersection of a context-free language (given by a grammar) with a regular language (the "input", which can be seen as a simple finite-state automaton) the importance of the notion of intersection for parsing purposes became apparent. Intersection is first of all defined on the *language level*: Intersect the (possibly infinite) set of strings which the grammar generates with the (possibly infinite) set of strings the finite-state automaton accepts. Since this may not be done effectively due to the infiniteness of the involved sets, the operation has to be lifted to the more compact level of the devices generating the sets.

In principle, there are at least two ways to intersect a context-free grammar G with a finite-state automaton A:

1. Convert G into a suitable pushdown automaton (PDA) M and intersect A with M to get M'. Then extract the result grammar G' from M'.
2. Intersect G and A directly.

With respect to 1., it is well known that the class of pushdown automata is closed under intersection with finite-state automata (henceforth FSA) (cf. Hopcroft and Ullman (1979)). The standard construction assumes a deterministic FSA (see next section) and operates both automata in parallel: Whenever the PDA makes a move on a certain input symbol a, this move is combined with a corresponding move of the FSA on a (see Hopcroft and Ullman (1979) for details of the construction).

Method 1 works most efficiently in case of grammars in *Greibach normal form* (GNF). Remember that a context-free grammar is in GNF if each of its rules conforms to the format $A \rightarrow aB_1 \ldots B_k$ where a is an alphabet symbol, A is a nonterminal (phrase) symbol and $B_1 \ldots B_k$ is a possibly empty sequence of nonterminals. Given a grammar in GNF, it is very easy to construct a pushdown automaton from it: when the PDA has A on its stack and next reads an a, it replaces A by $B_1 \ldots B_k$. Every context-free grammar can be converted into a weakly equivalent grammar in GNF (cf. Hopcroft and Ullman (1979)), but this changes the trees generated by the grammar and may lead to a substiantial increase in grammar size.

Method 2 was presented in Bar-Hillel et al. (1964) and works in the following way: Consider a grammar rule $X_0 \rightarrow X_1X_2 \ldots X_k$. Then choose an arbitrary state sequence $p_0 \ldots p_k$ from the state set Q of the FSA and create a new grammar rule

$$\langle p_0, X_0, p_k\rangle \rightarrow \langle p_0, X_1, p_1\rangle \langle p_1, X_2, p_2\rangle \ldots \langle p_{k-1}, X_k, p_k\rangle \ . \quad (1)$$

Proceedings of the 9th International Workshop on Finite State Methods and Natural Language Processing, pages 57–64,
Blois (France), July 12-15, 2011. ©2011 Association for Computational Linguistics

Leaving the grammar fixed, the time complexity of this method is in $\mathcal{O}(|Q|^{r+1})$ where r is the length of the longest right-hand side of a grammar rule. The drawback of the method is that it creates a great amount of useless nonterminals and rules. Nederhof and Satta (2008) improved the algorithm by adding simultaneous top-down and bottom-up filtering mechanisms to prevent the creation of useless symbols which of course does not change its worst-case complexity. This upper bound can be reduced to $\mathcal{O}(|Q|^3)$ by binarising the grammar rules (which naturally changes the generated trees). However, it is not clear how the algorithm behaves in practice on grammars with several thousands of rules ubiquitous in natural language processing.

In the present paper, we propose another algorithm based on the creation of a *GLR(0) automaton* which is subsumed by method 1 above. The rest of the paper is organised as follows: Section 2 briefly defines the relevant notions. Section 3 defines GLR(0) automata and presents an algorithm how to intersect them with FSAs. In Section 4 we report some experiments conducted with a big grammar extracted from a treebank.

2 Preliminaries

An alphabet Σ is a finite set of symbols. A string $x = a_1 \ldots a_n$ over Σ is a finite concatenation of symbols a_i taken from Σ. The length of a string $x = a_1 \ldots a_n$ – symbolically $|x|$ – is n. The empty string is denoted by ε and has length zero. Let Σ^* denote the set of all finite-length strings (including ε) over Σ.

A *finite-state automaton* (FSA) A is a 5-tuple $\langle Q, \Sigma, q_0, \delta, F\rangle$ with Q being a finite set of states; Σ, an *alphabet*, $q_0 \in Q$, the start state; $\delta : Q \times \Sigma \mapsto 2^Q$, the transition function; and $F \subseteq Q$, the set of final states.

Given two states $p, q \in Q$, a *path* from p to q in A – symbolically $p \underset{A}{\rightsquigarrow} q$ – is a sequence $s_0 s_1 \ldots s_k$ of states, such that $s_0 = p$, $s_k = q$, and for all $1 \leq i \leq k$: $\exists a \in \Sigma : s_i \in \delta(s_{i-1}, a)$. Given a path $\pi = p \underset{A}{\rightsquigarrow} q$, define $labels(\pi)$ as the concatenation of the symbols labeling the transitions along π. For an empty path $\pi = s_0$, $labels(\pi) = \varepsilon$. The length of path $\pi = s_0 s_1 \ldots s_k$ – symbolically $|\pi|$ – is k. We use $p \overset{k}{\underset{A}{\rightsquigarrow}} q$ to denote a path from p to q of length k in A.

An FSA is called *deterministic* if for all symbol-state pairs q, a, $|\delta(q,a)| \leq 1$. For a deterministic FSA, we may modify δ to be a partial function $Q \times \Sigma \mapsto Q$. When appropriate, we use δ as a total function by adding a special element $\perp$ to Q denoting failure. For deterministic FSA, we use sometimes the notation $p \overset{a}{\rightarrow} q$ to denote transitions: $p \overset{a}{\rightarrow} q$ if $\delta(p,a) = q$.

Define $\delta^* : Q \times \Sigma \mapsto G$ as the reflexive and transitive closure of δ: $\forall q \in Q, \delta^*(q, \varepsilon) = q$ and $\forall q \in Q, a \in \Sigma, w \in \Sigma^* : \delta^*(q, aw) = \delta^*(\delta(q,a), w)$.

Given a (deterministic) FSA $A = \langle Q, \Sigma, q_0, \delta, F\rangle$, the *language* $L(A)$ of A is defined as: $L(A) = \{x \in \Sigma^* \mid \delta^*(q_0, x) \in F\}$.

A *semiring* $\mathcal{K}$ is a 5-tuple $(W, \oplus, \otimes, \overline{0}, \overline{1})$ such that 1. W is a non-empty set, the *carrier set* of the semiring, 2. $(W, \oplus, \overline{0})$ is a commutative monoid, 3. $(W, \otimes, \overline{1})$ is a monoid, 4. $\otimes$ distributes over $\oplus$, and 5. $\overline{0}$ is an annihilator for $\otimes$: $\forall x \in W : x \otimes \overline{0} = \overline{0} \otimes x = \overline{0}$. In the following, we will identify a semiring $\mathcal{K}$ with its carrier set W. Common semirings are the tropical semiring $\mathcal{T} = \langle \mathbb{R}, min, +, \infty, 0\rangle$ and the probabilistic semiring $\mathcal{P} = \langle \mathbb{R}, +, \cdot, 0, 1\rangle$.

A *weighted context-free grammar* (WCFG) G over a semiring $\mathcal{K}$ is a 4-tuple $\langle N, \Sigma, S, P\rangle$: N is a finite set, the non-terminals, Σ is an alphabet, $S \in N$ the start symbol, and P a finite set of pairs $\langle A \rightarrow \beta, c\rangle \in (N \times (\Sigma \cup N)^*) \times \mathcal{K}$, the set of weighted rules. A WCFG without rule weights is called a *context-free grammar* (CFG).

In particular, if $\mathcal{K}$ is the probabilistic semiring and if we define an additional condition on σ:

$$\forall A \in N : \sum_{\langle A \rightarrow \beta, c\rangle \in P} c = 1 \ , \qquad (2)$$

then G is called a *probabilistic context-free grammar* (PCFG) (see also Nederhof and Satta (2008)). Fig. 1 shows a toy PCFG.

1: *S* → *NP VP* / 1.0	**2**: *NP* → *DET N* / 0.6
3: *NP* → *NE* / 0.3	**4**: *NP* → *NP PP* / 0.1
5: *PP* → *P NP* / 1.0	**6**: *VP* → *V* / 0.5
7: *VP* → *V NP* / 0.4	**8**: *VP* → *VP PP* / 0.1

Figure 1: *A toy PCFG with numbered rules. Probabilities are stated after /.*

Let $G = \langle \Sigma, N, S, P \rangle$ be a context-free grammar, and let V be $N \cup \Sigma$. Define a relation $\Rightarrow \subseteq V^* \times V^*$ as follows: $\alpha \Rightarrow \beta$ if $\alpha = xA\gamma, \beta = x\psi\gamma, x \in \Sigma^*, \gamma \in V^*$ and $A \rightarrow \psi \in P$.

Let $\overset{*}{\Rightarrow}$ be equal to $\bigcup_{k \geq 0} \overset{k}{\Rightarrow}$. A *leftmost derivation* of a string $w \in \Sigma^*$ is a sequence of elements from $\Rightarrow$ such that $S \Rightarrow X_1 \ldots X_k \Rightarrow \ldots \Rightarrow w$. We abbreviate this to $S \overset{*}{\Rightarrow} w$. The *language* of a CFG G – symbollically $L(G)$ – is defined as $L(G) = \{w \in \Sigma^* \mid S \overset{*}{\Rightarrow} w\}$. Finally, given a CFG G and an FSA A, define the intersection of G and A as follows: $G_\cap = G \cap A$ if $L(G) \cap L(A) = L(G_\cap)$.

The notion of a derivation and the language of a CFG carry over to WCFGs, as well as the notion of intersection. See Nederhof and Satta (2008) for details.

3 The Intersection Algorithm

The main idea to compute the intersection of a weighted context-free grammar G with a finite-state automaton A is stated in Algorithm 1.

Algorithm 1: INTERSECTION OF A WCFG AND AN FSA

Input: WCFG $G = \langle N, \Sigma, S, P \rangle$ over semiring $\mathcal{K}$
Input: FSA $A = \langle Q, \Sigma, q_0, \delta, F \rangle$
Output: WCFG $G_\cap = \langle N_\cap, \Sigma, S_\cap, P_\cap \rangle$ over semiring $\mathcal{K}$ with $N_\cap \subseteq N \times Q$ and $P_\cap \subseteq (N_\cap \times (N_\cap \cup \Sigma)^*) \times \mathcal{K}$

1 Construct GLR(0) automaton M for G
2 Compute $M_\cap$, the intersection of M and A
3 Extract $G_\cap$ from $M_\cap$

In line 1, the WCFG is converted into a GLR(0) automaton. Given a WCFG $G = \langle N, \Sigma, S, P \rangle$ over $\mathcal{K}$, a *GLR(0) automaton* (for *Generalised LR*) $M = \langle Q, \Delta, q_0, F, \delta, \tau \rangle$ over $\mathcal{K}$ is a finite-state automaton with Q, F and q_0 defined as for FSAs; Δ is $N \cup \Sigma$. Since M is required to be deterministic, $\delta : Q \times \Delta \mapsto Q$ is a partial transition function which maps – when defined – a state q and a symbol $a \in \Delta$ to a follow state. $\tau : Q \mapsto 2^P$ is a mapping from states to subsets of grammar rules (indices).[1]

GLR(0) automata are computed from grammars by an algorithm adapted from a standard algorithm (cf. Aho et al. (1986, p. 216ff.)) which will be explained in greater detail in Section 3.1.

Fig. 2 gives a example GLR(0) automaton for the grammar from Fig. 1. A GLR(0) recognizer is controlled by a GLR(0) automaton M. Given some input string w, it creates another GLR(0) automaton M' as a result by repeatedly applying its two main operations:[2]

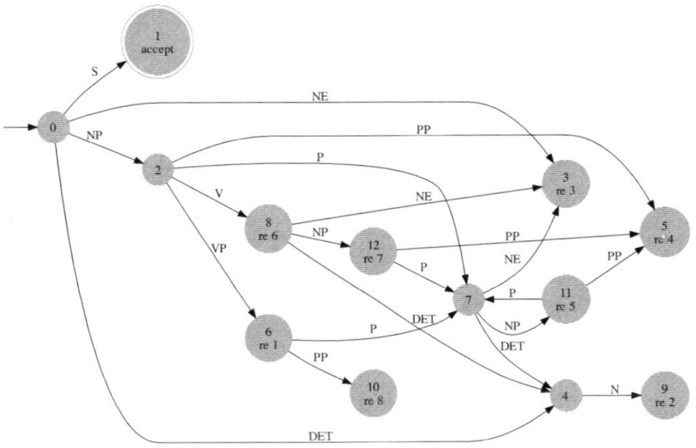

Figure 2: *The GLR(0) automaton for the grammar in Fig. 1. "re* n*"* means: "reduce with rule *n*". A transition from state p to state q corresponds to a (terminal or nonterminal) shift operation.

- **Shift**: When the recognizer reads an input symbol $a \in \Sigma$ in state q, it adds a transition $q \overset{a}{\rightarrow} \delta(q, a)$ to M'.

- **Reduce**: When while processing an input string, the parser reaches a state q for which $\tau(q)$ is defined, for each rule $A \rightarrow \alpha \in \tau(q)$, find all predecessor states p such that $labels(p \rightsquigarrow q) = \alpha$.[3] Then add a transition $p \overset{A}{\rightarrow} \delta(p, A)$ to M' (which may be interpreted as a nonterminal shift). $\delta(p, A)$ is also called a GOTO state.

The GLR(0) recognizer starts in state q_0 and scans the input string from left to right. It applies the operations *shift* and *reduce* until either an accepting state

[1]In the original definition of LR(k) automata, τ is a partial function $Q \mapsto P$. The presence of multiple reduce actions would indicate an ambiguity (a *reduce/reduce conflict*) which entails that the language of the underlying grammar G is not a LR(k)-language. See Aho and Ullman (1972).

[2]Actually, the LR(k) method was invented for parsing deterministic languages like programming languages. In these cases it is not necessary to create an output automaton. Instead, a simple stack is used on which state symbols are pushed and from which they a popped during a reduction.

[3]We momentarily disregard the rule weight here.

$f \in F$ is reached (in which case f is also marked as final in M') or the GLR(0) automaton blocks which causes an error to be signaled.

Continuing with Algorithm 1, line 2 intersects the GLR(0) automaton M with the FSA A, resulting in a GLR(0) automaton $M_\cap$.

Finally, in line 3, the WCFG $G_\cap$ generating $L(G) \cap L(A)$ is extracted from $M_\cap$.
The following subsections explain all three steps in greater detail.

3.1 Efficient Construction of GLR(0) Automata

The construction of a GLR(0) automaton M is based on the computation of the *collection of LR(0) item sets*. Here, the crucial notion is that one of a *dotted rule*. A *dotted rule* is a WCFG rule with a dot somewhere in its right-hand side. This dot indicates which part of the rule was already successfully applied and which part has yet to be matched. An example with respect to the grammar in Fig. 1 is: $NP \rightarrow NP \bullet PP$. A dotted rule is also called a *LR(0) item*. To compute M, we start with a set containing only the LR(0) item $S' \rightarrow \bullet S$ where S' is a new super start symbol. Then the main operation of the algorithm – *closure* – is applied to it. Basically, given a grammar $G = \langle N, \Sigma, S, P \rangle$, $closure(\{A \rightarrow \alpha \bullet B\beta\})$ (with $A, B \in N$ and $\alpha, \beta \in (N \cup \Sigma)^*$) computes on the basis of G the symbols which are expected next given that the automaton's expectation is to read a B.[4]
In our example case,

$$q_0 = closure(\{S' \rightarrow \bullet\, S\}) = \left\{ \begin{array}{l} S' \rightarrow \bullet\, S \\ S \rightarrow \bullet\, NP\ VP \\ NP \rightarrow \bullet\, DET\ N \\ NP \rightarrow \bullet\, NE \end{array} \right\} \quad (3)$$

The δ-function of M is computed as follows:

$$\delta(q, B) = closure(\{A \rightarrow \alpha B \bullet \beta \mid A \rightarrow \alpha \bullet B\beta \in q\}) \ . \quad (4)$$

For example, $\delta(q_0, \mathrm{NE}) = closure(\{\mathrm{NP} \rightarrow \mathrm{NE} \bullet\}) = \{\mathrm{NP} \rightarrow \mathrm{NE} \bullet\}$.

Let the state set Q of M be the set of all LR(0) item sets that can be reached by recursively applying δ and *closure* to q_0 and all item sets originating from it.

[4]Due to space limitations, we cannot state the definition of the closure algorithm. Please refer to Aho et al. (1986, p. 223) for the details.

If a state q contains an item $A \rightarrow \alpha\, \bullet$, the rule $A \rightarrow \alpha$ is added to $\tau(q)$. M reaches an accepting state f if the item set contains the LR(0) item $S' \rightarrow S\, \bullet$.

For grammars not having the LR(0) property (for example, ambiguous grammars), the construction introduces *conflicts*, see Aho and Ullman (1972). Nevertheless, the algorithm leads to deterministic GLR(0) automata for all grammars.

The naive approach representing LR(0) states as sets of dotted rules leads to increased computation times for bigger grammars, for example those extracted from treebanks. For example, the grammar extracted from the TiGer treebank (Brants et al. (2002)) has over 14,300 rules.

A better approach is replacing the dotted rule by a pair consisting of the rule index and the current position of the dot. But even then quite big item sets may result since treebank grammars often have several thousand rules for expanding a single nonterminal symbol.[5] Since the right hand sides of grammar rules expanding a given nonterminal symbol often share common prefixes, left-factoring the grammar (cf. Aho et al. (1986)) is an option when the structure of the parse tree is not of concern. In general, this is not the case in using (weighted) grammars for parsing natural languages.

Instead of altering the grammar, we prefer a more sophisticated representation of the dotted rules. All right hand sides α_i of a set of rules $\{B \rightarrow \alpha_i\}$ expanding B can be combined into a disjunctive regular expression $r = \alpha_1 + \alpha_2 + \ldots + \alpha_k$. r can be converted into a deterministic weighted finite-state machine by standard techniques (cf. Hopcroft and Ullman (1979)). The result is a trie-like left-factored automaton A_B representing the right hand sides of the rules for B. For the final states of A_B, we define a function $\rho : Q \rightarrow I$, where I is the set of rule indices of the WCFG. For a given final state q of A_B (representing a fully found right hand side α of a rule expanding B), $\rho(q) = i$ if $\exists c \in \mathcal{K} : \langle B \rightarrow \alpha, c\rangle$ is the ith rule of the grammar.

Fig. 3 shows the rule FSA A_{VP} for the toy grammar shown in Fig. 1.
An LR(0) item is then represented as a pair $\langle B, q\rangle$

[5]For example, the TiGer grammar used in Section 4 contains 2,378 rules for prepositional phrases and 3,475 rules for verbal phrases.

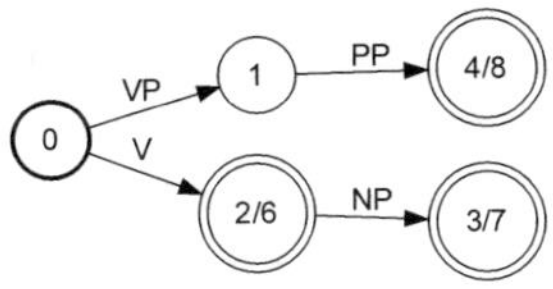

Figure 3: *The rule trie containing the right hand sides of VP of the grammar in Fig. 1. Double circles indicate final states and state the rule index after /.*

where B is a nonterminal and q a state in the FSA A_B associated with B. When during the closure operation a pair $\langle B, q\rangle$ is processed, the transitions $q \xrightarrow{X_i} p$ leaving q in A_B are enumerated and new items $\langle X_i, q0_{X_i}\rangle$ (if $X_i \in N$) are added to the closure items set.

3.2 Intersecting LR(0) Automata with Finite-state Automata

Algorithm 2 computes the intersection of M and A. The algorithm maintains a breadth-first queue L of state pairs $\in Q_M \times Q_A$. In line 4, a pair consisting of the two start states is inserted into L. In the **while**-loop between lines 5 and 31, a state pair $\langle q_M, q_A\rangle$ is removed from L. Then, two types of actions are applied to the current state pair $\langle q_M, q_A\rangle$: Reductions and shifts. Line 9 checks whether M defines reductions for state q_M. If true, the **for**-loop between lines 10 and 23 considers each rule $B \rightarrow \alpha$ with weight c. In line 11, the set of all ancestor nodes for current state $\langle q_M, q_A\rangle$ is computed for which there are paths π of length $|\alpha|$ to $\langle q_M, q_A\rangle$ (simultaneously, we also record the labels of the paths between an ancestor state and $\langle q_M, q_A\rangle$). By definition of the construction of a GLR(0) automaton, *labels*(π) equals α (disregarding the indices).

Then, the **for**-loop between lines 12 and 23 operates over each ancestor state $\langle q, q'\rangle$ of $\langle q_M, q_A\rangle$ and constructs new states and transitions which correspond to the GOTO-actions of the GLR(0) recognizer for nonterminal symbols. Before doing that, a rule $\langle B_{q_A} \rightarrow \alpha', c\rangle$ is added to the reduce actions of state $\langle q_M, q_A\rangle$ in line 13. Note that α' differs from the original α in rule $B \rightarrow \alpha$ in the indices carried by the nonterminals.[6] The subsequent steps are:

- In line 14, a new state $\langle \delta_M(q, B), q_A\rangle$ is created and checked whether it is present in the state set (and inserted if it is not). Here, $\delta_M(q, B)$ denotes the GOTO-state M defines for nonterminal B. Note that the second component q_A of $\langle \delta_M(q, B), q_A\rangle$ is copied from the current state pair $\langle q_M, q_A\rangle$ (the input index does not "move" on after a reduction, so to speak).

[6] We will discuss the necessity of indexed nonterminals B_{q_A} below.

Algorithm 2: INTERSECTION OF A GLR(0) AUTOMATON AND AN FSA

Input: GLR(0) automaton $M = \langle Q_M, \Delta_M, q0_M, F_M, \delta_M, \tau_M\rangle$ over a semiring $\mathcal{K}$
Input: Deterministic FSA $A = \langle Q_A, \Sigma, q0_A, \delta_A, F_A\rangle$
Output: GLR(0) automaton $M' = \langle Q_{M'}, \Delta_{M'}, q0_{M'}, F_{M'}, \delta_{M'}, \tau_{M'}\rangle$ over $\mathcal{K}$

1 $q0_{M'} \leftarrow \langle q0_M, q0_A\rangle$
2 $Q_{M'} \leftarrow \{q0_{M'}\}$
3 $F_{M'} \leftarrow \emptyset$
4 $Enqueue(q0_{M'}, L)$
5 **while** $L \neq \emptyset$ **do**
6 $\langle q_M, q_A\rangle \leftarrow Dequeue(L)$
7 **if** $q_M \in F_M \wedge q_A \in F_A$ **then**
8 $F_{M'} \leftarrow F_{M'} \cup \{\langle q_M, q_A\rangle\}$
9 **if** $\tau_M(q_M) \neq \bot$ **then**
// Perform reductions
10 **for** $\langle B \rightarrow \alpha, c\rangle \in \tau_M(q_M)$ **do**
11 $V_\alpha \leftarrow \{\langle q, q', labels(\pi)\rangle \mid \langle q, q'\rangle \in Q_{M'} \wedge \pi = \langle q, q'\rangle \overset{|\alpha|}{\underset{M'}{\rightsquigarrow}} \langle q_M, q_A\rangle\}$
12 **for** $\langle q, q', \alpha'\rangle \in V_\alpha$ **do**
13 $\tau_{M'}(\langle q_M, q_A\rangle) \leftarrow \tau_{M'}(\langle q_M, q_A\rangle) \cup \{\langle B_{q_A} \rightarrow \alpha', c\rangle\}$
14 **if** $\langle \delta_M(q, B), q_A\rangle \notin Q_{M'}$ **then**
15 $Q_{M'} \leftarrow Q_{M'} \cup \{\langle \delta_M(q, B), q_A\rangle\}$
16 $\delta_{M'}(\langle q, q'\rangle, B_{q_A}) \leftarrow \langle \delta_M(q, B), q_A\rangle$
17 $\Delta_{M'} \leftarrow \Delta_{M'} \cup \{B_{q_A}\}$
18 $Enqueue(\langle \delta_M(q, B), q_A\rangle, L)$
19 **else**
20 **if** $\delta_{M'}(\langle q, q'\rangle, B_{q_A}) = \bot$ **then**
21 $\delta_{M'}(\langle q, q'\rangle, B_{q_A}) \leftarrow \langle \delta_M(q, B), q_A\rangle$
22 **if** $\langle \delta_M(q, B), q_A\rangle \notin L$ **then**
23 $Enqueue(\langle \delta_M(q, B), q_A\rangle, L)$
// Perform shifts
24 **for** $a \in \Sigma$ **do**
25 **if** $\delta_M(q_M, a) \neq \bot \wedge \delta_A(q_A, a) \neq \bot$ **then**
26 $\Delta_{M'} \leftarrow \Delta_{M'} \cup \{a\}$
27 $p \leftarrow \langle \delta_M(q_M, a), \delta_A(q_A, a)\rangle$
28 $\delta_{M'}(\langle q_M, q_A\rangle, a) \leftarrow p$
29 **if** $p \notin Q_{M'}$ **then**
30 $Q_{M'} \leftarrow Q_{M'} \cup \{p\}$
31 $Enqueue(p, L)$
32 **return** M'

- In line 20, it is checked whether a transition leaving ancestor state $\langle q, q' \rangle$ with symbol B_{q_A} already exists. Here, there are two subcases to consider:
    1. $\langle \delta_M(q, B), q_A \rangle$ is a new state which entails that the transition $\langle q, q' \rangle \xrightarrow{B_{q_A}} \langle \delta_M(q, B), q_A \rangle$ also does not exist (lines 15–18). This happens when $\langle \delta_M(q, B), q_A \rangle$ is encountered for the first time. $\langle \delta_M(q, B), q_A \rangle$ is added to the state set (line 15) and a new transition leading to it is added to $\delta_{M'}$ (line 16). Finally, B_{q_A} is added to the alphabet of M' (line 17) and the new state $\langle \delta_M(q, B), q_A \rangle$ is inserted into the queue (line 18).
    2. $\langle \delta_M(q, B), q_A \rangle$ already existed, but not $\langle q, q' \rangle \xrightarrow{B_{q_A}} \langle \delta_M(q, B), q_A \rangle$ (lines 21–23). Here, we repeatedly encountered $\langle \delta_M(q, B), q_A \rangle$ during processing. This happens in case of local ambiguities where there exist multiple trees for some subpart of A headed by the same nonterminal. In terms of the graph structure of M', we create a *reentrant* node $\langle \delta_M(q, B), q_A \rangle$ with more than one incoming transition (line 21). Since $\langle \delta_M(q, B), q_A \rangle$ may trigger further reductions (its ancestor set was changed), it is reinserted into the queue (when not already present).

The shift operations performed in the **for**-loop between lines 24 and 31 are similar to the case of the intersection of two FSAs: For every transition leaving q_A labeled a it is tried to find a corresponding transition leaving q_M. If this transition exists, a new state pair $\langle \delta_M(q_M, a), \delta_A(q_A, a) \rangle$ is added to $Q_{M'}$ and L, if not already present (line 30). In addition, a transition $\langle q_M, q_A \rangle \xrightarrow{a} \langle \delta_M(q_A, a), \delta_A(q_A, a) \rangle$ is created (line 28).

Unsurprisingly, Algorithm 2 is simply a generalisation of Tomita's GLR algorithm (cf. Tomita and Ng (1991)) to the recognition of the language of an FSA instead of the recognition of a single sentence (which can be seen as a simple, linear FSA with a single final state). In the general case treated here, A may have several final states and may contain an infinite number of paths. Because of that, the nonterminal symbols of M' are indexed with the current state q_A of A. In that way, M' keeps track of the different reductions made for different paths in A.

Fig. 4(b) shows the result of applying Algorithm 2 to the GLR(0) automaton of Fig. 2 and the FSA of Fig. 4(a).

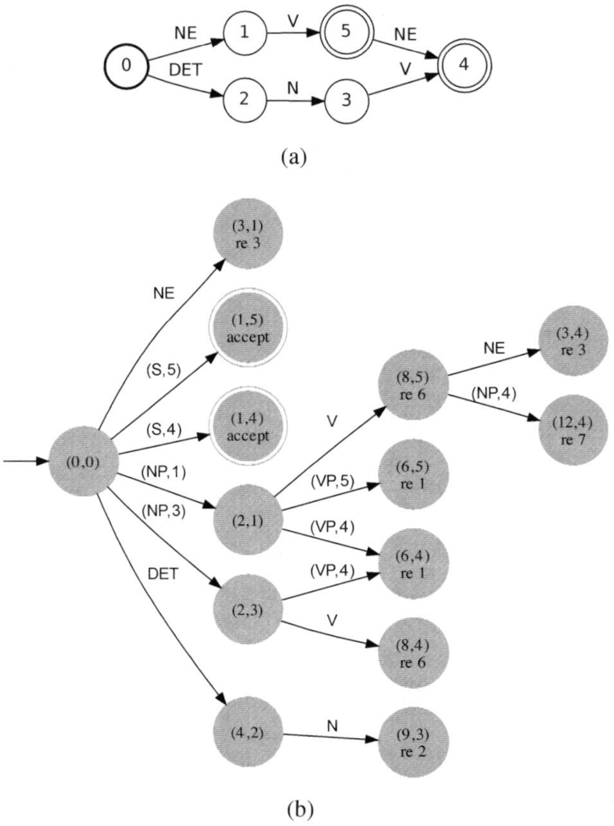

Figure 4: (a) *A deterministic FSA representing three sentences of the PCFG of Fig. 1.* (b) *The result of Algorithm 2 applied to the automata in Fig. 2 and Fig. 4(a). States are labeled with pairs* $\langle q_M, q_A \rangle$.

3.2.1 Complexity.

The outer **while**-loop of Algorithm 2 is bounded by $\mathcal{O}(|Q_M \times Q_A|)$. Since M and A are both deterministic, only a small subset of $Q_M \times Q_A$ will be actually created in the average case. Concerning the *shift*-actions (**for**-loop lines 24–31), each pair is inserted exactly once into the queue. Looking at the *reduce*-actions (lines 9–23), a state pair may be reinserted into the queue in case a new incoming transition is added for $\langle \delta_M(q, B), q_A \rangle$ (line 23). The number of reinsertions is bounded by the number of pos-

$S' \rightarrow S_4 \ / \ 1$	$S' \rightarrow S_5 \ / \ 1$
$S_4 \rightarrow NP_1 \ VP_4 \ / \ 1$	$S_4 \rightarrow NP_3 \ VP_4 \ / \ 1$
$S_5 \rightarrow NP_1 \ VP_5 \ / \ 1$	$NP_1 \rightarrow NE \ / \ 0.3$
$NP_3 \rightarrow DET \ N \ / \ 0.6$	$NP_4 \rightarrow NE \ / \ 0.3$
$VP_4 \rightarrow V \ NP_4 \ / \ 0.4$	$VP_4 \rightarrow V \ / \ 0.5$
$VP_5 \rightarrow V \ / \ 0.5$	

Figure 5: Rule set of the grammar extracted from Fig. 4(b).

sible reductions taking place at $\langle q_M, q_A \rangle$ which is in turn bounded by $|N|$, the number of nonterminals of G. The most expensive step is found in line 11. Let r be the length of the longest right-hand side of a rule in G. The number of state pairs $\langle q, q' \rangle$ created in line 11 and subsequently considered in the **for**-loop lines 12–23 is bounded by $\mathcal{O}(|Q_M \times Q_A|^r)$ (the number of ancestors increases exponentially with respect to the distance r). By applying the memoisation techniques proposed in Kipps (1991), this bound can be strengthend to $\mathcal{O}(|Q_M \times Q_A|^2)$. Putting everything together, the overall complexity of Algorithm 2 is in $\mathcal{O}(|Q_M \times Q_A|^3)$.

3.3 Extracting Grammar Rules

The last step, the extraction of $G_\cap = G \cap A$ is easy and stated in Algorithm 3.

Algorithm 3: EXTRACTING $G_\cap$.

Input: A GLR(0) automaton $M = \langle Q_M, \Delta_M, q_{0_M}, F_M, \delta_M, \tau_M \rangle$ over $\mathcal{K}$
Output: A WCFG $G_\cap = \langle N, \Delta_M \setminus N, S', P \rangle$ over $\mathcal{K}$

$N \leftarrow \{X_i \in \Delta_M \mid i \in \mathbb{N}\} \cup \{S'\}$

$$P \leftarrow \{\langle S' \rightarrow X_i, \bar{1} \rangle \mid \exists X_i \in N : \delta_M(q_{0_M}, X_i) \in F_M\} \cup \bigcup_{q \in Q_M \wedge \tau_M(q) \neq \perp} \tau_M(q)$$

Algorithm 3 simply extracts the grammar rules from the states q for which $\tau_M(q)$ is defined. Additionally, a new start symbol S' is introduced and trivially weighted rules $S' \rightarrow X_i$ are added to the rule set such that X_i is labeling a transition from q_{0_M} to a final state. Fig. 5 shows the grammar extracted from the automaton shown in Fig. 4(b).

Automaton	$\mathbf{A_1}$	$\mathbf{A_2}$	$\mathbf{A_3}$
$\lvert\mathbf{Q}\rvert$	8	56	173
$\lvert\delta\rvert$	9	64	259

Table 1: Sizes of the input FSA.

Phase	Operation	Time (ms)	Avg. time per sent	$\lvert\mathbf{Q}\rvert$	$\lvert\delta\rvert$
1	Constr. of M	$3,520$	-	$17,279$	$1,226,776$
2	$M \cap A_1$	47	47	$1,841$	$14,005$
2	$M \cap A_2$	$3,198$	320	$18,355$	$389,140$
2	$M \cap A_3$	$17,847$	178	$50,332$	$1,097,768$

Table 2: Results of the experiments with the TiGer grammar.

4 Experiments

We implemented the algorithm from the last section in the C++ programming language within the *fsm2* framework (see Hanneforth (2009)). The grammar used for the experiments has been extracted from the TiGer treebank (cf. Brants et al. (2002)). It contains 14,379 rules[7], and the sizes of the alphabet and the nonterminal sets are 51 and 25, resp. The length of the longest right-hand side of a rule is 17. For the FSA operand of the intersection algorithm, we created three minimal FSA accepting 1, 10 and 100 sentences (tag sequences) randomly taken from the TiGer corpus. The sizes of the automata are summarised in Table 1.

Table 2 shows the results of the experiments which were carried out on a 2.8 GHz CPU. The columns $|Q|$ and $|\delta|$ contain the sizes of the automata resulting from the operation mentioned before.

Since treebank grammars tend to avoid recursive rules and therefore assign flat structures to input strings, they create a lot of readings with spurious ambiguities. Johnson (1998) reports that approximately 9% of the rules of the Penn treebank are never used in a maximum likelihood setting since these rules are subsumed by combinations of other rules with a higher combined probability. We expect even better intersection timings in the face of more linguistically realistic grammars.

[7]Disregarding discontinous constructions like verb–particle rules which are not directly representable in the context-free grammar format.

5 Conclusion

Above, we presented a theoretical and practical algorithm to intersect weighted grammars with FSAs which can be used for parsing or language model training purposes (cf. Nederhof (2005)). No grammar transformation (for example, binarisation) is necessary to achieve optimal cubic complexity. Instead, the binarisation is implicit by using the dotted rule technique. However, the algorithm may suffer from a big grammar dependent constant for artificial grammars (see Johnson (1991) for details). This is due to the implicit subset construction present in the construction of M's δ-function in Eq. (4). An option to investigate for these artificial grammars would be considering the construction of *non-deterministic* GLR(0) automata.

References

Alfred V. Aho and Jeffrey D. Ullman. 1972. *The Theory of Parsing, Translation, and Compiling*. Prentice-Hall, Inc., Upper Saddle River, NJ, USA.

A. V. Aho, R. Sethi, and J. D. Ullman. 1986. *Compilers: Principles, Techniques, and Tools*. Addison-Wesley, Reading, Mass.

Y. Bar-Hillel, M. Perles, and E. Shamir. 1964. On Formal Properties of Simple Phrase Structure Grammars. In Y. Bar-Hillel, editor, *Language and Information: Selected Essays on their Theory and Application*, pages 116–150. Addison-Wesley, Reading, Massachusetts.

S. Billot and B. Lang. 1989. The Structure of Shared Forests in Ambiguous Parsing. In *Proceedings of the Twenty-Seventh Annual Meeting of the Association for Computational Linguistics*, pages 143–151, Vancouver (British Columbia). Association for Computational Linguistics (ACL).

Sabine Brants, Stefanie Dipper, Silvia Hansen, Wolfgang Lezius, and George Smith. 2002. The TIGER Treebank. In *Proceedings of the Workshop on Treebanks and Linguistic Theories*.

Thomas Hanneforth. 2009. *fsm2* - A Scripting Language Interpreter for Manipulating Weighted Finite-state Automata. In *Anssi Yli-Jyrä et al. (eds): Finite-State Methods and Natural Language Processing, 8th International Workshop*, pages 13–30, Berlin. Springer.

John E. Hopcroft and Jeffrey D. Ullman. 1979. *Introduction to Automata Theory, Languages and Computation*. Addison-Wesley.

M. Johnson. 1991. The Computational Complexity of GLR Parsing. In M. Tomita, editor, *Generalized LR Parsing*, pages 35–42. Kluwer, Boston.

Mark Johnson. 1998. PCFG Models of Linguistic Tree Representations. *Computational Linguistics*, 24(4):613–632.

J. R. Kipps. 1991. GLR Parsing in Time $\mathcal{O}(n^3)$. In M. Tomita, editor, *Generalized LR Parsing*, pages 43–60. Kluwer, Boston.

Mark-Jan Nederhof and Giorgio Satta. 2008. Probabilistic Parsing. In G. Bel-Enguix, M. Dolores Jimenez-Lopez, and C. Martin-Vide, editors, *New Developments in Formal Languages and Applications*, pages 229–258. Springer.

Mark-Jan Nederhof. 2005. A General Technique to Train Language Models on Language Models. *Computational Linguistics*, 31:173–186, June.

M. Tomita and S.-K. Ng. 1991. The Generalized LR Parsing Algorithm. In M. Tomita, editor, *Generalized LR Parsing*, pages 1–16. Kluwer, Boston.

Open Source WFST tools for LVCSR cascade development

Josef R. Novak, Nobuaki Minematsu, Keikichi Hirose
Graduate School of Information
Science and Technology
The University of Tokyo
{novakj,mine,hirose}@gavo.t.u-tokyo.ac.jp

Abstract

This paper introduces the Transducersaurus toolkit which provides a set of classes for generating each of the fundamental components of a typical WFST-based ASR cascade, including HMM, Context-dependency, Lexicon, and Grammar transducers, as well as an optional silence class WFST. The toolkit further implements a small scripting language in order to facilitate the construction of cascades via a variety of popular combination and optimization methods and provides integrated support for the T^3 and Juicer WFST decoders, and both Sphinx and HTK format acoustic models. New results for two standard WSJ tasks are also provided, and the toolkit is used to compare a variety of construction and optimization algorithms. These results illustrate the flexibility of the toolkit as well as the tradeoffs of various build algorithms.

1 Introduction

In recent years the Weighted Finite-State Transducer (WFST) paradigm has gained considerable popularity as a platform for Automatic Speech Recognition (ASR). The WFST approach provides an elegant, unified mathematical framework that can be utilized to train, generate, combine and optimize the many heterogenous knowledge sources that typically make up a modern Large Vocabulary Continuous Speech Recognition (LVCSR) system. This has lead to the development of several excellent general purpose software libraries devoted to the construction and manipulation of WFSTs, including the popular open source OpenFst C++ toolkit. Much research has also been conducted on the theoretical construction, integration and optimization of WFST models for ASR (Mohri, 1997; Mohri, 1999; Mohri, 2002; Allauzen, 2004; Mohri, 2008). Nevertheless to our knowledge at present there is no open source toolkit devoted to the construction of ASR-specific WFST models.

This lack of available tools represents an obstacle to the wider dissemination and adoption of WFST-based methods. In response to this, the current work introduces the Transducersaurus WFST toolkit (Novak, 2011), which aims to provide a unified, flexible and transparent approach to the construction of integrated WFST-based ASR cascades, while incorporating recent research results on this important topic. It includes a set of classes for constructing component models as well as a simple Domain Specific Language (DSL) suitable for specifying cascade integration and optimization commands. It provides integrated support for HTK (Young, 2006) and Sphinx (Walker, 2004) acoustic models and cascade construction support for both the T^3 (Dixon, 20007) and Juicer (Moore, 2005) WFST decoders. Where in past complicated development was required, with this toolkit input knowledge sources and a single command are sufficient to build a high-performance system. In addition to introducing the toolkit, this work contributes new experimental results for two LVCSR tasks from the Wall Street Journal (Paul, 1992) (WSJ) corpus, and provides discussion of alternative cascade build chains.

The remainder of the paper is structured as follows. Section 2 describes the main component models of a typical WFST-based ASR cascade. Section 3

Proceedings of the 9th International Workshop on Finite State Methods and Natural Language Processing, pages 65–73,
Blois (France), July 12-15, 2011.

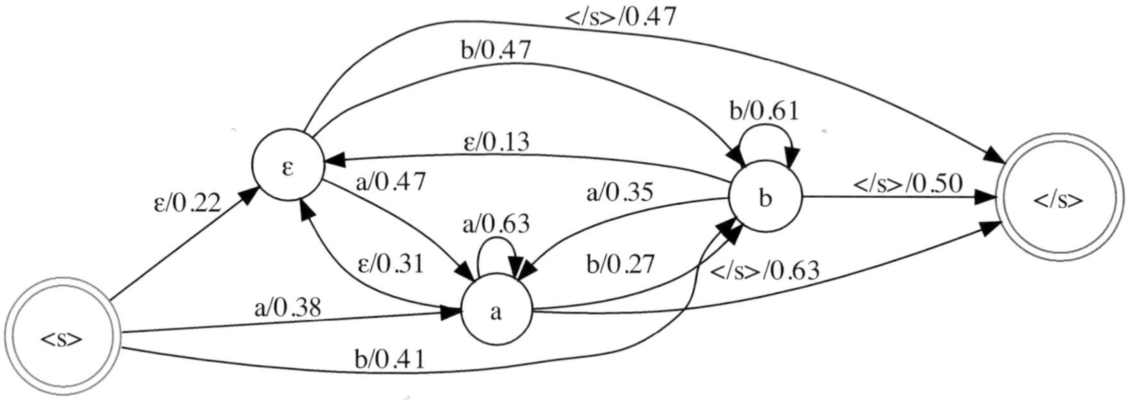

Figure 1: Detail of a bi-gram model for a simple two word LM.

describes the cascade integration tool and its capabilities. Section 4 describes new experimental results that explore the flexibility of the Transducersaurus toolkit. Section 5 provides additional analysis and explores the practical implications of various construction techniques. Finally, Section 6 concludes the paper.

2 Integrated LVCSR Cascades

The construction of WFST-based cascades for LVCSR tasks typically involves two major steps. The first step is to construct WFST-based representations of each of the component knowledge sources, and the second step is to integrate these components into either a single static cascade or, in the case of on-the-fly composition a smaller subset of integrated models. The most common component knowledge sources involved in the first step include a grammar **G**, in the form of a statistical language model, a pronunciation lexicon **L**, that maps monophone sequences to words, and a context-dependency transducer **C**,that maps context-dependent triphone sequences to corresponding monophone sequences. In addition to these three fundamental components, an HMM-level model **H**, that maps HMM state sequences to context-dependent triphone sequences is frequently utilized, and class-based silence models are also popular. The Transducersaurus toolkit provides integrated support for each of the **H**, **C**, **L**, **G**, and **T** component transducers, and these components are described in detail in the following subsections.

2.1 Grammar acceptor

The grammar component **G**, encodes information about word sequences, and typically represents a standard ARPA format statistical N-gram model. Several different approaches to transforming an N-gram model into an equivalent Weighted Finite-State Acceptor (WFSA) have been proposed in the literature (Allauzen, 2003). The simplest approach utilizes a single historyless back-off state, and uses normal ϵ-transitions to encode back-off arcs and associated back-off weights. This is the approach utilized currently in the Transducersaurus toolkit, and a small example of such a model is depicted in Figure 1.

The use of normal ϵ-transitions however, can lead to situations where back-off N-gram sequences may be less costly than the equivalent N-gram sequence. Strictly speaking this is incorrect, and (Allauzen, 2003) discusses two strategies for dealing with this problem. The first involves the use of special "failure" or ϕ-transitions for the back-off arcs. These ϕ-transitions encode the idea that the back-off arc should only be utilized in the event that an equivalent normal N-gram arc does not exist. The second strategy involves mutating the baseline ϵ-back-off configuration, adding additional back-off states and manipulating the back-off arcs so as to eliminate instances of path ambiguity. Transducersaurus utilizes the ϵ-transition approach mainly for the sake of simplicity, but support for the alternative strategies is planned for future work. The toolkit provides a python program, **arpa2fst.py** which may be used

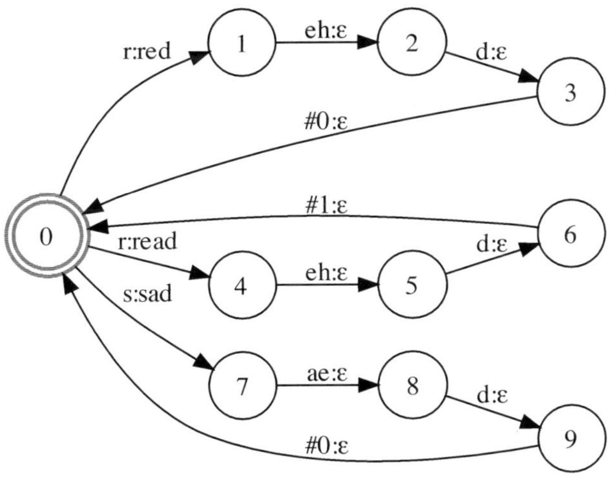

Figure 2: Example of a three-word lexicon transducer, L.

to transform a standard ARPA format LM into an equivalent WFSA. The tool also generates symbol tables as needed.

2.2 Lexicon transducer

The lexicon transducer **L**, maps monophone sequences or pronunciations to words. An example of a trivial lexicon transducer is described in Figure 2. In order to ensure that the lexicon can describe not just isolated words, but also word sequences, it is necessary to perform the closure of the resulting WFST prior to downstream composition. Furthermore, in order to handle the occurrence of homophones in the lexicon, it is necessary to augment the construction with auxiliary symbols as described in (Allauzen, 2004). If this step is not taken, the lexicon as well as any downstream cascades may become non-determinizable. The toolkit provides a lexicon generation tool in the form of **lexicon2fst.py**, and this tool supports closure, and auxiliary symbol generation natively. **lexicon2fst.py** provides support for generating HTK as well as Sphinx format lexicons, the latter of which typically utilizes positional triphones. The tool further generates necessary symbol tables, a list of monophones, and a list of any auxiliary symbols that are added during construction.

2.3 Context-dependency transducer

The Context-dependency WFST **C**, maps context-dependent triphone sequences to corresponding

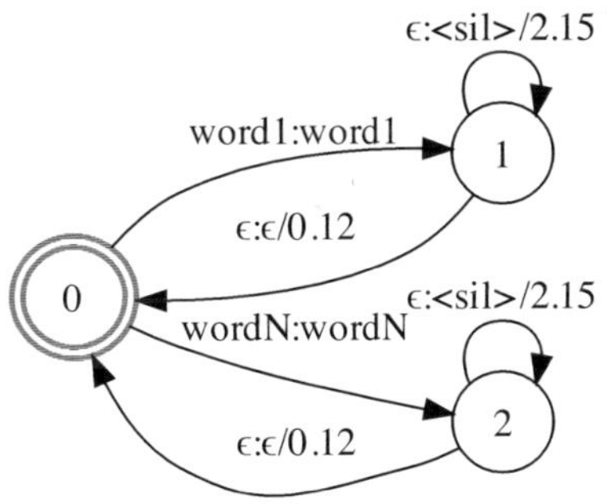

Figure 3: An N-word silence class model, **T**.

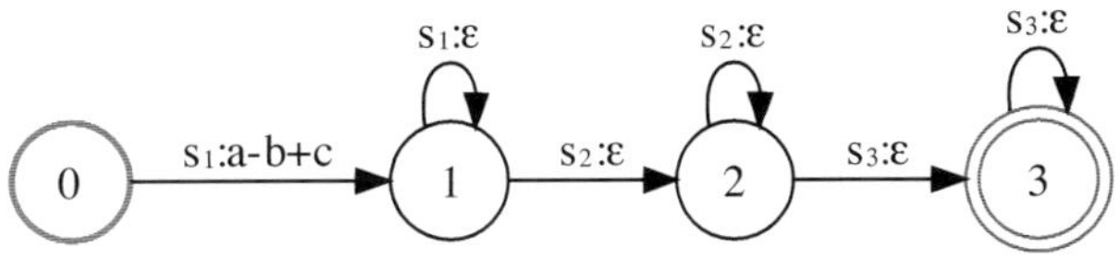

Figure 4: Example of a deterministic three-state HMM model for the triphone *a-b+c*.

context-independent monophone sequences. There are several methods of building this component as well, which are described and illustrated in detail in (Allauzen, 2004). The Transducersaurus toolkit implements a deterministic construction algorithm which results in a C transducer where the output symbols are delayed. There are two separate tools for building the **C** transducer, **cd2wfstHTK.py** and **cd2wfstSphinx.py** and as the names indicate, the first tool provides native support for the HTK format acoustic models, and the second provides native support for Sphinx format models. The **C** tools take as input a list of monophones, an optional list of auxiliary symbols, and an optional acoustic-model specific tied-list. The output consists of the text-format WFST and associated symbol tables. Both tools also provide support for an additional auxiliary WFST which can be used to replace auxiliary symbols or translate logical triphones to physical triphones found in the input acoustic model. This is important in situations where the user wishes to perform further optimizations on a CLG or $HCLG$ cascade.

2.4 Silence class transducer

As with most of the cascade components, there are several viable approaches to handling silence in a WFST-based LVCSR cascade. The Transducersaurus toolkit supports a special silence class transducer that can be utilized to transform a grammar by augmenting it with silence or filler arcs. Other alternatives include adding additional silence-trailing entries to the lexicon or utilizing forced-alignment to insert silences into existing speech transcripts. In the latter case the aligned transcripts can then be used directly to build an N-gram model with silence tokens. In the toolkit, the **silclass2fst.py** program can be used to generate a silence class transducer from a list of words. An example of the silence class transducer is depicted in Figure 3. Unlike the lexicon-based approach, the T approach permits long silences, and unlike the N-gram based approach, it encodes the idea that silences may follow any word without a context-sensitive penalty or boost. The trade-off between the silence loop and return ϵ-arc may be specified by the user but the toolkit supplies default values that were estimated from several hundred hours of spontaneous English conversation transcripts.

2.5 HMM level

The HMM-level transducer **H**, maps HMM state sequences from an acoustic model to context-dependent triphones. The toolkit currently focuses on a 3-state HMM configuration, although there are plans to extend this in future to more flexible configurations. An example of a deterministic, three-state **H** WFST for a single triphone, *a-b+c* is depicted in Figure 4. In practice the full **H** transducer describes the closure of the union of all triphones and monophones in the acoustic model. The structure is similar to the lexicon transducer, however the phonemes are replaced with HMM states, the words are represented by monophone and triphone labels, and the length of each entry is fixed to the number of HMM states used to train the models. In most acoustic models such as those produced by HTK and Sphinx, state-tying is used to share HMM states for under-represented models. With the above approach this can lead to non-determinism due to some triphones sharing the same underlying state sequences. This problem is handled by Transducersaurus by adding a second level of auxiliary symbols to the **H** transducer in order to guarantee determinizability. At present the **H** construction tool, **hmm2wfst.py** provides native support for Sphinx format *mdef* files, as well as support for the native AT&T text format. Native support for the HTK *hmmdefs* file format is also underway. Finally, the T^3 decoder provides online simulation of the HMM state self-loops, which eliminates the need to explicitly generate these during construction. Self-loop arc generation is however supported as an option.

3 Cascade integration with Transducersaurus

In most cases it is necessary to first combine the individual models described in the previous sections before they can be utilized for speech recognition. Much work has been done in the past in regards to theoretically optimal cascade optimization and compression methods, for example (Allauzen, 2004) describes several effective composition and optimization schemes and the impact that these have on WACC and decoding speed. Nevertheless the behavior of different construction and optimization schemes can vary considerably based on the size and complexity of the input models. The proposed toolkit provides a cascade integration tool, **transducersaurus.py** the aim of which is to facilitate learning and speed up the potentially tedious and time-consuming process of cascade generation. This tool calls the individual model construction classes described in Section 2 and automatically performs all required generation, compilation, integration and optimization algorithms. The tool further supports a wide selection of common features of WFST cascade generation including semiring selection, auxiliary symbol support, and fundamental WFST operations such as $composition$, $determinization$, and $minimization$ via the OpenFst library. The tool further provides integrated support for both HTK and Sphinx acoustic models. The flagship contribution of this toolkit however, is a simple WFST-oriented DSL which aims to streamline the specification of build algorithms and optimization procedures. This DSL is described in detail in the following section.

3.1 Cascade construction DSL

The DSL supported by the build tool allows the user to specify a build chain using a subset of the standard FST-based combination and optimization algo-

Table 1: A trivial cascade build command demonstrating several of the options available.

```
$ ./transducersaurus.py --tiedlist tiedlist --hmmdefs hmmdefs
--grammar my.lm --lexicon my.lex --amtype htk --convert tj
--command "min(det(H*det((C*det(L)).(G*T))))"
```

rithms, as well as shorthand for the component models described earlier. The user need only specify a simple chain for example,

```
--command "min(det(C*det(L*(G*T))))",
--command "(C*det(L)).(G*T)"
```

and the build tool will automatically tokenize and parse the command into the appropriate series of OpenFst commands, generating intermediate results as necessary along the way. At present the DSL is quite limited, but supports the min, det, $\circ$ (specified "$*$" on the command line) and "." operations as well as the construction of the **H**, **C**, **L**, **G**, and **T** component transducers. Here det refers to determinization, min to minimization, "$*$" to standard composition, and "." to Static Look-Ahead (SLA) composition, which was released in a recent version of OpenFst, and which implements the Look-Ahead composition algorithm proposed in (Allauzen, 2009). Auxiliary symbol replacement is handled automatically in a manner dependent on the set of build commands issued by the user.

The advantage of the DSL approach is that it permits very simple specification of the build chain, which in turn encourages experimentation and learning, and lends itself easily to further extension through the future addition of other standard operations. Thus the user only needs to prepare the component knowledge sources, and specify a build algorithm. For example the command in Table 1 will automatically construct an integrated recognition network utilizing a silence class model, SLA composition and an HTK-format acoustic model, and output an optimized $HCLGT$ cascade suitable for use in both Juicer and T^3.

4 Experiments

The proposed toolkit can be used to generate recognition networks for a variety of different tasks and inputs. In order to showcase this flexibility, several different experiments were carried out making use of different build chains and two test sets from the WSJ corpus. A selection of recent results are reported for HTK and Sphinx acoustic models and bot the Juicer and T^3 decoder. These results illustrate the correctness of the toolkit in reproducing previous baselines, and also confirm separate results encouraging the SLA-based build chains.

4.1 Experimental setup

All experiments for this work were performed on an 8 core Intel Xeon based machine running at 3GHz with a 6MB cache and 64GBs of main system memory running the RHEL OS. As with our previous results from (Novak, 2010), the experiments covered two popular tasks from the WSJ corpus. The first task, *nov92-5k*, focuses on the November 1992 ARPA WSJ test set which comprises 330 sentences, and was evaluated using the WSJ 5k non-verbalized vocabulary and the standard WSJ 5k closed bigram language model. The second task, *si_dt_s2-20k*, focuses on a subset of the WSJ1 Hub2 test set which comprises 207 sentences. The *si_dt_s2-20k* task, which is somewhat more difficult, was evaluated using a 64k vocabulary an a large 3-gram LM trained on 222M words from the CSR LM-1 corpus (Doddington, 1992). In order to help ensure the repeatability of our experiments, open source Sphinx and HTK acoustic models described in (Vertanen, 2006) were used throughout, and auxiliary parameter values for the T^3 and Juicer decoders were specified as in (Novak, 2010). Unless otherwise specified the log semiring was used for all constructions.

4.2 *Nov92-5k* LVCSR Experiments

The first set of experiments focused on the standard WSJ *Nov92-5k* test set, the default closed bigram language model and associated pronunciation lexicon. Open source Sphinx format acoustic models were used. The toolkit was utilized to generate six different cascades, which shared the same fundamental knowledge sources but differed in terms of the optimization procedures applied, and whether an

Table 2: WSJ-based WFST cascade characteristics for Sphinx acoustic models. Here min refers to minimization, det refers to determinization, the "$\circ$" operator refers to standard composition, and the "." operator refers to static look-ahead composition.

Cascade constructions	***Arcs***	***States***	***Size***
$(C \circ det(L)).G$	1,828,710	620,711	36 MB
$det((C \circ det(L)).G)$	3,588,184	726,782	64 MB
$min(det((C \circ det(L)).G))$	3,260,139	654,008	58 MB
$det(H \circ ((C \circ det(L)).G))$	4,226,328	2,729,896	96 MB
$det(H \circ det((C \circ det(L)).G))$	6,981,130	3,528,195	147 MB
$min(det(H \circ det((C \circ det(L)).G)))$	6,318,302	3,107,984	132 MB

H-level transducer was utilized in the cascade. Recent work such as (Allauzen, 2010) as well as our own recent experiments have shown that SLA composition, which omits the $det(LG)$ operation, performs equally well, thus SLA composition was utilized in all six cascade constructions.

The command used to generate these cascades was specified as

```
$ ./transducersaurus.py --tiedlist mdef
--amtype sphinx --grammar bcb05cnp-2g.arpa
--lexicon bcb05cnp.dic --convert t
--base auto --prefix bcb05s
--command "(C*det(L)).G"
```

and the value of the `--command` parameter was simply modified to generate each of the six different variations. The properties of each of the resulting cascades are described in detail in Table 2. The variation in terms of the number of arcs, states and total size clearly indicates the relative effects of applying different optimization operations to the construction process. The simplest construction, $(C \circ det(L)).G$ results in the smallest cascade in this case. Subsequent application of determinization increases the initial size of the cascade, while miniminization again reduces the overall size. This pattern is repeated with the addition of the HMM-level WFST. The set of Sphinx format cascades generated with the **transducersaurus.py** tool were subsequently evaluated inside of the T^3 decoder and the results of these evaluations are described in Figure 5.

Although small in this simple task, the effect of optimization techniques can nonetheless still be clearly seen in the difference between the $(C \circ det(L)).G$ construction and the determinized and minimized variants. In general the impact of these optimizations is increased for larger and more complicated models. Nevertheless the gains are not achieved without a cost. In particular each additional call to the determinization and minimization algorithms consumes significant additional computing resources and time. These requirements grow rapidly as the size and complexity of the input models increases. Thus it is pragmatic to strike a balance between development time, resource requirements and achievable RTF versus WACC. In order to help illustrate this trade-off we also looked at the memory consumption versus time characteristics of the $det(LG)$ determinization operation, the standard $C \circ (LG)$ composition, and the SLA composition, $CL.G$. The results for the bcb05 cascade used to evaluate the *Nov92-5k* test set are depicted in Figure 6, and unequivocally show that the determinization operation is by far the most costly, but also indicate the advantages of SLA composition over the standard variant.

4.3 *si_dt_s2-20k* LVCSR Experiments

The second set of experiments involved the *si_dt_s2* test set, and a much larger 3-gram language model based on the CSR corpus. These experiments were carried out to show that the toolkit is a viable choice not just for small models, but can be used in a straightforward manner to also build very large, efficient cascades. This experiment also illustrates the ability of the toolkit to generate both HTK, and Sphinx based recognition networks and to construct working cascades for both Juicer and the T^3 decoder. In this case experiments focused on a single construction scheme; the simple yet effective $(C \circ det(L)).G$ and the commands utilized to build the cascades are described in Table 4 and informa-

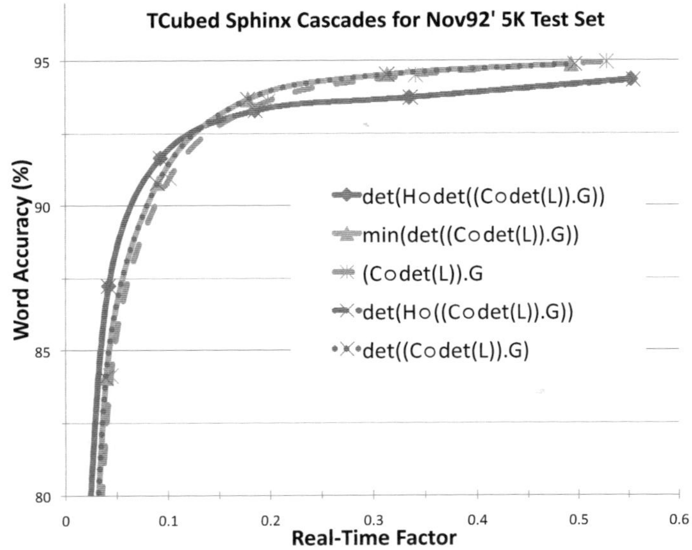

Figure 5: Cascade build comparison for the Nov92-5k task using the T^3 and Sphinx format acoustic models.

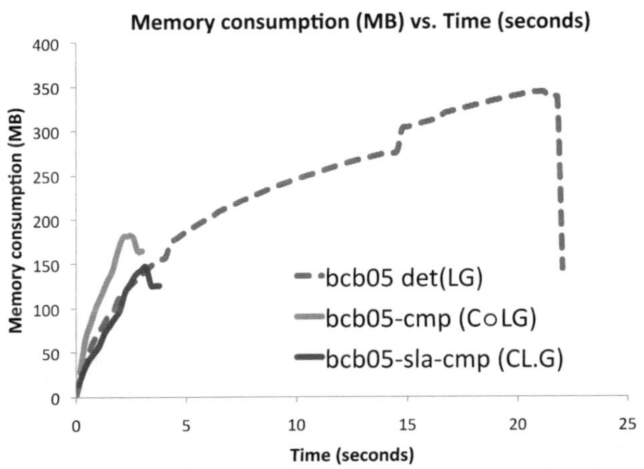

Figure 6: Memory consumption versus time comparison of the $det(LG)$ operation and SLA versus standard composition for the bcb05 CLG cascade.

tion regarding arc and state counts as well as overall size is described in Table 3 while RTF versus WACC results for the three tests are illustrated in Figure 7.

5 Discussion

The results from the two experiments provide new empirical evidence supporting previous research results in this area. Results from Subsection 4.2 show that the toolkit can be utilized to quickly and simply develop a variety of different LVCSR cascades and that build results accurately and reliably re-

Table 3: CSR-based WFST cascade characteristics for HTK and Sphinx models. Both cascades employed a $(C \circ det(L)).(G \circ T)$ construction scheme.

Cascade	*Arcs*	*States*	*Size*
CSR-64k-HTK	146.4M	92.4M	3.3GB
CSR-64k-Sphinx	143.8M	88.8M	3.2GB

flect previously reported findings. We note that the $HCLG$ builds converge more slowly, but achieve the same best WACC at approximately 2x real-time. The SLA composition algorithm is an improvement over standard composition (Allauzen, 2010), but the most substantial gains from the alternative $(C \circ det(L)).G$ build chain result from the ability to avoid the otherwise costly $det(LG)$ determinization operation in a simple CLG construction. In the experiments described in Subsection 4.2, using SLA composition provided roughly a 50% memory savings, and an average overall time savings of nearly 80%. The cross-comparison results described in Subsection 4.3 replicate previous results from (Novak, 2010), this time utilizing the SLA build. Notably, in this case the SLA build produces significantly smaller cascades and furthermore the relative sizes of the Sphinx versus the HTK format models is reversed. The latter result is likely a consequence of the positional triphones utilized by the Sphinx mod-

Table 4: Cascade build commands for the si_dt_s2-20k LVCSR experiments.

```
$ ./transducersaurus.py --tiedlist mdef --amtype sphinx --grammar
lm_csr_64k_nvp_3gram.arpa --base auto --lexicon lm_csr_64k_nvp.dic
--prefix bcb05s --convert t  --command "(C*det(L)).G"

$ ./transducersaurus.py --tiedlist tiedlist --hmmdefs hmmdefs
--amtype htk --grammar lm_csr_64k_nvp_3gram.arpa  --base auto
--lexicon lm_csr_64k_nvp_3gp-htk.dic --prefix csr64kh
--convert t --command "(C*det(L)).G"
```

els, which permit a smaller degree of sharing, thus resulting in a larger increase in size following determinization in the $C \circ det(L \circ G)$ construction. The small performance variation among the AM types and T^3 versus Juicer again suggest that there is not much technical motivation to overtly favor any particular combination. Rather the availability of resources and existing expertise should guide development choices.

Finally, the T^3 decoder also supports GPU-based computation of acoustic likelihood scores, and these results have been reported in several previous works. We note however, that application of GPU-based acoustic scoring, when available tends to provide the strongest single speedup, and that use of the more computationally intensive $logsum$ operation versus the standard $logmax$ also tends to boost maximum accuracy. This implies that SLA composition, combined with GPU-based acoustic scoring and a comparatively simple $(C \circ det(L)).G$ build chain provides highly competitive results. This strikes a strong balance between RTF, WACC, memory and storage requirements and overall build time. Further savings in terms of memory requirements, storage and build time can be gained from performing the lookahead composition on-the-fly at decoding time.

6 Conclusion and Future Work

In this work we have introduced Transducersaurus, a new open source software toolkit for building and manipulating WFST-based ASR cascades. The toolkit provides integrated support for the T^3 and Juicer WFST decoders and both HTK and Sphinx acoustic models, and supports construction of the **H**, **C**, **L**, **G**, and **T** component WFSTs. We showed the effectiveness of the toolkit on a variety of different tasks, looking at both construction variants on a simple set of inputs, and performing a decoder and acoustic model cross comparison on a much larger task. Furthermore we have provided a detailed explanation of the SLA build process as it is supported by the toolkit along with its merits. The ASR application development process is often iterative, and these results reinforce the idea that by utilizing a simplified build chain and the SLA composition approach, overall efficiency can be greatly improved at little or no cost to either the RTF or WACC of a particular recognition network.

In future we plan to further expand the range of available operations, and expand the current limited DSL build syntax, provide integrated support for out-of-vocabulary words, and introduce parallel support for the AT&T fsmtools. Experiments looking at a much wider variety of languages and model inputs currently in the planning phase. Although the toolkit is still in the early stage of development we hope that it will facilitate learning as well as more efficient work in this area, and promote further discussion.

At present the Transducersaurus toolkit can be downloaded freely from the location listed in (Novak, 2011), and is available under the terms of the liberal BSD license.

References

Mehryrar Mohri 1997. *Finite-State Transducers in Language and Speech Processing*, in Computational Linguistics, Vol. 23, Issue 2.

Mehryar Mohri and Michael Riley. 1999. *Network optimizations for large-vocabulary speech recognition*, Speech Communication, Vol. 28, Issue 1.

Mehryar Mohri, Fernando Pereira and Michael Riley. 2002. *Weighted finite-state transducers in speech recognition*, Computer Speech and Language, Vol. 16, Issue 1.

Cyril Allauzen, Mehryar Mohri, Michael Riley and Brian

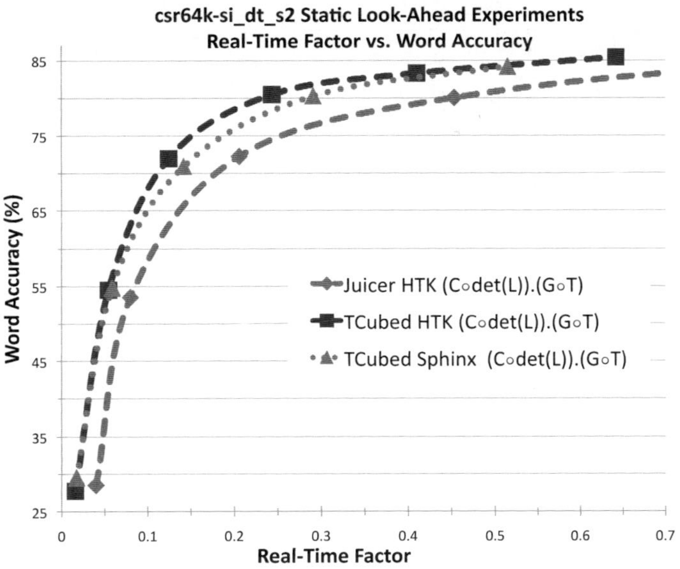

Figure 7: Cross comparison for the si_dt_s2-20k task using the T^3 and Juicer decoders, Sphinx and HTK format acoustic models on the 3-gram CSR LM-1 language model.

Roark. 2004. *A Generalized Construction of Integrated Speech Recognition Transducers*, in Proc. ICASSP, pp. 761-764.

Mehryar Mohri, Fernando Pereira and Michael Riley. 2008. *Speech recognition with weighted finite-state transducers*, Springer Handbook of Speech Processing, pp. 1-31.

Josef Novak. 2011. `code.google.com/p/transducersaurus/`

Steve Young, Gunnar Evermann, Dan Kershaw, Gareth Moore, Julian Odell, Dave Ollason, Valtcho Valtchev and Phil Woodland. 2006. *The HTK Book (for HTK Version 3.2)," Cambridge University Engineering Department.*

Willie Walker, Paul Lamere, Philip Kwok, Bhiksha Raj, Rita Singh, Evandro Gouvea, Peter Wolf and Joe Woelfel. 2004. *Sphinx-4: A flexible open source framework for speech recognition*, Sun Microsystems Technical Report, TR-2004-139.

Paul Dixon, Diamantino Caseiro, Tasuka Oonishi and Sadaoki Furui. 2007. *The Titech Large Vocabulary WFST Speech Recognition System*, in Proc. ASRU, pp. 1301-1304.

Darren Moore, John Dines, Mathew Magimai Doss, Jithendra Vepa, Octavian Cheng and Thomas Hain. 2005. *Juicer: A Weighted Finite State Transducer Speech Decoder*, in Proc. Interspeech, pp. 241-244.

Douglas Paul and James Baker. 1992. *The Design for the Wall Street Journal-based CSR Corpus*, in Proc. ICSLP 92, pp. 357-362.

Cyril Allauzen, Mehryar Mohri and Brian Roark. 2003. *Generalized Algorithms for Constructing Language Models*, in Proc. ACL, pp.40-47.

Josef Novak, Paul Dixon and Sadaoki Furui. 2010. *An Empirical Comparison of the T^3, Juicer, HDecode and Sphinx3 Decoders*, in Proc. InterSpeech 2010, pp. 1890-1893.

Cyril Allauzen, Michael Riley and Johan Schalkwyk. 2009. *A Generalized Composition Algorithm for Weighted Finite-State Transducers*, InterSpeech 2009, pp. 1203-1206.

George Doddington. 1992. *CSR Corpus Development*, DARPA SLS Workshop," pp. 363-366.

Keith Vertanen. 2006. *Baseline WSJ Acoustic Models for HTK and Sphinx: Training Recipes and Recognition Experiments*, Cavendish Laboratory, University of Cambridge.

Cyril Allauzen and Michael Riley. 2010. *OpenFst: A General and Efficient Weighted Finite-State Transducer Library*, tutorial, SLT.

Intersection of Multitape Transducers vs. Cascade of Binary Transducers: The Example of Egyptian Hieroglyphs Transliteration

François Barthélemy
CNAM (Cédric),
292 rue Saint-Martin, Paris, France
INRIA (Alpage),
Rocquencourt, France
francois.barthelemy@cnam.fr

Serge Rosmorduc
CNAM (Cédric),
292 rue Saint-Martin, Paris, France
serge.rosmorduc@cnam.fr

Abstract

This paper uses the task of transliterating an Egyptian Hieroglyphic text into the latin alphabet as a model problem to compare two finite-state formalisms : the first one is a cascade of binary transducers; the second one is a class of multitape transducers expressing simultaneous constraints. The two systems are compared regarding their expressivity and readability. The first system tends to produce smaller machines, but is more tricky, whereas the second one leads to more abstract and structured rules.

1 Introduction

In the eighties, two models of Finite State computations were proposed for morphological descriptions: two-level morphology (Koskenniemi, 1983) where simultaneous constraints are described using two-level rules, and rewrite rule systems where rules apply sequentially (Kaplan and Kay, 1994). From a computational point of view, both kinds of rules are compiled into binary transducers. The transducers are merged using *intersection* in the simultaneous model whereas transducer *composition* is used by the sequential model.

Two-level grammars appeared difficult to write because of rule conflicts: the different two-level rules are not independent. Their semantics is not compositional: the semantics of a set of rule is not the composition of the semantics of each rule.

In the last decade, a new kind of simultaneous finite state model has been proposed which does not use two-level rules and avoids rule conflicts. The model uses multitape transducers (Barthélemy, 2007). The present paper is devoted to an application written successively with a cascade of transducers and an intersection of multitape transducers.

The application consists in transliterating Egyptian Hieroglyphs without resorting to a lexicon. The transliteration task is a transcription from the original writing to an extended latin alphabet used to write consonantal skeleton of words. This task is far from obvious, as we explain in 2.2.

The next section gives more details about hieroglyphs. Then, a transliteration grammar using a cascade of weighted rewrite rules is presented. Section 4 presents the *multigrain multitape transducers* and the *Karamel language* used to define them. Then comes a description of a Karamel grammar for hieroglyph transliteration adapted from the rewrite rule cascade. The last section compares the two grammars and their respective strengths and weaknesses.

2 Egyptian hieroglyphs

2.1 Hieroglyphic encoding and transliteration

The systems we are about to describe take as input an ASCII description of hieroglyphic texts, based on a system called "le manuel de codage" (Buurman et al., 1988), and output a transliteration of the text, that is, a transcription in latin characters of the *consonants* (the Egyptians did not write vowels). Meanwhile, we do also determine word frontiers. An example is given in figure 1.

The letter used in the transliteration layer are conventional signs used in ASCII computer-encoding

Proceedings of the 9th International Workshop on Finite State Methods and Natural Language Processing, pages 74–82,
Blois (France), July 12-15, 2011.

<table>
<tr><td>hierogl.</td><td></td><td></td><td></td><td></td><td></td><td></td><td></td><td></td><td></td><td></td><td></td><td></td><td></td><td></td><td></td></tr>
<tr><td>input</td><td>M17</td><td>G43</td><td>D21</td><td>Z1</td><td>N35</td><td>O34</td><td>A1</td><td>Z1</td><td>N35</td><td>N42</td><td>G17</td><td>D36</td><td>I9</td><td>M23</td><td>G43</td></tr>
<tr><td>output</td><td colspan="2">iw</td><td colspan="2">rA</td><td>n</td><td colspan="3">z</td><td colspan="4">nHm</td><td>f</td><td colspan="2">sw</td></tr>
<tr><td rowspan="2">trans-
lation</td><td colspan="2">part</td><td colspan="2">mouth</td><td>of</td><td colspan="3">man</td><td colspan="4">save</td><td>it</td><td colspan="2">him</td></tr>
<tr><td colspan="15">the mouth of a man saves him</td></tr>
</table>

Figure 1: example of sentence transliteration

of Egyptian texts. In this encoding, uppercase and lowercase letters note different consonants. Besides, ‘A’, ‘a’ and ‘i’ are used to represent consonantic signs (which the Egyptological tradition renders as vowel in scholarly pronunciation). The above sentence would be pronounced “iu ra en se neḥem ef su”.

2.2 The Egyptian hieroglyphic writing system

In this section, we explain the basics of the hieroglyphic system (Allen, 2010) , and we detail a number of problems met when trying to transliterate it.

Hieroglyphs can be written in lines or columns, right-to-left or left-to-right and are typically grouped to fill the available space, as in this text : . In this work, we will neglect the exact position of signs and deal with their sequence.

Another characteristic is that there are no real word separators. The present work will address this issue.

2.2.1 Kinds of signs

The hieroglyphic system used a mix of phonetic and ideographic signs to note the language. Many signs may have more than one possible value.

The *phonograms* note a number of *consonants*, typically one, two or three. For instance, the owl stands for the consonant “m”, and the chessboard for the sequence of consonant “mn”. Vowels are not written, so egyptologists would insert arbitrary “e” between the consonant, and thus, is conventionally pronounced “men”. Those phonograms are classified as uniliteral, biliteral, and triliteral signs, depending on the number of consonants they represent.

Ideograms are more or less word-sign. Usually, they are followed by a stroke, to mark this specific use. For instance, writes the word “kA”, bull.

Determinatives are semantic classifiers which have no phonetic realisation, but give the general semantic class of a word. As they tend to occur at word endings, they ease the word separation problem too. For instance, in , “mooring pole”, the sign classifies the word as a “wooden thing”.

2.2.2 Word formation

Egyptian word spellings tend to contain a phonetic part followed by a determinative.

In the phonetic part, signs which represent more than one consonant come usually with “phonetic complements”, which are uniliteral signs, representing one, two or three consonants of the multiconsonantic sign. For instance, in the group , “nDm”, the phonetic sign has the value n + D + m. But it is nonetheless supplemented by the “m” sign. The group is to be read “nDm” and not “nDmm”.

To give a complete example, the word , “snDm” ,“to seat”, is to be understood as

s	nDm+m=nDm	determinative

2.2.3 A few specific problems

Word formation, as we have just described it, is only a general principle. The presence of determinatives is optional, and very usual words (especially grammatical words) have usually none. This makes word separation a complex task.

More, single signs may have multiple values. The frontiers between types of signs are fuzzy; the basis of the phonetic system is the rebus, and an ideogram, which represents a given word with a given consonantic skeleton, can often be used phonetically. For instance, the “house” sign, , can stand both for the word “house, “pr”, or as phonogram in the verb “to go out”, which happens to have the same transliteration, “pr”. The same sign can be abstracted the other way, losing any phonetic value, and be used as determinative for “house-like” places, like , “kAp”, “shelter”.

This fuzziness makes it difficult to give a clear-cut description of signs, even in context. Some signs, which have the behaviour of both determinatives (they tend to stand at word endings) and of phonetic signs (they have still a very definite phonetic value) have been coined as "phonetic determinatives". They pose specific problems, because the word, as in many languages, may have grammatical inflections standing after the word root. Those inflections are usually written *before* the phonetic determinative, and make the phonetic part non-continuous. For instance, in the word "sr.t", "what has been predicted", the root of the verb, "sr", is written phonetically , then we have an intrusive , "t" , which is a feminine/neutral inflection, then, the phonetic-determinative "sr" , for the verb "to predict" , and finally, the determinative for "mouth actions". We want to limit the number of rules which deal with this phenomenon.

Other signs have simply a number of unrelated phonetic values. For instance, can be either "Ab" or "mr". Usually, the context, and in particular, the phonetic complements, help to choose.

Apart from the present work, a number of systems dealing with transliteration have been created: S. Billet (?) has written an transliteration agent-oriented system, and M.-J. Nederhof (?) has described an algorithm for *aligning* hieroglyphic encoding and transliteration.

3 A first solution : a cascade of transducers

In (Rosmorduc, 2008), we introduced a system based on a cascade of weighted finite-state transducers with variables. Basically, each weighted transducer applies a set of rewriting rules of the form:

$$t_1, ...t_n \rightarrow u_1...u_m/c$$

where c is the cost of the rule (a real number) and t_i and u_j are terms. Terms can be either a variable (of the form `$X`), a constant identifier or integer, e.g. `A1` or `100`, or a functional term, whose argument can be either constants or variables, e.g. `P(i, $A, $B)`. Variables on the right side must also appear on the left side.

The text entry (which is variable-free) is used as input for the first transducer in the cascade. Variables values are lazily matched with the input - as a result, the rules representation is compact, while the final transducer can be quite large (e.g. for a text of 1300 words, the last resulting transducer contains over 1 000 000 nodes).

The costs are attached to the last link of a rule representation. When the cascade is computed, they are combined by a simple addition. When all transducers have been used to process the input, one of the least-cost path is selected as "the" best path, and the transliteration can be read on the output layer. The actual costs are quite ad-hoc, with low values indicating likely rules, and high values, unlikely ones. With equally valued rules, the system tends to prefer the rules which encourage the grouping of signs.

The current system is compounded of five transducers. We will first explain the main purpose of each one, and then concentrate on exceptional uses.

First transducer, normalization: this is a rather simple technical layer, as we need to normalize the entry, because the encoding often proposes a choice of codes for the same sign.

Second layer, sign values: The second layer replaces the sign codes with their values. Values are expressed using functors. Each functor corresponds to a particular kind of value, and the functor's arguments represent the value.

phonetic values are expressed as P(X), P(X,Y) or P(X,Y,Z), depending on the number of consonants in a given sign. For instance, the following rules.

```
A17 => P(X,r,d) / 100
A17 => P(n,m,H) / 300
```

states that sign A17 can have the phonetic value "Xrd" or "nmH", "Xrd" being preferred with a cost of 100 over nmH (cost 300).

determinatives are expressed as DET(MEANING), where "MEANING" is (occasionally) used to keep track of the determinative's value. E.g.

```
A17 => DET(child) / 100
```

states that A17 can be a determinative for "child".

phonetic determinatives and ideograms are expressed with the same system as phonetic signs:

```
A17 => IP(X,r,d) / 100
D56 => ID(r,d) / 100
```

plural and ideogram markers which can be found as word endings, are expressed using `END()`, which takes as argument “P1” if the word is singular, or “P3” if it is plural.

Third layer, groups: this layer build “groups” aggregating a complex phonetic sign with its phonetic complements. Note that groups are not words, as a word can contain more than one group.

```
P($x,$y), P($x), P($y) =>
        G($x,$y), endGroup / 10
```

states that a biliteral sign of value `P($x,$y)`, can be completed with two uniliteral signs representing both `$x` and `$y`, and that they form a group of phonetic value `G($x,$y)`. The symbol `endGroup`, which is inserted after the group, will be used in the next layer when gluing the phonetic parts and the word endings.

The layer also recognises the possible forms of word endings, which include some inflections, determinative, and possibly plural markers :

```
P(w), P(t), DET($x), END($y) =>
  b3,L(w),L(t),DET($x),endWord/100
```

The "b3" is a marker which will be combined with "endGroup" in the following layers.

Fourth layer, words phonetics: This forth layer deals mainly with the phonetic shape of words. Not all consonantic sequence, nor all group sequences, can form a word with equal probability. Egyptian has mostly bi and tri-consonantal roots, so shorter and longer words (ignoring the inflections) are not that likely. Two typical rules are:

```
G($x,$y), endGroup, G($z) =>
     L($x), L($y), L($z) / 100
G($x,$y), endGroup, G($x,$y) =>
     L($x), L($y), L($x), L($y)
     / 100
```

The first states that building a triliteral word with two groups, a biliteral one and a uniliteral one, is quite possible. The other concerns quadriliteral rules. Arbitrary combinations resulting in a quadriliteral root are usually given a high cost, but in this rule, we represent a reduplicated[1] root of the form XYXY, which is a rather usual way of building intensive words in Egyptian.

Word endings and groups are also attached by rules which erase at no cost the sequence `endGroup, b3`, which ensures that a “phonetic part” followed by a word ending is the favoured way of building a word. Erasing `endGroup` on its own, which amounts to allowing a word with only a phonetic part (which is still possible), is given a large cost of 1000.

Fifth layer, cleanup and ending attachment This last part does some cleanup, and removes data which was copied from layer to layer, in order to keep only relevant analysis. It also deals with *phonetic determinatives*, for which the previous layer is a bit too early.

3.1 Cross layers issues and discussions

3.1.1 The so-called phonetic determinatives

The problem of phonetic determinative is that we are going to combine them, not with a group, but with the word's phonetics. Let's consider the following example :

glyphs					
codes	O34	D21	X1	E27	A2
groups	s	r	t	IP(s,r)	det
	phonetics		word ending		

Here, the root part of the word phonetics is compounded of two uniliteral signs, making two groups. The word ending contains a “t” which is the feminine inflection, the phonetic determinative E27, and the determinative of mouth actions.

The problem is that we need to combine the first part with the ending, while keeping a low number of rules. This is done in two steps. First, in the group layer, we re-order the signs, in order to put the phonetic determinative before the inflections. We introduce a token, “b4”, which will be consumed in the last layer.

```
P(t), IP($x,$y), DET($a) =>
```

[1]this is the technical word used by the scholars, even though *duplicated* would probably suffice.

```
    b4, IP($x,$y), L(t), DET($a),
    e4 / 10
```

The word layer will simply copy the result of the group layer. Then, in the "cleanup" layer, as we do have a representation of the word, we can combine it with the IP if needed :

```
L($X), L($Y), b4, IP($X,$Y) =>
    L($X), L($Y) / 10
```

Note that this rule is agnostic about the way the L() readings were produced.

3.1.2 Word separation

Word separation is a by-product of our system. Basically, we explicitly mark certain sequences of signs as word endings, plus, we can transform any group ending into a word ending. The possible phonetic structures of a word (as a group sequence) are also listed. The combination of those systems, along with their associated cost, is used to produce a reasonable words separation.

3.1.3 Exceptions

The idea of the system was to try to experiment on transliteration without a lexicon, which can be useful for unknown word. Basically, no extensive lexicon is used; however, grammatical words, and some very frequent verbs don't respect the usual word-formation rules. For instance, the verb "Dd" "to say" is written with 𓆓 (I10) and 𓂧 (D46), which are respectively uniliteral signs we will render "D" and "d". The nice thing with automata here is that they lend to a graceful representation of those exceptions. We directly map the signs to the final output in one of our levels, and the result will be copied by each level until the last one :

```
I10, D46 => startWord, L(D),
            L(d), endWord / 100
```

4 Intersection-oriented multitape transducers

This section is devoted to Karamel, a language used to define multitape finite state transducers (Barthélemy, 2009).

The definition of multi-tape machines is done using regular expressions extended with *tuples*. Tuples are somehow Cartesian products which glue together independent regular expressions read on different tapes, but unlike Cartesian product, tuples are not distributive with respect to concatenation. The theoretical basis of the language is the *multigrain relations* (Barthélemy, 2007). The tuples used in regular expressions are instances of *tuple types* which must be declared beforehand. The tuples are written using curly braces and begin with the type name, followed by the components. Components of the tuples are both named and ordered, so two syntaxes are allowed to write them: with the name or using the order. Default values are defined for each component.

Embedded tuples are used to give tree-structure to tuples in the relations. There is a constraint: a tape appears in *at most one* of the components of the tuple. Recursive structures are therefore not allowed. The regular sets defined by regular expressions extended with tuples are closed under intersection and difference. So these two operations are available for writing extended regular expressions.

Here are a couple of concrete examples written using Karamel syntax. The value of a sign is expressed using a tuple type called val which has 4 tapes: for hieroglyph signs, for phonetic values written with the latin alphabet, for the semantic value and one for a subtype of values used in composition rules. The tapes are called respectively tsig, tphon, tsem and vtype. An instance of a purely phonetic sign value:

```
{val: tsig=<P17>, tphon=nmh,
      tsem=<>, vtype=<phon>}
```

The notation <> stands for the empty string and <P17> for the single symbol P17, whereas nmh is a string of three symbols. The notation {val} is used when no value is specified for the components of a val tuple. In this case, all the components take their respective default values.

Phonetic values are sometimes composed in groups where some consonants are redundantly written. Groups are implemented by 2-tuples where the first component contains a string of phonetic values and the second one is the transliteration (on tape trans). Here is an example:

```
{group: vals=
    {val: tsig=<F28>, tphon=ab,
               vtype=<phon>}
    {val: tsig=<D58>,tphon=b,
          vtype=<phon> },
```

```
    trans= ab}
```

The examples given above are string tuples. Extended regular expression may use regular operators to describe regular sets of tuples, like in the following example: {wend: ({det}|{phon}|{tend})+} which describes the set of all tuples of type wend where the first component is a non-empty string of tuples of types det, phon and tend.

A Karamel grammar begins with some declarations: symbols, classes of symbols, tapes and tuple types. A class of symbol is a finite set of symbols which has a name. A class name may be used in regular expressions and stands for the disjunction of the symbols in the class. Variables are available and take values in such classes. Occurrences of a variable within a given regular expression must take the same value. Variables express long-distance dependencies. Here is an example of expression using a variable:

```
{group:
    vals={phon: $x in (<letter>)},
    trans= $x}
```

This may be read: the letter found in the phon tuple on tape tphon is the same as the letter found on the trans tape of the same group tuple.

It is possible to define abbreviations for tuples where the order and the default value of the components may be different from the ones in the type definition. For example, an abbreviation called phon is defined for instances of the type val where the component tsem is set to the empty string and the component vtype is set to the value <phon>. This abbreviation is used to define purely phonetic values. For instance {phon: tsig=<F28>, tphon=ab} is just another notation for the tuple

```
{val: tsig=<F28>, tphon=ab,
      vtype=<phon>, tsem=<>}.
```

A machine already defined may be used in an extended regular expression, using its name written between << and >>. E.g. {group: <<some_vals>>*} uses the machine some_vals.

The extended regular expressions may include weights which are arbitrary floating numbers. Weights are written in expressions enclosed by two exclamation marks. The operations on transducers combine weights using the *tropical semiring*. Operations such as concatenation, composition and intersection compute sums of weights of both operands. The *n-best* operation is available to select the paths having the smallest weights in a machine.

The *external composition* is a binary operation which combines a multitape machine and a regular language, considered as an input on a given tape. The *external projection* projects a multitape machine on one tape and then removes all the tuple boundaries. These two operations are the interface of a multitape machine with the outer world.

5 Transliteration using multitape transducers

A Karamel Grammar has been written by translating the cascade of binary transducers presented in section 4. The classes of symbols defined include the hieroglyphs (class sign), the letters used in the transliteration (class letter), a set of semantics values (class sem), divided in two subclasses, generic values (class gensem) and regular values (class regsem). There are also several classes of auxiliary symbols such as subtype names. The tapes include one tape for the text written with hieroglyphs (tape tsig), one tape contains the transliteration (tape trans), two tapes contain respectively the phonetic and the semantic values of the signs (tapes tphon and tsem). There are several auxiliary tapes for information such as subtypes and rule identifiers.

There are a number of different tuple types with up to four levels of embedding. A tuple type is used to represent sign values on four tapes. One tape is used for the hieroglyphs, possibly a sequence of several signs, another for the phonetic value which is a sequence of latin letters, another tape contains the semantic value. The last tape called vtype contains a value type which is important to separate subclasses of values which play a different role and appear in different places of the forms. There are six subtypes: pure phonetic values, ideograms, phonetic ideograms, determinatives and numbers. Six abbreviations are defined for these subtypes, which set the vtype value and some other tapes. For instance, for the determiners, the phonetic value (tape phon) is set to the empty string.

The tuple type `group` is used for groups of phonetic values where some consonants are written redundantly. A sequence of such groups is used to write the phonetic part of a form which is represented using a `core` tuple.

There are also tuples to write frozen forms, directly from hieroglyphs. These forms do not use embedded `val` tuples. The type `wend` is used to describe the word endings which usually follow the phonetic parts. Word endings contain the inflection written phonetically and determinatives. The types `idform`, `number` and `gram` describe forms and their main component is a sequence of values (`val` tuples). They describe respectively an ideographic notation, a number and a grammatical word such as a pronoun or a preposition. With all these tuple types, there are several possible structures for forms :

```
{cpform: {core: {group: {val}*}*}
         {wend: {val}*}+}|
{idform: {val}*}|{number:{val}*}|
{gram: {val}*}|{frozen};
```

An instance of the most complex structure :

```
{cpform:
  {core:
    {group: {phon: s, <S29>}, s}
    {group: {phon: nDm, <M29>}
            {phon: m, <G17>}, nDm}}
  {wend:{det: <seat>, <A17>}}}
```

This corresponds to the analysis of nDm :

S29=𓋴	M29+G17=𓆼𓅓	A17=𓀔
s	nDm+m=nDm	determinative

Each tuple type is described in the grammar using two transducers: one which describes all the possible values for one occurrence of the tuple type, the second one describes the context in which sequences of the tuple types may appear to make a form. The second transducers uses the definition of the first one. For instance, the word endings follow a number of patterns including phonetic values and determiners. These patterns are described in a machine called `all_word_endings`. The context of the patterns is described in a machine called `actual_word_endings`. Part of the code of the two machines is given below. Note that the second machine uses the first one in its definition.

```
let all_word_endings =
   {wend: seq = {phon: y},
          trans = y};!1000!
  |{wend: seq = {det}{phon: y},
          trans = y};!100!
  |{wend: seq = {phon: y}{det},
          trans = y};!100!
  | ...

let actual_word_endings =
  {cpform:{core:{group:{val}*}*}
       <<all_word_endings>>+}|
  {idform:{val}*}|{number:{val}*}|
  {gram:{val}*}|{frozen};
```

Each pattern in a machine `all_XXX` corresponds to one rule of the rewrite rule system of the original grammar. The excerpt above translates the rules :

```
P(y) => b3, L(y), endWord / 1000
DET($x), P(y) => b3, L(y),
           DET($x), endWord / 100
P(y), DET($x) => b3, L(y),
           DET($x), endWord / 100
```

The auxiliary symbols `b3` and `endWord` used in the rewrite rules correspond to the opening and closing of a `wend` tuple in Karamel.

The description of all written forms is potentially given by the intersection of all the machines `actual_XXX`, one machine for each tuple type. This intersection is statically computable, and the result is a large transducer. It is also possible to compute the intersection dynamically: the text represented by a sequence of hieroglyphs is first combined with one of the machines using an `external composition` operation, then the result is intersected successively with all the other transducers. The best transliteration is computed by an n-best computation and the transliteration is finally extracted using an `external projection`.

6 Comparison of the two approaches

The two grammars represent the structure of forms using different means: the cascade grammar uses pairs of auxiliary symbols whereas the Karamel grammar uses tuples. The structure described is almost identical in both grammars. Some tuples of the grammar are not represented in the cascade grammar: it is the case of the smallest tuples (type `val`) and some of the largest tuples (type `cpform`).

Values in the cascade grammars are rewritten either phonetically or semantically. The sign and the corresponding value are never simultaneously represented in the intermediate strings.

The multitape grammar puts homogeneous information on each tape: there is a tape for hieroglyphs, two for phonetic values, one for semantics, several for auxiliary values. The cascade concatenates different kind of symbols, especially at the intermediate levels. The input consists in hieroglyphs and the output in latin letters, but the intermediate strings have not only both kind of representations (hieroglyph and latin letters), but also semantic values and auxiliary symbols.

Some of the rewrite rules change the order of signs with respect to the text order. This is used for two purposes: in word ending, determinatives which sometime appear before the inflection marked using phonetic values, are pushed to the end of the word in such a way that all the determinatives of a word ending are contiguous. This is important for the next layer of the cascade which rewrites pairs of determinatives with various weights, depending on semantics constraints. The other case of reordering deals with the phonetic determinatives which are put at the beginning of word endings. This is done to check that the phonetic value of the sign is coherent with the transliteration of the phonetic part.

The Karamel grammar does not need to change the order of symbols. The constraints on multiple determinatives and the coherence between phonetic ideograms and the phonetic part transliteration are expressed as long-distance dependencies using Karamel variables.

The formalism used in the cascade consists in rewrite rules without context: a center is rewritten regardless of the surrounding symbols. There is no way to express long-distance dependencies within the formalism. On the other hand, long-distance dependencies are costly: they result in larger transducers.

There are also some cases of changes in the structure proposed for a form in the cascade grammar: two word endings are collapsed into one by removing the symbols marking the end of the first and beginning of the second. In the Karamel grammar, this rule is not implemented as a change of the structure, but by allowing under conditions a second word ending after the first one. The structures are never changed once built.

step	states		arcs	
step	binary	multitape	binary	multitape
values	75	12 723	2 095	61 581
groups	8 675	165 286	20 234	277 812
words	10 383	104 844	23 605	7 458 881
cleanup	923	821 031	5 001	924 514

Figure 2: sizes of binary and multitape machines

The multitape transducers are larger than binary transducers for a couple of reasons. They contain more information because they keep all the information whereas in the cascade, some symbols are forgotten after they have been rewritten. Another reason is that there is an overhead due to representation of tapes and tuples, which are compiled using auxiliary symbols. The third reason is that some long distance dependencies are implemented in the multitape machines. These long-distance dependencies do not appear in one binary transducer, but they appear when statically composing the transducers of the cascade. Figure 2 gives the sizes of comparable machines of the two grammars.

7 Conclusion

The comparison done here is not completely fair because the second grammar has been translated from the first one, almost rule by rule. This does not give the best possible implementation of the application in Karamel. Some features available in Karamel are not used.

The Karamel language provides a more abstract description of the forms, using an explicit tree structure and separating the different pieces of information on different tapes, according to semantic criteria. On the other hand, the Karamel machine is much larger. Karamel is a high-level declarative formalism whereas non contextual rewrite rules are an efficient low-level language.

Some trade-off is possible: cascade of transducers may be expressed using a richer language (e.g. XFST (Beesley and Karttunen, 2003)) whereas the Karamel language has some contextual rewrite rules which have not been presented in this paper because they are not used in the Egyptian transliteration grammar.

References

James P. Allen. 2010. *Middle Egyptian: An Introduction to the Language and Culture of Hieroglyphs*. Cambridge University Press.

François Barthélemy. 2007. Multi-grain relations. In *Implementation and Application of Automata, 12th International Conference (CIAA)*, pages 243–252, Prague, Czech Republic.

François Barthélemy. 2009. A testing framework for finite-state morphology. In *Implementation and Application of Automata, 14th International Conference (CIAA)*, volume 5642 of *Lecture Notes in Computer Science (LNCS)*, pages 75–83, Sydney, Australia.

Kenneth R. Beesley and Lauri Karttunen. 2003. *Finite State Morphology*. CSLI Publications.

Jan Buurman, Nicolas Grimal, Michael Hainsworth, Jochen Hallof, and Dirk Van Der Plas. 1988. *Inventaire des signes hieroglyphiques en vue de leur saisie informatique*. Mémoires de l'Académie des Inscriptions et Belles Lettres. Institut de France, Paris.

Ronald M. Kaplan and Martin Kay. 1994. Regular models of phonological rule systems. *Computational Linguistics*, 20:3:331–378.

Kimmo Koskenniemi. 1983. Two-level model for morphological analysis. In *IJCAI-83*, pages 683–685, Karlsruhe, Germany.

Serge Rosmorduc. 2008. Automated transliteration of egyptian hieroglyphs. In Nigel Strudwick, editor, *Information Technology and Egyptology in 2008, Proceedings of the meeting of the Computer Working Group of the International Association of Egyptologists (Informatique et Egyptologie), Vienna, 811 July 2008*, pages 167–183. Gorgias Press.

A Note on Sequential Rule-Based POS Tagging

Sylvain Schmitz
LSV, ENS Cachan & CNRS, Cachan, France
schmitz@lsv.ens-cachan.fr

Abstract

Brill's part-of-speech tagger is defined through a cascade of leftmost rewrite rules. We revisit the compilation of such rules into a single sequential transducer given by Roche and Schabes (*Comput. Ling.* 1995) and provide a direct construction of the minimal sequential transducer for each individual rule.

Keywords. Brill Tagger; Sequential Transducer; POS Tagging

1 Introduction

Part-of-speech (POS) tagging consists in assigning the appropriate POS tag to a word in the context of its sentence. The program that performs this task, the *POS tagger*, can be learned from an annotated corpus in case of supervised learning, typically using hidden Markov model-based or rule-based techniques. The most famous rule-based POS tagging technique is due to Brill (1992). He introduced a three-parts technique comprising:

1. a *lexical tagger*, which associates a unique POS tag to each word from an annotated training corpus. This lexical tagger simply associates to each known word its most probable tag according to the training corpus annotation, i.e. a unigram maximum likelihood estimation;

2. an *unknown word tagger*, which attempts to tag unknown words based on suffix or capitalization features. It works like the contextual tagger, using the presence of a capital letter and bounded sized suffixes in its rules: for instance in English, a *-able* suffix usually denotes an adjective;

3. a *contextual tagger*, on which we focus in this paper. It consists of a cascade of string rewrite rules, called *contextual rules*, which correct tag assignments based on some surrounding contexts.

In this note, we revisit the proof that contextual rules can be translated into sequential transducers[1] proposed by Roche and Schabes (1995): whereas Roche and Schabes give a separate proof of sequentiality and exercise it to show that their constructed non-sequential transducer can be determinized (at the expense of a worst-case exponential blow-up), we give a direct translation of a contextual rule into the minimal normalized sequential transducer, by adapting Simon (1994)'s string matching automaton to the transducer case. Our resulting sequential transducers are of linear size (before their composition). A similar construction can be found in (Mihov and Schultz, 2007), but no claim of minimality is made there.

2 Contextual Rules

We start with an example by Roche and Schabes (1995): Let us suppose the following sentences were tagged by the lexical tagger (using the Penn Treebank tagset):

*Chapman/NNP killed/VBN John/NNP Lennon/NNP
*John/NNP Lennon/NNP was/VBD shot/VBD by/IN Chapman/NNP
He/PRP witnessed/VBD Lennon/NNP killed/VBN by/IN Chapman/NNP

[1] Historically, what we call here "sequential" used to be called "subsequential" (Schützenberger, 1977), but we follow the more recent practice initiated by Sakarovitch (2009).

Proceedings of the 9th International Workshop on Finite State Methods and Natural Language Processing, pages 83–87,
Blois (France), July 12-15, 2011. ©2011 Association for Computational Linguistics

There are mistakes in the first two sentences: *killed* should be tagged as a past tense form "VBD", and *shot* as a past participle form "VBN".

The contextual tagger learns contextual rules over some tagset Σ of form $uav \rightarrow ubv$ (or $a \rightarrow b \,/\, u\_v$ using phonological rule notations (Kaplan and Kay, 1994)), meaning that the tag a rewrites to b in the context of u_v, where the context is of length $|uv|$ bounded by some fixed $k+1$; in practice, $k = 2$ or $k = 3$ (Brill (1992) and Roche and Schabes (1995) use slightly different *templates* than the one parametrized by k we present here). For instance, a first contextual rule could be "$\mathrm{nnp\,vbn} \rightarrow \mathrm{nnp\,vbd}$" resulting in a new tagging

Chapman/NNP killed/VBD John/NNP Lennon/NNP
*John/NNP Lennon/NNP was/VBD shot/VBD by/IN Chapman/NNP
*He/PRP witnessed/VBD Lennon/NNP killed/VBD by/IN Chapman/NNP

A second contextual rule could be "$\mathrm{vbd\,in} \rightarrow \mathrm{vbn\,in}$" resulting in the correct tagging

Chapman/NNP killed/VBD John/NNP Lennon/NNP
John/NNP Lennon/NNP was/VBD shot/VBN by/IN Chapman/NNP
He/PRP witnessed/VBD Lennon/NNP killed/VBN by/IN Chapman/NNP

As stated before, our goal is to compile the entire sequence of contextual rules learned from a corpus into a single sequential function.

Let us first formalize the semantics we will employ in this note for Brill's contextual rules.[2] Let $\mathcal{C} = r_1 r_2 \cdots r_n$ be a finite sequence of string rewrite rules in $\Sigma^* \times \Sigma^*$ with Σ a POS tagset of *fixed size*. In practice the rules constructed in Brill's contextual tagger are *length-preserving* and 1*-change-bounded*, i.e. they modify a single letter, but this is not a useful consideration for our transducer construction. Each rule $r_i = u_i \rightarrow v_i$ defines a *leftmost rewrite relation* $\xRightarrow[\mathrm{lm}]{r_i}$ defined by

$$w \xRightarrow[\mathrm{lm}]{r_i} w' \text{ iff } \exists x, y \in \Sigma^*, w = xu_iy \wedge w' = xv_iy$$
$$\wedge\, \forall z, z' \in \Sigma^*, w \neq zu_iz' \vee x \leq_{\mathrm{pref}} z$$

where $x \leq_{\mathrm{pref}} z$ denotes that x is a prefix of z. Note that the domain of $\xRightarrow[\mathrm{lm}]{r_i}$ is $\Sigma^* \cdot u_i \cdot \Sigma^*$. The *behavior* of a single rule is then the relation $[\![r_i]\!]$ included in $\Sigma^* \times \Sigma^*$ defined by $[\![r_i]\!] = \xRightarrow[\mathrm{lm}]{r_i} \cup \mathrm{Id}_{\Sigma^* \setminus (\Sigma^* \cdot u_i \cdot \Sigma^*)}$, i.e. it applies $\xRightarrow[\mathrm{lm}]{r_i}$ on $\Sigma^* \cdot u_i \cdot \Sigma^*$ and the identity on its complement $\Sigma^* \setminus (\Sigma^* \cdot u_i \cdot \Sigma^*)$. The behavior of $\mathcal{C}$ is then the composition $[\![\mathcal{C}]\!] = [\![r_1]\!] \fatsemi [\![r_2]\!] \fatsemi \cdots \fatsemi [\![r_n]\!]$. Note that this behavior does *not* employ the transitive closure of the rewriting rules.

A naive implementation of $\mathcal{C}$ would try to match each u_i at every position of the input string w in Σ^*, resulting in an overall complexity of $O(|w| \cdot \sum_i |u_i|)$. One often faces the problem of tagging a *set* of sentences $\{w_1, \ldots, w_m\}$, which yields $O((\sum_i |u_i|) \cdot (\sum_j |w_j|))$. As shown in Roche and Schabes' experiments, compiling $\mathcal{C}$ into a single sequential transducer $\mathcal{T}$ results in practice in huge savings, with overall complexities in $O(|w| + |\mathcal{T}|)$ and $O(|\mathcal{T}| + \sum_j |w_j|)$ respectively.

Each $[\![r_i]\!]$ is a rational function, being the union of two rational functions over disjoint domains. Let $|r_i|$ be the length $|u_iv_i| \leq k$. Roche and Schabes (1995, Sec. 8.2) provide a construction of an exponential-sized transducer $\mathcal{T}_{r_i}$ for each $[\![r_i]\!]$, and compute their composition $\mathcal{T}_\mathcal{C}$ of size $|\mathcal{T}_\mathcal{C}| = O(\prod_{i=1}^n 2^{|r_i|})$. As they show that each $[\![r_i]\!]$ is actually a sequential function, their composition $[\![\mathcal{C}]\!]$ is also sequential, and $\mathcal{T}_\mathcal{C}$ can be determinized to yield a sequential transducer $\mathcal{T}$ of size doubly exponential in $\sum_{i=1}^n |r_i| \leq nk$ (see Roche and Schabes, 1995, Sec. 9.3). By contrast, our construction directly yields linear-sized minimal sequential transducers for each $[\![r_i]\!]$, resulting in a final sequential transducer of size $O(\prod_{i=1}^n |r_i|) = O(2^{n \log k})$.

3 Sequential Transducer of a Rule

Intuitively, the sequential transducer for $[\![r_i]\!]$ is related to the *string matching automaton* (Simon, 1994; Crochemore and Hancart, 1997) for u_i, i.e. the automaton for the language $\Sigma^* u_i$. This insight yields a *direct* construction of the minimal sequential transducer of a contextual rule, with at most $|u_i| + 1$ states. Let us recall a few definitions:

[2] This is not exactly the semantics assumed by either Brill nor Roche and Schabes, who used iterated-application semantics, resp. contextual and non contextual, instead of the single-application semantics we use here. This has little practical consequence.

3.1 Preliminaries

Overlaps, Borders (see e.g. Crochemore and Hancart, 1997, Sec. 6.2). The *overlap* $\mathrm{ov}(u,v)$ of two words u and v is the longest suffix of u which is simultaneously a prefix of v. A word u is a *border* of a word v if it is both a prefix and a suffix of v, i.e. if there exist v_1, v_2 in Σ^* such that $v = uv_1 = v_2u$. For $v \neq \varepsilon$, the longest border of v different from v itself is denoted $\mathrm{bord}(v)$.

Fact 1. *For all u, v in Σ^* and a in Σ, $\mathrm{ov}(ua,v) = \mathrm{ov}(u,v)\cdot a$ if $\mathrm{ov}(u,v)\cdot a \leq_{\mathrm{pref}} v$ and $\mathrm{ov}(ua,v) = \mathrm{bord}(\mathrm{ov}(u,v)\cdot a)$ otherwise.*

Sequential Transducers (see e.g. Sakarovitch, 2009, Sec. V.1.2). Formally, a sequential transducer from Σ to Δ is a tuple $\mathcal{T} = \langle Q, \Sigma, \Delta, q_0, \delta, \eta, \iota, \rho\rangle$ where $\delta : Q\times\Sigma \to Q$ is a partial transition function, $\eta : Q \times \Sigma \to \Delta^*$ a partial transition output function with the same domain as δ, i.e. $\mathrm{dom}(\delta) = \mathrm{dom}(\eta)$, $\iota \in \Delta^*$ is an initial output, and $\rho : Q \to \Delta^*$ is a partial final output function. $\mathcal{T}$ defines a partial *sequential function* $[\![\mathcal{T}]\!] : \Sigma^* \to \Delta^*$ with $[\![\mathcal{T}]\!](w) = \iota\cdot\eta(q_0,w)\cdot\rho(\delta(q_0,w))$ for all w in Σ^* for which $\delta(q_0,w)$ and $\rho(\delta(q_0,w))$ are defined, where $\eta(q,\varepsilon) = \varepsilon$ and $\eta(q,wa) = \eta(q,w)\cdot\eta(\delta(q,w),a)$ for all w in Σ^* and a in Σ.

Let us note $\mathcal{T}_{(q)}$ for the sequential transducer with q for initial state. We write $u\wedge v$ for the longest common prefix of strings u and v; the longest common prefix of all the outputs from state q can be written formally as $\bigwedge_{v\in\Sigma^*}[\![\mathcal{T}_{(q)}]\!](v)$. A sequential transducer is *normalized* if this value is ε for all $q \in Q$ such that $\mathrm{dom}([\![\mathcal{T}_{(q)}]\!]) \neq \emptyset$, i.e. if the transducer outputs symbols as soon as possible; any sequential transducer can be normalized. The *translation* of a sequential function f by a word w in Σ^* is the sequential function $w^{-1}f$ with $\mathrm{dom}(w^{-1}f) = w^{-1}\mathrm{dom}(f)$ and $w^{-1}f(u) = (\bigwedge_{v\in\Sigma^*} f(wv))^{-1}\cdot f(wu)$ for all u in $\mathrm{dom}(w^{-1}f)$. As in the finite automata case where minimal automata are isomorphic with residual automata, the minimal sequential transducer for a sequential function f is defined as the *translation transducer* $\langle Q, \Sigma, \Delta, q_0, \delta, \eta, \iota, \rho\rangle$, where $Q = \{w^{-1}f \mid w \in \Sigma^*\}$ (which is finite), $q_0 = \varepsilon^{-1}f$, $\iota = \bigwedge_{v\in\Sigma^*} f(v)$ if $\mathrm{dom}(f) \neq \emptyset$ and $\iota = \varepsilon$ otherwise, $\delta(w^{-1}f,a) = (wa)^{-1}f$, $\eta(w^{-1}f,a) = \bigwedge_{v\in\Sigma^*}(w^{-1}f)(av)$ if $\mathrm{dom}((wa)^{-1}f) \neq \emptyset$ and $\eta(w^{-1}f,a) = \varepsilon$ otherwise, and $\rho(w^{-1}f) = (w^{-1}f)(\varepsilon)$ if $\varepsilon \in \mathrm{dom}(w^{-1}f)$, and is otherwise undefined.

3.2 Main Construction

Here is the definition of our transducer for a contextual rule (see Fig. 1):

Definition 2 (Transducer of a Contextual Rule). The sequential transducer $\mathcal{T}_r$ associated with a contextual rule $r = u \to v$ with $u \neq \varepsilon$ is defined as $\mathcal{T}_r = \langle \mathrm{pref}(u), \Sigma, \Sigma, \varepsilon, \delta, \eta, \varepsilon, \rho\rangle$ with the set of prefixes of u as state set, ε as initial state and initial output, and for all a in Σ and w in $\mathrm{pref}(u)$,

$$\delta(w,a) = \begin{cases} wa & \text{if } wa \leq_{\mathrm{pref}} u \\ w & \text{if } w = u \\ \mathrm{bord}(wa) & \text{otherwise} \end{cases}$$

$$\rho(w) = \begin{cases} \varepsilon & \text{if } w \leq_{\mathrm{pref}} (u\wedge v) \\ (u\wedge v)^{-1}w & \text{if } (u\wedge v) <_{\mathrm{pref}} w <_{\mathrm{pref}} u \\ \varepsilon & \text{otherwise, i.e. if } w = u \end{cases}$$

$$\eta(w,a) = \begin{cases} a & \text{if } wa \leq_{\mathrm{pref}} (u\wedge v) \\ \varepsilon & \text{if } (u\wedge v) <_{\mathrm{pref}} wa <_{\mathrm{pref}} u \\ (u\wedge v)^{-1}v & \text{if } wa = u \\ a & \text{if } w = u \\ \rho(w)a\cdot\rho(\mathrm{bord}(wa))^{-1} & \\ & \text{otherwise.} \end{cases}$$

It remains to show that this sequential transducer is indeed the minimal normalized sequential transducer for $[\![r]\!]$.

Proposition 3 (Correctness). *Let $r = u \to v$ with $u \neq \varepsilon$. Then $[\![\mathcal{T}_r]\!] = [\![r]\!]$.*

Proof. Let us first consider the case of input words in $\Sigma^*\backslash(\Sigma^*\cdot u\cdot\Sigma^*)$:

Claim 3.1. For all w in $\Sigma^*\backslash(\Sigma^*\cdot u\cdot\Sigma^*)$, $\delta(\varepsilon,w) = \mathrm{ov}(w,u)$ and $\eta(\varepsilon,w) = w\cdot\rho(\mathrm{ov}(w,u))^{-1}$.

By induction on w: since $u \neq \varepsilon$, the base case is $w = \varepsilon$ with $\delta(\varepsilon,\varepsilon) = \varepsilon = \mathrm{ov}(\varepsilon,u)$ and $\eta(\varepsilon,\varepsilon) = \varepsilon = \varepsilon\cdot\varepsilon^{-1} = \varepsilon\cdot\rho(\varepsilon)^{-1}$. For the induction step, we consider wa in $\Sigma^*\backslash(\Sigma^*\cdot u\cdot\Sigma^*)$ for some w in Σ^*

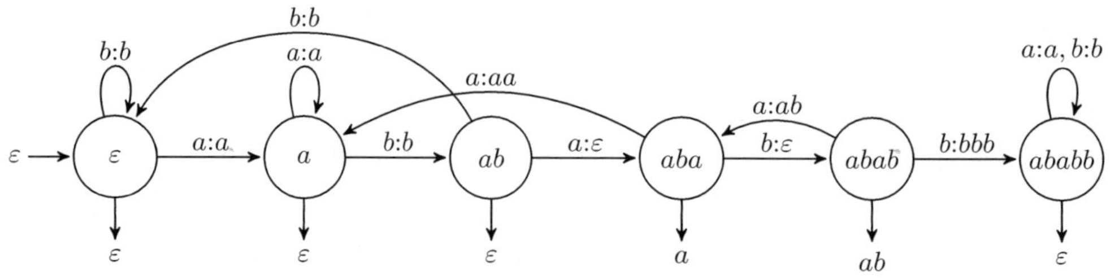

Figure 1: The sequential transducer constructed for $ababb \to abbbb$.

and a in Σ:

$$\begin{aligned}\delta(\varepsilon, wa) &= \delta(\delta(\varepsilon, w), a) \overset{i.h.}{=} \delta(\mathrm{ov}(w,u), a)\\ &\overset{\text{Fact 1}}{=} \mathrm{ov}(wa, u)\\ \eta(\varepsilon, wa) &= \eta(\varepsilon, w)\cdot \eta(\delta(\varepsilon, w), a)\\ &\overset{i.h.}{=} w\cdot\rho(\delta(\varepsilon,w))^{-1}\cdot\eta(\delta(\varepsilon,w),a)\\ &= w\cdot\rho(w')^{-1}\cdot\eta(w',a)\ ;\\ &\qquad\text{(by setting } w' = \delta(\varepsilon, w))\end{aligned}$$

we need to do a case analysis for this last equation:

Case $w'a \not\leq_{\mathrm{pref}} u$ Then $\eta(w', a) = \rho(w')\cdot a\cdot\rho(\mathrm{border}(w'a))^{-1}$, which yields $\eta(\varepsilon, wa) = w\cdot\rho(w')^{-1}\cdot\rho(w')\cdot a\cdot\rho(\delta(\varepsilon,wa))^{-1} = wa\cdot\rho(\delta(\varepsilon,wa))^{-1}$.

Case $w'a <_{\mathrm{pref}} u$ Then $\delta(\varepsilon, wa) = w'a$, and we need to further distinguish between several cases:

- **$w'a \leq_{\mathrm{pref}} (u\wedge v)$** then $\rho(w') = \varepsilon$, $\eta(w',a) = a$, and $\rho(w'a) = \varepsilon$, thus $\eta(\varepsilon, wa) = wa = wa\cdot\varepsilon^{-1} = wa\cdot\rho(w'a)^{-1}$,
- **$w' = (u\wedge v)$** then $\rho(w') = \varepsilon$, $\eta(w',a) = \varepsilon$, and $\rho(w'a) = (u\wedge v)^{-1}\cdot w'a = a$, $\eta(\varepsilon, wa) = w = wa\cdot a^{-1} = wa\cdot\rho(w'a)^{-1}$,
- **$(u\wedge v) <_{\mathrm{pref}} w'$** then $\rho(w') = (u\wedge v)^{-1}\cdot w'$, $\eta(w',a) = \varepsilon$, and $\rho(w'a) = (u\wedge v)^{-1}\cdot w'a$, thus $\eta(\varepsilon, wa) = w\cdot((u\wedge v)^{-1}\cdot w')^{-1} = wa\cdot a^{-1}\cdot((u\wedge v)^{-1}\cdot w')^{-1} = wa\cdot\rho(w'a)^{-1}$. □

The claim yields that $[\![\mathcal{T}_r]\!]$ coincides with $[\![r]\!]$ on words in $\Sigma^*\backslash(\Sigma^*\cdot u\cdot\Sigma^*)$, i.e. is the identity over $\Sigma^*\backslash(\Sigma^*\cdot u\cdot\Sigma^*)$. Then, since $u \neq \varepsilon$, a word in $\Sigma^*\cdot u\cdot\Sigma^*$ can be written as waw' with w in $\Sigma^*\backslash(\Sigma^*\cdot u\cdot\Sigma^*)$, a in Σ with wa in $\Sigma^*\cdot u$, and w' in Σ^*. Let $u = u'a$; the claim implies that $\delta(\varepsilon, w) = u'$ and $\eta(\varepsilon, w) = w\cdot\rho(u')^{-1}$. Thus, by definition of $\mathcal{T}_r$, $\delta(\varepsilon, wa) = u'a = u$ and thus $\eta(\varepsilon, wa) = \eta(\varepsilon, w)\cdot\eta(u', a) = w\cdot\rho(u')^{-1}\cdot(u\wedge v)^{-1}\cdot v$;

if $(u\wedge v) <_{\mathrm{pref}} u'$ $\eta(\varepsilon, wa) = w\cdot((u\wedge v)^{-1}\cdot u')^{-1}\cdot(u\wedge v)^{-1}\cdot v = w\cdot u'^{-1}\cdot v = wa\cdot u^{-1}\cdot v$;

otherwise i.e. if $u' = (u\wedge v)$: $\eta(\varepsilon, wa) = w\cdot u'^{-1}\cdot v = wa\cdot u^{-1}\cdot v$.

Thus in all cases $[\![\mathcal{T}_r]\!](wa) = [\![r]\!](wa)$, and since $\mathcal{T}_r$ starting in state u (i.e. $\mathcal{T}_{r(u)}$) implements the identity over Σ^*, we have more generally $[\![\mathcal{T}_r]\!] = [\![r]\!]$. □

Lemma 4 (Normality)**.** *Let $r = u \to v$. Then $\mathcal{T}_r$ is normalized.*

Proof. Let $w \in \mathrm{Prefix}(u)$ be a state of $\mathcal{T}_r$; let us show that $\bigwedge[\![\mathcal{T}_{r(w)}]\!](\Sigma^*) = \varepsilon$.

If $(u\wedge v) <_{\mathrm{pref}} w <_{\mathrm{pref}} u$ let $u' = w^{-1}u \in \Sigma^+$, and consider the two outputs $[\![\mathcal{T}_{r(w)}]\!](u') = \eta(w, u')\rho(u) = (u\wedge v)^{-1}v$ and $[\![\mathcal{T}_{r(w)}]\!](\varepsilon) = \rho(w) = (u\wedge v)^{-1}w$. Since $(u\wedge v) <_{\mathrm{pref}} u$ we can write u as $(u\wedge v)au''u'$, and either $v = (u\wedge v)bv'$ or $v = u\wedge v$, for some $a \neq b$ in Σ and u'', v' in Σ^*; this yields $w = (u\wedge v)au''$ and thus $[\![\mathcal{T}_{r(w)}]\!](u')\wedge[\![\mathcal{T}_{r(w)}]\!](\varepsilon) = \varepsilon$.

otherwise $\rho(w) = \varepsilon$, which yields the lemma. □

Proposition 5 (Minimality)**.** *Let $r = u \to v$ with $u \neq \varepsilon$ and $u \neq v$. Then $\mathcal{T}_r$ is the minimal sequential transducer for $[\![r]\!]$.*

Proof. Let $w <_{\mathrm{pref}} w'$ be two different states in $\mathrm{Prefix}(u)$; we proceed to prove that $[\![w^{-1}\mathcal{T}_r]\!] \neq [\![w'^{-1}\mathcal{T}_r]\!]$, hence that no two states of $\mathcal{T}_r$ can be merged. By Thm. 4 it suffices to prove that $[\![\mathcal{T}_{r(w)}]\!] \neq [\![\mathcal{T}_{r(w')}]\!]$, thus to exhibit some $x \in \Sigma^*$

such that $[\![\mathcal{T}_{r(w)}]\!](x) \neq [\![\mathcal{T}_{r(w')}]\!](x)$. We perform a case analysis:

if $w' \leq_{\mathbf{pref}} (u \wedge v)$ then $w <_{\text{pref}} (u \wedge v)$ thus $[\![\mathcal{T}_{r(w)}]\!](x) = x$ for all $x \notin w^{-1} \cdot \Sigma^* \cdot u \cdot \Sigma^*$; consider $[\![\mathcal{T}_{r(w)}]\!](w'^{-1}u) = w'^{-1}u \neq w'^{-1}v = [\![\mathcal{T}_{r(w')}]\!](w'^{-1}u)$;

if $w \leq_{\mathbf{pref}} (u \wedge v)$ and $w' = u$ then $[\![\mathcal{T}_{r(w')}]\!](x) = x$ for all x and we consider $[\![\mathcal{T}_{r(w)}]\!](w^{-1}u) = w^{-1}v \neq w^{-1}v = [\![\mathcal{T}_{r(w')}]\!](w^{-1}u)$;

otherwise that is if $w \leq_{\text{pref}} (u \wedge v)$ and $(u \wedge v) <_{\text{pref}} w' <_{\text{pref}} u$, or $(u \wedge v) <_{\text{pref}} w <_{\text{pref}} w' \leq_{\text{pref}} u$, we have $\rho(w) \neq \rho(w')$ thus $[\![\mathcal{T}_{r(w)}]\!](\varepsilon) \neq [\![\mathcal{T}_{r(w')}]\!](\varepsilon)$. □

4 Conclusion

The results of the previous section yield (the cases $u = \varepsilon$ and $u = v$ are trivial):

Theorem 6. *Given a contextual rule $r = u \to v$, one can construct directly the minimal normalized sequential transducer $\mathcal{T}_r$ of size $O(|r|)$ for $[\![r]\!]$.*

The remaining question is whether we can obtain better upper bounds on the size of the sequential transducer $\mathcal{T}_{\mathcal{C}}$ for a cascade $\mathcal{C} = r_1 \cdots r_n$ than $O(2^{n \log k})$. It turns out that there are cascades of length n for which no sequential transducer with a subexponential (in n) number of states can exist, thus our construction is close to optimal.

References

Eric Brill. 1992. A simple rule-based part of speech tagger. In *ANLP '92*, pages 152–155. ACL Press.

Maxime Crochemore and Christophe Hancart. 1997. Automata for matching patterns. In Grzegorz Rozenberg and Arto Salomaa, editors, *Handbook of Formal Languages*, volume 2. Linear Modeling: Background and Application, chapter 9, pages 399–462. Springer.

Ronald M. Kaplan and Martin Kay. 1994. Regular models of phonological rule systems. *Comput. Linguist.*, 20(3):331–378.

Stoyan Mihov and Klaus U. Schultz. 2007. Efficient dictionary-based text rewriting using subsequential transducers. *Nat. Lang. Eng.*, 13(4):353–381.

Emmanuel Roche and Yves Schabes. 1995. Deterministic part-of-speech tagging with finite-state transducers. *Comput. Linguist.*, 21(2):227–253.

Jacques Sakarovitch. 2009. *Elements of Automata Theory*. Cambridge University Press.

Marcel-Paul Schützenberger. 1977. Sur une variante des fonctions séquentielles. *Theor. Comput. Sci.*, 4(1):47–57.

Imre Simon. 1994. String matching algorithms and automata. In Juliani Karhumäki, Hermann Maurer, and Grzegorz Rozenberg, editors, *Results and Trends in Theoretical Computer Science: Colloquium in Honor of Arto Salomaa*, volume 812 of *LNCS*, pages 386–395. Springer.

FTrace: a Tool for Finite-State Morphology

James Kilbury
Heinrich-Heine-Universität Düsseldorf
kilbury@phil.uni-duesseldorf.de

Katina Bontcheva
Heinrich-Heine-Universität Düsseldorf
bontcheva@phil.uni-duesseldorf.de

Younes Samih
Heinrich-Heine-Universität Düsseldorf
samih@phil.uni-duesseldorf.de

Abstract

In this paper we describe our work in progress on FTrace, a tool for finite-state morphology that provides a tracing facility for developers of applications for synchronic and diachronic language descriptions. We discuss not only the current tool for downward tracing, but also the challenges that we face in the further development of FTrace, especially in upward tracing. Finally, we present an example, draw some conclusions, and outline our future work. **Keywords:** FTrace, tracing, finite-state morphology, xfst, foma, SWI Prolog, Prolog network-interpreter, diachronic language descrip-tion.

1 Introduction

In this paper we describe FTrace, a tool for finite-state morphology that provides a tracing facility for developers of applications for synchronic and diachronic language descriptions. It constitutes work in progress, and we therefore will discuss not only the current tool for downward tracing, but also the challenges that we face in the further development of FTrace, especially in upward tracing.

In Section 2 we explain our motivation for creating FTrace, in Section 3 we describe the overall architecture of the system and outline briefly the language-description module and the visualization environment. In Section 4 we describe in detail the module for compiling and exporting the individual networks for replacement rules into Prolog notation before we describe the Prolog network-interpreter and the specific problems we face in downward and upward tracing in Section 5. Finally, in Section 6 we illustrate the tool with an example, and in Section 7 we draw some conclusions and outline our future work.

2 Motivation

In the past decade software systems like xfst and foma (cf. Beesley and Karttunen, 2003; Hulden, 2009, respectively) based on finite-state technology have greatly facilitated the use of replacement rules (Karttunen, 1995) in computational descriptions of natural languages. The vast majority of such applications have been purely synchronic and often employ replacement rules to capture morphophonemic alternations within lexical paradigms.

The replacement format, however, makes the rules equally attractive as a framework in which the phonology of a language can be modelled diachronically. The formal process is essentially the same, whether we synchronically derive surface forms from underlying lexical representations with morphophonemic rules, or diachronically derive later representations from corresponding earlier forms. In both cases we have a binary relation consisting of pairs $<w_0, w_n>$ of an upper-level string w_0 and a lower-level string w_n defined in the description by a sequence of replacement rules $R_1, \ldots, R_n$ and implicitly by the corresponding derivation $w_0, w_1, \ldots, w_n$, where each string w_j for $j \geq 1$ is produced from string w_{j-1} by the application of R_j.

So much for the elementary formal language theory. The whole point of systems like xfst is that the entire sequence $R_1, \ldots, R_n$ of replacement rules is composed and compiled into a single network encoding the binary relation. So we don't see any of the intermediate strings w_j of the derivation, and

Proceedings of the 9th International Workshop on Finite State Methods and Natural Language Processing, pages 88–92, Blois (France), July 12-15, 2011.

that is precisely what makes finite-state technology so efficient.

Once an application has been correctly developed, we normally have no need or desire to see derivations, but the situation is different if we have difficulty formulating replacement rules in a way that gives us the results we want. This is especially the case for students learning to use xfst or foma to encode linguistic descriptions. Then it is very helpful to be able to follow entire derivations in terms of the individual rule applications. This is just what a tracing facility would provide, but neither xfst nor foma has one. Vi-xfst (cf. Oflazer and Yilmaz, 2004) has a very useful dependency-tracking tool that we can use to visualize relationships between rules, but it includes no tracing facility that meets our requirements.

A first glance this appears to be a job that the developers of xfst or foma should do in order to produce the best tracing tool, but there is a short cut that requires no changes in the source code or involvement of the original developers. A feature of both systems is that they allow individual networks to be exported in Prolog notation. If each rule R_j is exported as a corresponding network N_j, then it is easy for a user to write his own Prolog program to interpret the individual networks as governed by a "play list" of the names of rule networks in their order of application. Such Prolog programming is described, e.g., in (Gazdar and Mellish, 1989, p. 37 ff.) and serves as the basis for our Prolog code which we specify below in 5.2 for the benefit of readers unfamiliar with (Gazdar and Mellish, 1989).

In our own work we have adopted the latter strategy.

3 Architecture of the Tool

There are four modules in FTrace:

1. the language-description module,
2. the module for export of xfst/foma networks in Prolog notation,
3. the Prolog interpreter,
4. the visualisation environment (SWI Prolog).

3.1 The Language-Description Module

The language-description module can consist of a single xfst script that contains the (continuation) lexicons and the replacement rules as well as variable declarations that define natural classes of segments and clusters of morphological tags. However, it can be a full-fledged lexicon that contains an xfst script with the variable declarations, the replacement rules, etc., a lexc master lexicon, and several (lexicographic) text files that contain the stems belonging to different inflectional classes.

It is very important to mention that the xfst script must comply with a number of special conventions.

Since we are not interested in the individual networks of tag clusters or natural classes of segments but want to export only the individual networks of the replacement rules, we need to introduce different naming conventions. Thus, the names of tag clusters or natural classes of segments begin with a capital letter (e.g., **VowFrt**, **Vowfrt**, **TAGS**), while the names of the rules begin with a lower-case letter (e.g., **r2**, **jerFrtVoc**).

The second convention refers to the play list that is needed by the Prolog network-interpreter (cf. above, Section 2, Motivation). The play list can be a part of the language-description module and have the form of a regular expression that denotes a cascade of replacement rules and has xfst syntax. It is possible, however, for the play list to be omitted from the language-description module. In this case the developer writes the play list as an xfst comment. In both cases the name of the regular expression must begin with a lower-case letter and the line must contain an xfst comment '# ... **QQ**', which marks the play list for Perl (cf. Section 4). We have chosen this particular string because it is highly unlikely to be a substring of any reserved or natural-language word.

3.2 The XFST/Foma-Specific Module(s)

Of the four modules only the export module is specific to either xfst or foma. This is necessary since there are some important differences between xfst and foma:

- an xfst script cannot be started from outside the application environment but can make calls to the system;
- a foma script can be started from outside the application environment but cannot make calls to the system (last tested version: 0.9.14alpha).

In Section 4 we explain in detail an export module for xfst.

3.3 The Visualisation Environment

Since the Prolog network-interpreter will be described in detail in Section 5, we still need to say a few words about the visualisation environment. Our interpreter is compatible with most distributions of Prolog. However, we have chosen SWI Prolog for the following reasons:

- SWI Prolog is widely used for research and in instruction, it offers a comprehensive environment and is free;
- It is very easy to type UTF8 characters in the console and to display them. This makes SWI Prolog an ideal environment for tracing with language descriptions that use various writing systems such as, e.g., Cyrillic and Arabic.

4 The Module for Compiling and Exporting the Prolog Networks

The module consists of several xfst and Perl files. The task is to print the Prolog networks for each replacement rule and to export the rules to a separate Prolog UTF8 file that will be used by the network interpreter. In addition, the play list that is specified in the language description has to be extracted and added to that file. All tasks in this module run automatically; the user just needs to provide the name of the language-description file.

The main element of this module is an xfst script *ftrace.xfst*. First it starts an interactive Perl script *GetName.perl.pl*[1] that asks the user to type in the name of the language description file and saves it to a text file[2] *LDSrc.txt*. In the next steps the language description file is compiled, and the names of the defined variables are printed and saved to a file *defined.txt*.

The second Perl script *PrintNwks.perl.pl* selectively extracts from *defined.txt* only the names of variables that (according to the convention) begin with a lower-case letter, and dynamically creates an xfst script *print-prolog-source.xfst* that prints the corresponding Prolog networks. However, the names that are assigned to the networks by xfst have nothing to do with the names given to the rules by the linguist. The original names of the rules are restored automatically before the networks are saved to a Prolog file *<filenameoflang-descr>-Nwks.pl*.

The third Perl script *PrintPlList.perl.pl* extracts the play list and rewrites it in Prolog syntax. Then the play list is appended to the file (*<filenameoflangdescr>-Nwks.pl*) that contains the Prolog networks.

Finally, the Perl script reminds the user that his files are saved to a temporary directory and will be deleted with the next execution of FTrace. The name and the location of the file that contains the Prolog networks and the play list are also displayed.

5 The Prolog Network-Interpreter

The complexity of the tracing interpreter depends chiefly on the sublanguage of xfst or foma we wish to cover for tracing. For the time being we have excluded special features such as flag diacritics and merge in xfst (cf. Beesley and Karttunen, 2003: 339 ff., 401 ff.) and assume simply (1) variable definitions to specify natural segment classes, (2) elementary regular expressions to define the distribution of segments in the upper-level language (i.e. "(mor)-phonotactics" of the proto-language), and (3) replacement rules. Crucially, we want our tracing facility to provide not only apply-down traces of derivations from upper to lower forms, but also of apply-up derivations from lower to upper.

5.1 Special Problems

Special problems of programming the trace interpreter are posed by some reserved symbols. In particular, '**?**' for "any symbol" and '**0**' or '**[]**' and '**[..]**' for deletion and epenthesis rules, respectively, require attention. '**?**' is familiar enough and need not be discussed here.

The null-symbols '**0**' or '[]' and '[..]', however, can lead to difficulties with termination. For downward tracing there is no problem with deletion rules using '**0**' or '[]', whether they are conditioned by an environment or not, and tracing apply-down application of epenthesis rules with an

[1] Since both Perl and Prolog files have extension 'pl', the Perl scripts additionally have 'perl' in the filename before the 'pl' extension.

[2] All files that are created by the export module are saved to a temp directory and are deleted with the next execution of *ftrace.xfst*

environment is likewise unproblematic. An unconditioned epenthesis rule would be disastrous for a description and for tracing, but we assume one normally would not want to write such a rule in the first place for a natural language. This is all fairly obvious.

The situation is less transparent, however, when it comes to apply-up tracing. Again, there is no problem with deletion or epenthesis rules with environments, and – symmetrically to the apply-down application of deletion rules – even apply-up application of unconditioned epenthesis rules could in principle be handled, but we don't want such rules, anyway.

The real problem arises with unconditioned deletion rules. We have just seen that apply-down application is unproblematic, but their apply-up application is equivalent to apply-down application of unconditioned epenthesis, which we have excluded. So we appear to be faced with a dilemma: For many descriptions it appears attractive to have unconditioned rules to delete, e.g., symbols for morpheme boundaries, and in any case, we would not want to *disallow* their use by linguists; on the other hand, apply-up tracing seems inevitably to lead to an infinite or at least unacceptably large number of possible antecedent strings from which a given string could arise through uncondtioned deletion of a segment.

In order to deal with this we have developed a strategy based on the notion of distributional filtering. Consider the above-mentioned example of a rule ''+' -> 0' to delete all instances of a morpheme boundary '+' after it has served its function, e.g. in conditioning other morphophonemic rules. If our description consisted merely of a sequence of replacement rules *R1*, … , *Rn* including the deletion rule, then not only apply-up tracing with single rules, but also apply-up applications with the overall network in general would lead to an explosion in the computation of upper forms from which a lower form could arise. The problem dissolves, however, if we compose a network *N0* constraining the distribution of symbols in the ultimate upper language with the total network R arising from the composition of all replacement rules; if *N0* correctly specifies where '+' can occur in the first place, then it can only be deleted from these positions, and the problem is solved for apply up in a single, composite network.

We now need to carry over the filtering idea to upward tracing. The upper language defined by the network of a single unconditioned deletion rule must be restricted in order to ensure that the set of possible antecedent strings is highly constrained. Consider the sequence of networks *N0*, *N1*, …, *Nn* where each *Ni* except *N0* arises from *Ri*. For each *Nj* stemming from an unconditioned deletion rule, we can define *Nj'* as the composition *N0* .o. *N1* .o. … *Nj-1*. Then in upward tracing of the application of *Nj* to produce string *w*, not [*Nj* .o. *w*].u , but rather [*Nj'*.l .o. *Nj* .o. *w*].u is computed to get the set of possible antecedent strings. This gives us the desired filtering effect and solves the problem for tracing.

5.2 Downward tracing

The implementation of downward tracing is simple. Given replacement rules defined like these

```
define r1 [ k -> c || _ i ] ;
define r2 [ i -> 0 || _ .#. ] ;
```

xfst or foma constructs the network encoded in Prolog, which is exported to a file (cf. the example in Section 6 below).

Following the techniques of Gazdar and Mellish mentioned above, a Prolog network-interpreter for downward tracing can then be implemented easily. Due to limitations of space we omit the listings here. The interpreter has been tested extensively.

6 An Example

The following example already given above is very simple and transforms a fictitious proto-language *PL* into a daughter language *DL* with two ordered sound changes: palatalization of the velar *k* to *c* before the front vowel *i*, followed by the deletion of *i* in final position. Here, again, is the code of the language description:

```
# LgDL.txt
define r1 [ k -> c || _ i ] ;
define r2 [ i -> 0 || _ .#. ] ;
# define lgdl [r1 .o. r2] ; QQ
```

After the compilation of the language description, the Prolog networks of replacement rules **r1** and **r2** and the play list are exported to *LgDL-Nwks.pl*. Here is part of the content of this file:

```
:- encoding(utf8).
network(r1).
arc(r1, 0, 0, "?").
arc(r1, 0, 0, "c").
arc(r1, 0, 0, "i").
arc(r1, 0, 1, "k").
arc(r1, 0, 2, "k":"c").
arc(r1, 1, 0, "?").
arc(r1, 1, 0, "c").
arc(r1, 1, 1, "k").
arc(r1, 1, 2, "k":"c").
arc(r1, 2, 0, "i").
final(r1, 0).
final(r1, 1).
network(r2).
arc(r2, 0, 0, "?").
arc(r2, 0, 1, "i").
arc(r2, 0, 2, "i":"0").
arc(r2, 1, 0, "?").
arc(r2, 1, 1, "i").
arc(r2, 1, 2, "i":"0").
final(r2, 0).
final(r2, 2).
rule_list(lgdl, [r1, r2]).
```

The Prolog downward tracing interpreter *applydn.pl* is compiled in the SWI Prolog console, and then *LgDL-Nwks.pl* is consulted. Now the developer can test pairs of words from the proto-language and the daughter language:

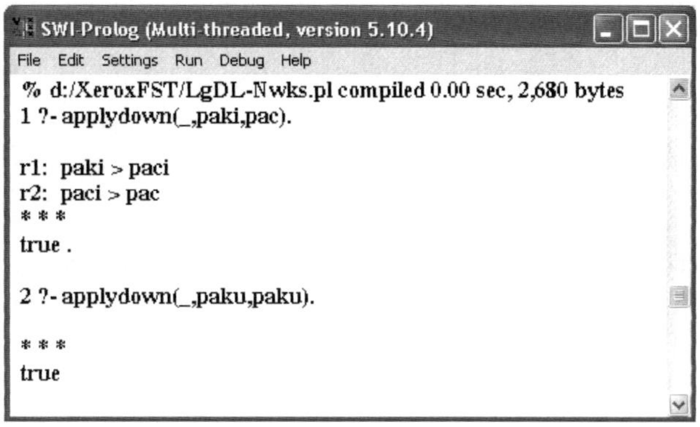

7 Conclusion

We believe that FTrace can be useful and help developers of synchronic and diachronic language descriptions to debug their applications. In teaching historical linguistics it makes it possible to show the historical development of the phonological system of a language in detail and to test the proposed rules for derivations of individual forms. The same tool can equally well be used to produce explicit synchronic derivations from underlying forms to surface forms.

References

Kenneth R. Beesley and Lauri Karttunen. 2003. Finite State Morphology. CSLI, Stanford

Gerald Gazdar and Chris Mellish. 1989. Natural Language Processing in Prolog. Addison-Wesley, Wokingham et al.

Mans Hulden. 2009. Foma: a finite-state compiler and library. In: Proceedings of the EACL 2009 Demonstrations Session, pp. 29-32.

Lauri Karttunen. 1995. The replace operator. In: 33rd ACL Proceedings, 16-23.

Kemal Oflazer and Yasin Yılmaz. 2004. Vi-xfst: a visual regular expression development environment for Xerox finite state tool. In: SIGPHON 2004: Proceedings of the Seventh Meeting, Barcelona, Spain.

Incremental Construction of Millstream Configurations Using Graph Transformation

Suna Bensch
Department of Computing Science
Umeå University (Sweden)
suna@cs.umu.se

Frank Drewes
Department of Computing Science
Umeå University (Sweden)
drewes@cs.umu.se

Helmut Jürgensen
Department of Computer Science
The University of Western Ontario (Canada)
hjj@csd.uwo.ca

Brink van der Merwe
Department of Computing Science
Stellenbosch University (South Africa)
abvdm@cs.sun.ac.za

Abstract

Millstream systems are a non-hierarchical model of natural language. We describe an incremental method for building Millstream configurations while reading a sentence. This method is based on a lexicon associating words and graph transformation rules.

1 Introduction

Language processing is an incremental procedure. This is supported by various psycholinguistic and cognitive neuroscience-based studies (see e.g. (Taraban and McClelland, 1988)). We do not postpone the analysis of an utterance or sentence until it is complete, but rather start to process immediately hearing the first words (or word parts). We present ongoing work regarding the incremental syntactic and semantic analysis of natural language sentences. We base this work on Millstream systems (Bensch and Drewes, 2010), (Bensch et al., 2010), a generic mathematical framework for the description of natural language. These systems describe linguistic aspects such as syntax and semantics in parallel and provide the possibility to formalise the relation between them by interfaces. Millstream systems are motivated by contemporary linguistic theories (see e.g. (Jackendoff, 2002)). A Millstream system consists of a finite number of *modules* each of which describes a linguistic aspect and an *interface* which describes the dependencies among these aspects. The interface establishes links between the trees given by the modules, thus turning unrelated trees into a meaningful whole called a *configuration*. For simplicity, we just consider Millstream systems containing only two modules, for syntax and semantics. With this simplifying assumption, a configuration of the Millstream system consists of two trees with links between them and represents the analysis of the sentence that is the yield of the syntax tree. An obvious question is how such a configuration can be constructed from a given sentence. Such a procedure would be a step towards automatic language understanding based on Millstream systems. We propose to use graph transformations for that purpose. By expressing language processing in terms of graph transformation we can employ a wealth of theoretical results relating graph transformations and monadic second-order logic. We mimic the incremental way in which humans process language, thus constructing a Millstream configuration by a step-by-step procedure while reading the words of a sentence from left to right. The idea is that the overall structure of a sentence is built incrementally, word-by-word. With each word, one or more lexicon entries are associated. These lexicon entries are graph transformation rules the purpose of which is to construct an appropriate configuration. For a sentence like *Mary likes Peter*, for example, we first apply a lexicon entry corresponding to *Mary*, which results in a partial configuration that represents the syntactic, semantic and interface structure of *Mary*. We continue by applying the lexicon entry for *loves*, which yields a partial configuration representing *Mary loves*. Finally, a lexicon entry representing *Peter* is applied, resulting in the overall Millstream configuration for the entire sentence.

Proceedings of the 9th International Workshop on Finite State Methods and Natural Language Processing, pages 93–97,
Blois (France), July 12-15, 2011.

2 Millstream Configurations as Graphs

A configuration in a Millstream system is a tuple of ranked and ordered trees (in our restricted case, a pair consisting of the syntactic and the semantic representation of a sentence) with links between them. The (labelled) links indicate relations between the nodes. A typical link establishes a relation between two nodes belonging to different trees. In this paper, we want to represent configurations in a way which is suitable for graph transformation. For this, we first define the general type of graphs considered. For modelling convenience, we work with hypergraphs in which the hyperedges (but not the nodes) are labelled. For simplicity, we call hypergraphs graphs and their hyperedges edges. Edge labels are taken from a doubly ranked alphabet Σ, meaning that Σ is a finite set of symbols in which every symbol a has *source* and *target ranks* $rank_{src}(a), rank_{tar}(a) \in \mathbb{N}$ determining the number of sources and targets, respectively, that an edge label's a is required to have.

Definition 1 *Let Σ be a doubly ranked alphabet. A Σ-graph is a quadruple (V, E, src, tar, lab) consisting of finite sets V and E of* nodes *and* edges, source *and* target functions $src, tar\colon E \to V^*$, *and an* edge labelling function $lab\colon E \to \Sigma$ *such that $rank_{src}(lab(e)) = |src(e)|$ and $rank_{tar}(lab(e)) = |tar(e)|$ for all $e \in E$. The components of a graph G will also be referred to as $V_G, E_G, src_G, tar_G, lab_G$. By $\mathcal{G}_\Sigma$ we denote the class of all Σ-graphs.*

A *Millstream alphabet* is a doubly ranked alphabet Σ in which the target rank of each symbol is either 1 or 0. Symbols of target rank 1 are *tree symbols*; edges labelled with these symbols are *tree edges*. Symbols of target rank 0 are *link symbols*; edges labelled with link symbols are *links*. A tree or link symbol a may be denoted by $a_{(k)}$ to indicate that $rank_{src}(a) = k$. In the following, the term *tree* refers to an acyclic graph in which all edges are tree edges, each node is the target of exactly one edge, and there is exactly one node (the root) that is not a source of any edge. A Σ-*configuration* is a graph $G \in \mathcal{G}_\Sigma$ such that the deletion of all links from G results in a disjoint union of trees.

Figure 1 depicts a tree, built using the tree symbols $\mathsf{S}_{(2)}, \mathsf{VP}_{(2)}, \mathsf{NP}_{(1)}, \mathsf{V}_{(1)}, Mary_{(0)}, loves_{(0)}, Peter_{(0)}$. To save space we use the drawing style shown in Figure 2 instead. The links pointing to tree

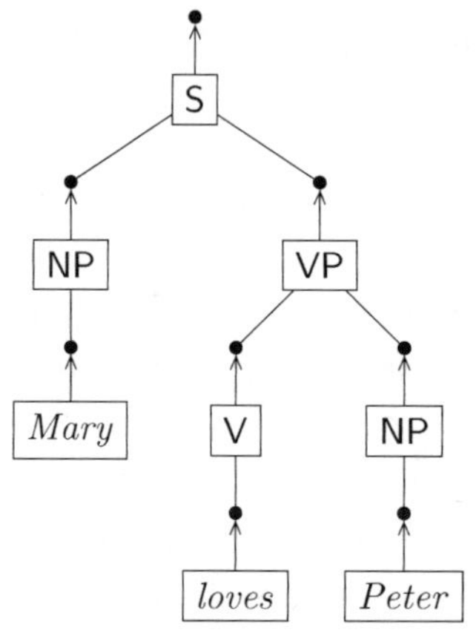

Figure 1: A tree in its (hyper)graph representation

symbols point to the target nodes of the tree edge representing that symbol.

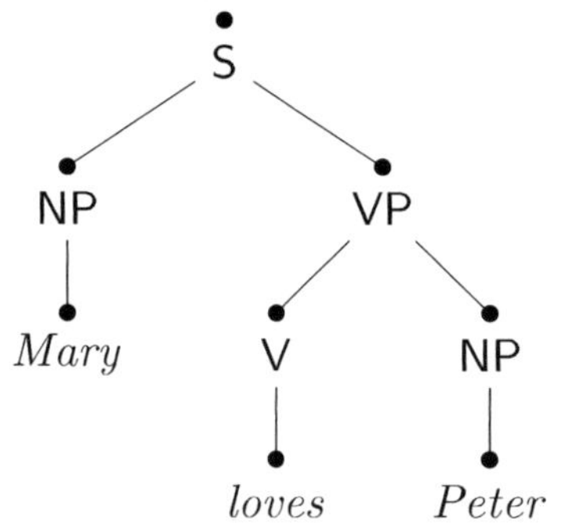

Figure 2: A more condensed representation of the tree in Figure 1

A k-ary link establishes a relation between k nodes by arranging them in a tuple. In this paper there is only one link symbol, this link symbol is of source rank 2, and connects nodes across the two trees every configuration consists of. These links are drawn as unlabelled dashed lines. With these conventions, a complete configuration looks as shown in Figure 3. This configuration consists of two trees, representing the (extremely simplified) syntactic and semantic structures of the sentence *Mary loves Peter*. The symbols in the semantic tree are interpreted as functions from a many-sorted algebra. The sorts of the algebra are the semantic domains of interest, and the evaluation of a (sub-) tree yields an element of one of these sorts. In the semantic tree shown in the figure, we assume that Mary and Peter are (interpreted as) functions without arguments (i.e., constants) returning elements of the sort *name*. The

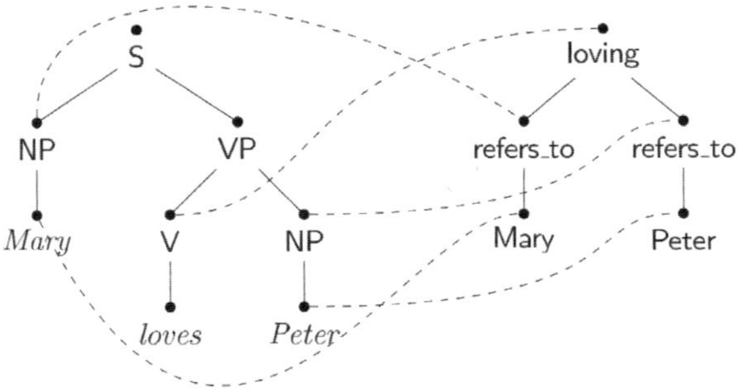

Figure 3: A sample configuration that relates a syntactic and a semantic tree

function refers_to takes a name as its argument and returns, say, an element of the domain *person*. Finally, loving is a function that takes two persons as arguments and returns an element of the domain *state*, namely the state that the first argument (commonly called the *agent*) loves the second (the *patient*). The links establish correspondences between nodes in the two trees showing that, e.g., the verb of the sentence corresponds to the function loving, whose two arguments correspond to the two noun phrases of the sentence. In realistic settings, one would of course use more elaborate trees. However, since we primarily want to convey the idea behind our proposed approach, we use this simple type of configuration as our running example.

3 Incremental Construction of Configurations

In a Millstream system, we are given k *modules* for each of the k trees in a configuration. These modules are tree grammars or any other kind of device generating trees. Furthermore, we are given a logical *interface* that describes which configurations (consisting of k trees generated by the modules and a set of links between them) are considered to be correct. In the current paper, we take a more pragmatic point of view and investigate how configurations can be built up "from scratch" along a sentence using an approach based on implementing a lexicon by graph transformation.

We use graph transformation in the sense of the so-called double pushout (DPO) approach (Ehrig et al., 2010) (with injective morphisms). A rule r is a span $r = (L \supseteq K \subseteq R)$ of graphs L, K, R. The rule applies to a graph G if

1. L is isomorphic to a subgraph of G (for simplicity, let us assume that the isomorphism is the identity) and
2. no edge in G is attached to a node in $V_L \setminus V_K$.

In this case, applying r means to remove all nodes and edges from G that are in L but not in K, and to add all nodes and edges that are in R but not in K. Thus, the so-called glueing graph K is not affected by the rule, but rather used to "glue" the new nodes and edges in the right-hand side R to the existing graph. The second condition for applicability ensures well-formedness, as it makes sure that the deletion of nodes does not result in so-called dangling edges, i.e., edges with an undefined attachment. If the result of the application of r to G is G', this may be denoted by $G \underset{r}{\Rightarrow} G'$. Moreover, if R is a set of graph transformation rules, and $G \underset{r}{\Rightarrow} G'$ for some $r \in R$, we denote this fact by $G \underset{R}{\Rightarrow} G'$.

Compared to general DPO rules, our lexicon rules are quite restricted as they never delete anything. In other words, we always have $L = K$, and hence the rules only glue new subgraphs to the existing (partial) configuration. We call rules of this kind *incremental* and denote the set of all incremental rules over a Millstream alphabet Σ by $\mathcal{R}_\Sigma$. In addition to the conditions 1 and 2 above, we restrict the applicability of rules further, by introducing a third condition:

3. $tar_G(e) \neq tar_R(e')$ for all tree edges $e \in E_G$ and $e' \in E_R \setminus E_K$.

This condition merely avoids useless nondeterminism leading into dead ends.

Derivations start with a common start graph. Since our example is extremely simple, it suffices to choose the graph that consists of the edge labelled with the root symbol $\mathsf{S}_{(2)}$ of the syntactic tree (together with the three attached nodes). The fact that all our rules satisfy $L = K$ means that we can depict a rule as just one graph, namely R, where the nodes and edges in L are drawn in blue. Graph transformation rules of this type are called lexicon entries. Figures 4, 5 and 6 show sample lexicon entries for the words *Mary*, *loves*, and *Peter*, respectively. Starting with the start graph (the blue subgraph in Figure 4) and applying the three rules in the order in which the words appear in the sentence takes us to the configuration in Figure 3. Note that the complete lexicon should contain another entry similar to the one in Figure 4, but with *Mary* and Mary being replaced by *Peter* and Peter, respectively. Similarly, there should be a variant of Figure 6 for the name Mary. This would make it possible to read the sentence *Peter loves Mary*. The reader should also note that, when reading the third word of the sentence, *Peter*, the corresponding variant of Figure 4 cannot be applied, because the first child of S is already present.

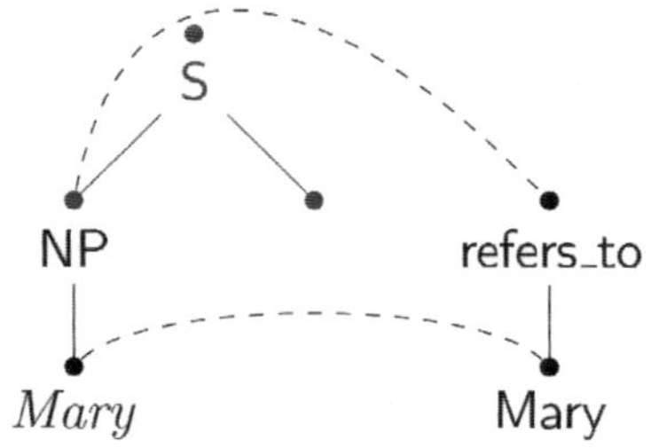

Figure 4: Lexicon entry for *Mary*

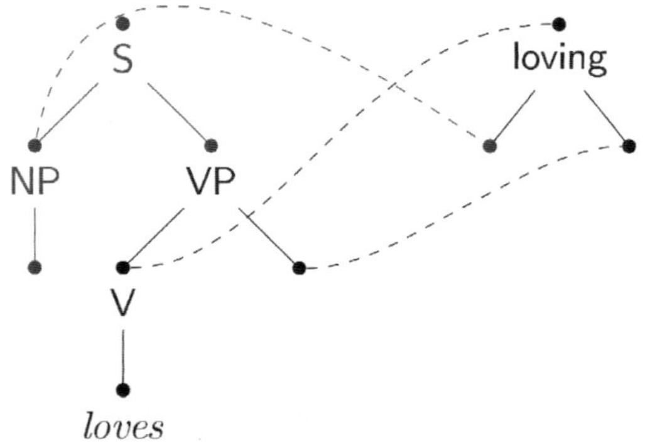

Figure 5: Lexicon entry for *loves*

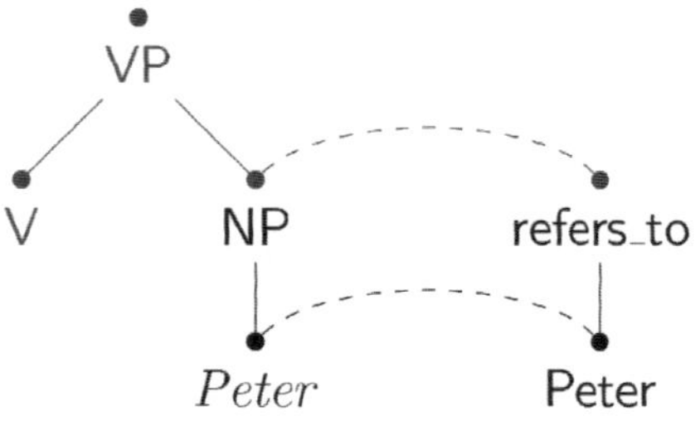

Figure 6: Lexicon entry for *Peter*

Definition 2 *A* reader *is a quadruple* $R = (\Sigma, W, \Lambda, S)$ *consisting of a finite set* W *of words (the input words), a Millstream alphabet* Σ, *a mapping* Λ *called the* lexicon, *and a start graph* $S \in \mathcal{G}_\Sigma$. *The lexicon assigns to every* $w \in W$ *a finite set* $\Lambda(w) \subseteq \mathcal{R}_\Sigma$ *of rules, the* lexicon entries.

A reading *of an input sentence* $w_1 \cdots w_n$ *by* R *is a derivation*

$$S \underset{\Lambda(w_1)}{\Rightarrow} G_1 \underset{\Lambda(w_1)}{\Rightarrow} \cdots \underset{\Lambda(w_n)}{\Rightarrow} G_n$$

such that G_n *is a* Σ*-configuration. The set of all* Σ*-configurations that result from readings of* $w = w_1 \cdots w_n$ *is denoted by* $R(w)$, *and the language (of* Σ*-configurations) generated by* R *is* $L(R) = \bigcup_{w \in W^*} R(w)$.

Future work will have to develop methods for proving the correctness of readers with respect to a given Millstream system. This notion of correctness is given in the next definition.

Definition 3 *Let* MS *be a Millstream system having a distinguished syntactic module* M *(i.e., every configuration of* MS *contains a syntactic tree.) The set of all configurations of* MS *is denoted* $L(MS)$. *A reader* $R = (\Sigma, W, \Lambda, S)$ *is* correct with respect to MS *if* $L(R) = L(MS)$ *and, for every* $w \in W^*$ *and every* $G \in R(w)$, *the yield of the syntactic tree of* G *is equal to* w.

4 Future Work

More research will be necessary to find out whether the type of lexicon entries proposed is most appropriate. Bigger lexica to treat a greater variety and complexity of sentences need to be considered, and an implementation is required. An extension to render the readers of Section 3 more powerful might introduce nonterminal (hyper-)edges to act as indicators of "construction sites". These nonterminals would be consumed when a lexicon entry is applied. An important question for future research is how to build lexica in a systematic way, possibly distinguishing lexica with different strategies, to accommodate different behaviours of readers. Future research will also have to study efficient algorithms for constructing lexica and readings. In particular, it should be possible to "learn". For large lexica, efficient pattern matching algorithms are needed and optimisation algorithms would need to be examined.

References

Suna Bensch and Frank Drewes. 2010. Millstream systems – a formal model for linking language modules by interfaces. In F. Drewes and M. Kuhlmann, editors, *Proc. ACL 2010 Workshop on Appl. of Tree Automata in Natural Lang. Proc. (ATANLP 2010)*, 28–36. The Association for Computer Linguistics.

Suna Bensch, Frank Drewes, and Henrik Björklund. 2010. Algorithmic properties of Millstream systems. In Y. Gao, H. Lu, S. Seki, and S. Yu, editors, *Proc. 14th Intl. Conf. on Developments in Language Theory (DLT 2010)*, volume 6224 of *LNCS*, pages 54–65. Springer.

Hartmut Ehrig, Karsten Ehrig, Ulrike Prange, and Gabriele Taentzer. 2006. *Fundamentals of Algebraic Graph Transformation*. Monogr. in Theor. Comp. Sci. An EATCS Series. Springer.

Ray Jackendoff. 2002. Foundations of Language: Brain, Meaning, Grammar, Evolution. Oxford University Press.

Roman Taraban and James McClelland. 1988. Constituent attachment and thematic role assignment in sentence processing: Influences of content-based expectations. *Journal of Memory and Language*, 27:597–632.

Stochastic K-TSS bi-languages for Machine Translation

M. Inés Torres
Depto. de Electricidad y Electrónica
Universidad del País Vasco
Bilbao, Spain
manes.torres@ehu.es

Francisco Casacuberta
Instituto Tecnológico de Informática
Universidad Politécnica de Valencia
Valencia, Spain
fcn@iti.upv.es

Abstract

One of the approaches to statistical machine translation is based on joint probability distributions over some source and target languages. In this work we propose to model the joint probability distribution by stochastic regular *bi-languages*. Specifically we introduce the stochastic k-testable in the strict sense *bi-languages* to represent the joint probability distribution of source and target languages. With this basis we present a reformulation of the GIATI methodology to infer stochastic regular *bi-languages* for machine translation purposes.

1 Introduction

The goal of *statistical machine translation* (SMT) is to search for the sentence $\hat{\mathbf{t}}$ that maximizes the a-posteriori probability $P(\mathbf{t}|\mathbf{s})$ of the target sentence $\mathbf{t}$ being the translation of a given sentence $\mathbf{s}$ from the source language. The translation models in SMT are automatically learned from bilingual samples. In the early nineties machine translation was tackled as a pure probabilistic process by the IBM research group (Brown et al., 1993). Within the SMT framework, *stochastic-finite-state transducers* (SFSTs) have also been proposed for machine translation purposes (Bangalore and Riccardi, 2002) (Shankar et al., 2005) (Casacuberta and Vidal, 2004) (Casacuberta and Vidal, 2007) (Blackwood et al., 2009). In such a context, SMT can be viewed as the problem of computing the joint probability distribution of some source and target languages. i.e. $P(\mathbf{t}, \mathbf{s})$, inferred from a bi-lingual corpus. The joint probability distributions of pairs of strings may be modeled by a probability distribution on a set of strings based on bi-lingual units as proposed in (Bangalore and Riccardi, 2002) for SFSTs. Alternatively (Casacuberta and Vidal, 2004) (Mariño et al., 2006) proposed n-grams models of bi-lingual units. However, only a few techniques to learn finite-state transducers for machine translation purposes can be found (Bangalore and Riccardi, 2002) (Oncina et al., 1993) (Knight and Al-Onaizan, 1998) (Casacuberta and Vidal, 2007). On the other hand, a method of inference of SFST based on the inference of stochastic finite-state automata (Casacuberta and Vidal, 2004) was proposed and then used in machine translation applications (Casacuberta and Vidal, 2007) (Pérez et al., 2008) (González and Casacuberta, 2009). This method was called *grammatical inference and alignments for transducer inference* (GIATI) and is based on some important properties relating regular translations generated by finite-state-transducers and regular languages over some bi-lingual alphabet (Berstel, 1979).

On the other hand, different stochastic regular *bi-languages* can be introduced to model $P(\mathbf{s}, \mathbf{t})$ distribution. Turning to stochastic regular languages, let us note that the class of stochastic *k-testable in the strict sense* (k-TSS) languages is a subclass of stochastic regular languages that can be inferred from a set of positive training data (Torres and Varona, 2001) (Vidal et al., 2005a) (Torres and Casacuberta, 2011) by some stochastic extension of the inference algorithm in (García and Vidal, 1990). Thus, they belong to the subset of regular languages that can be used to characterize some pattern recog-

Proceedings of the 9th International Workshop on Finite State Methods and Natural Language Processing, pages 98–106,
Blois (France), July 12-15, 2011. ©2011 Association for Computational Linguistics

nition tasks. In particular, stochastic k-TSS has been used in many natural language processing tasks such as phone recognition (Galiano and Segarra, 1993), speech recognition (Torres and Varona, 2001), language identification (Guijarrubia and Torres, 2010), language modeling (Justo and Torres, 2009) or machine translation (Pérez et al., 2008).

In this work we propose to model the joint probability distribution $P(\mathbf{t}, \mathbf{s})$ by stochastic regular *bi-languages*. A first contribution of our work is the reformulation of the GIATI methodology to infer stochastic regular *bi-languages* for machine translation purposes. This proposal allows the use of some stochastic *bi-automaton* to get the sentence $\hat{\mathbf{t}}$ that corresponds to the source sentence $\hat{\mathbf{s}}$. This stochastic *bi-automaton* need to be inferred from a sample set of *bi-strings*. As a consequence, this methodology does not required any SFST as original GIATI did. Thus, there is no need to any property relating stochastic regular translations and stochastic regular languages to support the proposed method. On the other hand, different stochastic regular *bi-languages* can be introduced to model the joint probability distribution. As a second contribution we propose in this work the use of stochastic k-TSS *bi-languages* to model $Pr(\mathbf{s}, \mathbf{t})$. For this purpose we extend definitions and theorems of stochastic k-TSS languages (Vidal et al., 2005a) (Torres and Casacuberta, 2011) to stochastic k-TSS *bi-languages* and then write a corollary to the stochastic extension of the morphism theorem.

We contribute in Section 2 with some definitions of *bi-strings*, stochastic *bi-languages* and stochastic *bi-automata*. In Section 3 we propose to model the joint probability distribution through stochastic *bi-language* and then use stochastic *bi-automaton* for translation purposes. In Section 4 we deal with stochastic k-TSS *bi-languages* and *bi-automaton*, introducing some definitions and theorem applications. Then we present in Section 5 the inference of stochastic k-TSS *bi-automata* for machine translation as a reformulation of the GIATI methodology. Finally Section 6 deals with some concluding remarks and future work.

2 Stochastic regular bi-languages

In this Section we first provide the basic definitions of bi-string, stochastic regular bi-language and stochastic and deterministic finite state bi-automata proposed in this work.

Let Σ and Δ be two finite alphabets and $\Sigma^{\leq m}$ and $\Delta^{\leq n}$, the finite sets of sequences of symbols in Σ and Δ of length up to m and n respectively. Let $\Gamma \subseteq (\Sigma^{\leq m} \times \Delta^{\leq n})$ be a finite alphabet (*extended alphabet*) consisting of pairs of strings, that we call *extended symbols*, $(s_1 \ldots s_i : t_1 \ldots t_j) \in \Gamma$ such that $s_1 \ldots s_i \in \Sigma^{\leq m}$ and $t_1 \ldots t_j \in \Delta^{\leq n}$ with $0 \leq i \leq m$ and $0 \leq j \leq n$.

Definition 2.1. *A bi-language is a set of strings over an extended alphabet Γ, i.e., a set of strings of the form $\mathbf{b} = b_1 \ldots b_k$ such that $b_i \in \Gamma$ for $0 \leq i \leq k$. A string over an extended alphabet Γ will be called bi-string.*

Alternatively (Kornai, 2008) defines a *bi-string* as composed by two strings and an association relation. In the same way, *bi-languages* are defined as sets of well-formed *bi-strings* that undergo the usual set-theoretic operations of intersection, union and complementation. Concatenation of such *bi-strings* is also defined in (Kornai, 2008). In this context, regular *bi-languages* were previously defined in (Kornai, 1995). In the context of machine translation, (Mariño et al., 2006) defines a *bi-language* as composed of bi-lingual units which were referred to as *tuples* extracted from alignments of a bilingual corpus. This definition could be consistent with the one provided in definition 2.1. Also in machine translation, (Bangalore and Riccardi, 2002) defines a *bi-language* corpus as consisting of source-target symbol pair sequences $(s_1 : t_1) \ldots (s_i : t_i) \ldots (s_n : t_n)$ such that $s_i \in L_s \cup \{\lambda\}$ and its aligned symbol $t_i \in L_t \cup \{\lambda\}$ where L_s and L_t are a couple of related languages. This definition allows for pairs of symbols by contrast with definition 2.1 where pairs of finite-length strings are considered. Finally, let us note that regular tree languages were also been referred as bilanguages (Pair and Quere, 1968) (Berger and Pair, 1978).

We are now referring to the work by (Vidal et al., 2005a). This work is a survey of probabilistic finite-state machines and related definitions and properties. In this survey, the authors provide a definition of probabilistic automata that corresponds to *generative* models. Note that in classical (and non probabilistic) formal theory strings are generated by *grammars*. In this paper we are using the formalism developed in (Vidal et al., 2005a).

Given a finite alphabet Σ, a *stochastic language* is defined in (Vidal et al., 2005a) as a probability distribution over Σ^*. Let us extend this definition to consider *bi-strings* and then get stochastic *bi-languages*.

Definition 2.2. *Given two finite alphabets Σ and Δ, a stochastic bi-language $\mathcal{B}$ is a probability distribution over Γ^* where $\Gamma \subseteq (\Sigma^{\leq m} \times \Delta^{\leq n})$, $m, n \geq 0$. Let $\mathbf{z} = z_1 \dots z_{|\mathbf{z}|}$ be a bi-string such that $z_i \in \Gamma$ for $1 \leq i \leq |\mathbf{z}|$. If $Pr_{\mathcal{B}}(\mathbf{z})$ denotes the probability of the bi-string $\mathbf{z}$ under the distribution $\mathcal{B}$ then $\sum_{\mathbf{z} \in \Gamma^*} Pr_{\mathcal{B}}(\mathbf{z}) = 1$.*

Let now define a deterministic and probabilistic finite-state *bi-automaton* (DPFBA) by extending the standard definition of a deterministic and probabilistic finite-state automaton (DPFA) as follows:

Definition 2.3. *A DPFBA is a probabilistic finite-state bi-automaton $\mathcal{BA} = (Q, \Sigma, \Delta, \Gamma, \delta, q_0, P_f, P)$ if Q is a finite set of states, Σ and Δ are two finite alphabets, Γ is an extended alphabet such that $\Gamma \subseteq (\Sigma^{\leq m} \times \Delta^{\leq n})$, $m, n \geq 0$, $\delta \subseteq Q \times \Gamma \times Q$ is a set of transitions of the form $(q, (\tilde{s}_i : \tilde{t}_i), q')$ where $q, q' \in Q$ and , $(\tilde{s}_i : \tilde{t}_i) \in \Gamma$, $q_0 \in Q$ is the unique initial state, $P_f : Q \rightarrow [0, 1]$ is the final-state probabilistic distribution and $P : \delta \rightarrow [0, 1]$ defines transition probabilistic distributions ($P(q, b, q') \equiv Pr(q', b|q)$ for $b \in \Gamma$ and $q, q' \in Q$) such that:*

$$P_f(q) + \sum_{b \in \Gamma, q' \in Q} P(q, b, q') = 1 \quad \forall q \in Q \qquad (1)$$

where a transition (q, b, q') is completely defined by q and b. Thus, $\forall q \in Q$, $\forall b \in \Gamma$ $|\{q' : (q, b, q')\}| \leq 1$

Finally let $\mathbf{z} \in \Gamma^*$ and let $\theta = (q_0, z_1, q_1, z_2, q_2, ..., q_{|\mathbf{z}|-1}, z_{|\mathbf{z}|}, q_{|\mathbf{z}|})$ be a path for $\mathbf{z}$ in $\mathcal{BA}$. The probability of generating θ is:

$$Pr_{\mathcal{BA}}(\theta) = \left(\prod_{j=1}^{|\mathbf{z}|} P(q_{j-1}, z_j, q_j) \right) \cdot P_f(q_{|\mathbf{z}|}) \qquad (2)$$

$\mathcal{BA}$ is a DPFBA and thus unambiguous. Then, a given *bi-string* $\mathbf{z}$ can only be generated by $\mathcal{BA}$ through a unique valid path $\theta(\mathbf{z})$. Thus, the probability of generating $\mathbf{z}$ with $\mathcal{BA}$ is $Pr_{\mathcal{BA}}(\mathbf{z}) = Pr_{\mathcal{BA}}(\theta(\mathbf{z}))$.

3 Statistical translation with bi-automata

Let us consider a source and a target languages from a source vocabulary Σ and a target vocabulary Δ, respectively. The goal of machine translation is to map a sentence in the source language, i.e. a string of symbols $\mathbf{s} = s_1 \dots s_{|\mathbf{s}|}$, $s_i \in \Sigma$ into a sentence in the target language $\mathbf{t} = t_1 \dots t_{|\mathbf{t}|}$, $t_i \in \Delta$. Statistical machine translation (SMT) is based on the *noisy channel* approach (Shannon, 1948) where $\mathbf{t}$ is considered to be a noisy version of $\mathbf{s}$ (Brown et al., 1993). Thus, the translation of a given string $\mathbf{s} \in \Delta^*$ in the source language is a string $\hat{\mathbf{t}} \in \Delta^*$ in the target language such that:

$$\hat{\mathbf{t}} = \arg\max_{\mathbf{t} \in \Delta^*} Pr(\mathbf{t}|\mathbf{s})$$

Alternatively, a joint probability distribution can be used by developing $Pr(\mathbf{t}|\mathbf{s})$ in previous Equation as follows:

$$\hat{\mathbf{t}} = \arg\max_{\mathbf{t} \in \Delta^*} \frac{Pr(\mathbf{s}, \mathbf{t})}{Pr(\mathbf{s})} = \arg\max_{\mathbf{t} \in \Delta^*} Pr(\mathbf{s}, \mathbf{t}) \qquad (3)$$

since, $Pr(\mathbf{s})$ does not depend on $\mathbf{t}$. Distribution $Pr(\mathbf{s}, \mathbf{t})$ can be modeled by a stochastic finite state transducer (Bangalore and Riccardi, 2002) (Casacuberta and Vidal, 2004). Alternatively in this paper we model this distribution by a stochastic regular *bi-language*.

To this end, let $\mathbf{z}$ be a *bi-string* over the extended alphabet $\Gamma \subseteq \Sigma^{\leq m} \times \Delta^{\leq n}$ such as $\mathbf{z} : \mathbf{z} = z_1 \dots z_{|\mathbf{z}|}$, $z_i = (\tilde{s}_i : \tilde{t}_i)$ where $\tilde{s}_i = s_1 \dots s_{|\tilde{s}_i|} \in \Sigma^{\leq m}$ and $\tilde{t}_i = t_1 \dots t_{|\tilde{t}_i|} \in \Delta^{\leq n}$. Extended symbols $(\tilde{s}_i : \tilde{t}_i) \in \Gamma$ have been obtained through some alignment between $\Sigma^{\leq m}$ and $\Delta^{\leq n}$. String $\mathbf{s} \in \Sigma^*$ is a sequence of substrings $\tilde{s}_i$ such as $\mathbf{s} = \tilde{s}_1 \dots \tilde{s}_{|\mathbf{z}|}$ that has been obtained through a previously segmentation procedure. In the same way string $\mathbf{t} \in \Delta^*$ is a sequence of substrings $\tilde{t}_i$ such as $\mathbf{t} = \tilde{t}_1 \dots \tilde{t}_{|\mathbf{z}|}$. Then $Pr(\mathbf{s}, \mathbf{t})$ can be calculated as follows:

$$Pr(\mathbf{s}, \mathbf{t}) = \sum_{\forall \mathbf{z} \in \Gamma^* : (h_\Sigma(\mathbf{z}), h_\Delta(\mathbf{z})) = (\mathbf{s}, \mathbf{t})} Pr(\mathbf{z}) \qquad (4)$$

In such a case, $Pr(\mathbf{s},\mathbf{t})$ can be modeled by a DPFBA $\mathcal{BA}$ such as the one defined in Definition 2.3. Thus, the probability $Pr(\mathbf{s},\mathbf{t})$ according to $\mathcal{BA}$ is defined as

$$\begin{aligned} Pr_{\mathcal{BA}}(\mathbf{s},\mathbf{t}) &= \sum_{\forall \mathbf{z}\in\Gamma^*:(h_\Sigma(\mathbf{z}),h_\Delta(\mathbf{z}))=(\mathbf{s},\mathbf{t})} Pr_{\mathcal{BA}}(\mathbf{z}) \\ &= \sum_{\forall\theta\in g(s,t)} Pr_{\mathcal{BA}}(\theta) \end{aligned}$$

where $g(s,t)$ denotes the set of all possible paths in $\mathcal{BA}$ matching $(\mathbf{s},\mathbf{t})$ and $Pr_{\mathcal{BA}}(\theta)$ is calculated according to Equation 2.

3.1 The search through a stochastic finite state bi-automaton

The main goal of SMT according to Equation 3 is to find the optimal target string $\hat{\mathbf{t}}$ given a source string $\hat{\mathbf{s}}$ and given a stochastic model of the involved joint probability. When $Pr(\mathbf{s},\mathbf{t})$ is modeled by a DPFBA $\mathcal{BA}$ we need to be able to get the string $\hat{\mathbf{t}} = \tilde{t}_1\ldots\tilde{t}_{|\mathbf{z}|}$ that corresponds to the source sequence $\mathbf{s} = \tilde{s}_1\ldots\tilde{s}_{|\mathbf{z}|}$, given $Pr_{\mathcal{BA}}(\mathbf{s},\mathbf{t})$ through Equation 5. A *bi-automaton* $\mathcal{BA}$ is ambiguous with respect to the input sequence s. Thus, all pairs $(\mathbf{s},\mathbf{t})$ matching the given input sequence s are considered, i.e the maximization is carried out $\forall\mathbf{t}\in\Delta^*$ instead of $\forall(\mathbf{s},\mathbf{t})\in\Gamma^*$. As a consequence $\hat{\mathbf{t}}$ is obtained as follows:

$$\begin{aligned} \hat{\mathbf{t}} &= \arg\max_{\mathbf{t}\in\Delta^*} Pr_{\mathcal{BA}}(\mathbf{s},\mathbf{t}) \\ &= \arg\max_{\mathbf{t}\in\Delta^*} \sum_{\forall\theta\in g(s,t)} Pr_{\mathcal{BA}}(\theta) \end{aligned}$$

This search for the optimal $\hat{\mathbf{t}}$ through Equation 5 has proved to be a difficult computational problem (Casacuberta and de la Higuera, 2000). In practice Equation 5 can be computed by the so-called *maximum approximation*, which assume that the sum close the maximum term. In such a case we first estimate the optimal path $\hat{\theta}$ is obtained as:

$$\hat{\theta} = \arg\max_{\forall\theta\in g(\mathbf{s})} Pr_{\mathcal{BA}}(\theta)$$

where $g(\mathbf{s})$ denotes the set of possible paths in $\mathcal{BA}$ matching s and $Pr_{\mathcal{BA}}(\theta)$ is calculated by Equation 2. The approximate translation $\hat{\mathbf{t}}$ is then computed as the concatenation of the target substrings associated to the estimated path $\hat{\theta}$: $(q_0,(\tilde{s}_1 : \tilde{t}_1),q_1)(q_1,(\tilde{s}_2 : \tilde{t}_2),q_2)\ldots..(q_{m-1},(\tilde{s}_m : \tilde{t}_m),q_m)$ and $\hat{\mathbf{t}} = \tilde{t}_1,\tilde{t}_2,\ldots,\tilde{t}_m$ by the recursive algorithm proposed in (Casacuberta and Vidal, 2004) adapted now to a *bi-automaton*.

4 Stochastic k-TSS bi-languages

Different stochastic regular *bi-languages* can be introduced to model $Pr_{\mathcal{BA}}(\mathbf{s},\mathbf{t})$ distribution in Equation 5. In particular we propose in this work the use stochastic k-TSS DPFBA. In this Section we deal with stochastic k-TSS *bi-languages* as a particular case of stochastic *bi-languages* defined in Section 2.

To this end, let us now turn to stochastic k-TSS languages which are a subclass stochastic regular languages. Stochastic k-TSS languages are defined in (Vidal et al., 2005a) and (Torres and Casacuberta, 2011) as a four-tuple $Z_k = (\Sigma, P_{I_k}, P_{F_k}, P_{T_k})$, where Σ is a finite alphabet; $P_{I_k} : \Sigma^{<k} \to [0,1]$ are the *initial* probabilities, i.e. the probability that a string $a_1\ldots a_j \in I_k \subseteq \Sigma^{<k}$ is a starting segment of a string in the language; $P_{F_k} : \Sigma^{<k} \to [0,1]$ are the *final* probabilities, i.e. the probability that a string $a_1\ldots a_j \in F_k \subseteq \Sigma^{<k}$ is a final segment of a string in the language and $P_{T_k} : \Sigma^k \to [0,1]$ are the allowed-segments probabilities, i.e. the probability that a string $a_1\ldots a_k \in (\Sigma^k - T_k)$ according to the corresponding normalization conditions. Thus, strings in the stochastic k-TSS language L_{Z_k} start with segments in I_k of length up to $k-1$, they end with segments in F_k of length up to $k-1$ and do not include segments in T_k of length k. This definition can be straightforwardly extended to consider *bi-languages* as follows:

Definition 4.1. *A stochastic k-TSS bi-language* $Z_{B_k} = (\Gamma, P_{I_{B_k}}, P_{F_{B_k}}, P_{T_{B_k}})$ *is a stochastic k-TSS language defined on a extended alphabet* $\Gamma \subseteq \Sigma^{\leq m} \times \Delta^{\leq n}$.

Z_{B_k} defines a probability distribution $\mathcal{B}_{Z_{B_k}}$ on Γ^*, simplified as $\mathcal{B}_k$ from now, such as for any string of *bi-strings* $\mathbf{z}\in\Gamma^*$ of size $|\mathbf{z}|$, i.e. $\mathbf{z} = z_1\ldots z_{|\mathbf{z}|}$ the probability $Pr_{\mathcal{B}_k}(\mathbf{z})$ is calculated according to:

$$\begin{cases} P_{I_k}(z_1\ldots z_{|\mathbf{z}|})\cdot P_{F_k}(z_1\ldots z_{|\mathbf{z}|}) & \text{if } |\mathbf{z}|<k \\ P_{I_k}(z_1\ldots z_{k-1})\cdot \prod_{i=k}^{|\mathbf{z}|} P_{T_k}(z_{i-k+1}\ldots z_{i-1},z_i)\cdot & \\ P_{F_k}(z_{|z|-(k-2)}\ldots z_{|\mathbf{z}|}) & \text{if } |\mathbf{z}|\geq k \end{cases}$$

$Pr_{\mathcal{B}_k}(\mathbf{z})$ is the probability of the string $z \in \Gamma^*$ under the k-TSS distribution $\mathcal{B}_k$. Thus:

$$\sum_{\mathbf{z} \in \Gamma^*} Pr_{\mathcal{B}_k}(\mathbf{z}) = 1 \qquad (5)$$

Let us now fall back to classical k-TSS to bear in mind some important theorems. An interesting subclass of k-TSS is the class of 2-TSS languages, which are known as *local languages*. There is an important generative property which relates local languages and general regular languages given by the morphism theorem (García et al., 1987), which establish that any regular language can be generated by a local language. A stochastic extension of the morphism theorem was introduced in (Vidal et al., 2005b). A stochastic regular *bi-language* is a particular case of stochastic regular languages for an *extended* alphabet $\Gamma \subseteq (\Sigma^{\leq m} \times \Delta^{\leq n})$. As a consequence, we can apply the stochastic extension of the morphism theorem in (Vidal et al., 2005b) to stochastic regular *bi-languages* and then write a corollary for this theorem as follows:

Corollary 4.1. *Let Σ and Δ be two finite alphabets, $\Gamma \subseteq (\Sigma^{\leq m} \times \Delta^{\leq n})$ be an extended alphabet and $\mathcal{B}$ a stochastic regular bi-language on Γ^*. There exists then a finite alphabet Γ', an alphabetic morphism $h : \Gamma'^* \rightarrow \Gamma^*$ and a stochastic local language $\mathcal{D}_2$ over Γ'^* such that $\mathcal{B} = h(\mathcal{D}_2)$; i.e.,*

$$\begin{aligned} Pr_{\mathcal{B}}(\mathbf{z}) &= Pr_{\mathcal{D}_2}(h^{-1}(\mathbf{z})) \\ &= \textstyle\sum_{\mathbf{y} \in h^{-1}(\mathbf{z})} Pr_{\mathcal{D}_2}(\mathbf{y}) \quad \forall \mathbf{z} \in \Gamma^* \end{aligned}$$

where $h^{-1}(\mathbf{z}) = \{\mathbf{y} \in \Gamma'^* | \mathbf{z} = h(\mathbf{y})\}$. Thus, any stochastic regular *bi-language* defined over Γ^* can be generated by a local language over some Γ'^* where Γ and Γ' are finite alphabets of *extended symbols* such that $\Gamma, \Gamma' \subseteq \Sigma^{\leq m} \times \Delta^{\leq n}$

We need now to deal with stochastic k-TSS *bi-automata* as well as with the way to get them from a training corpus. The inference of k-TSS automata was first addressed in (García and Vidal, 1990). Given a set of positive sample set R^+ of an unknown language, an efficient algorithm obtains a deterministic finite-state automaton that recognizes the smallest k-TSS language containing the sample set R^+. A preliminary form of a stochastic extension was presented in (Segarra, 1993) and then fully formalized in (Torres and Casacuberta, 2011). In that work a k-TSS DPFA is defined as a class of DPFA able to generate stochastic k-TSS languages where the unambiguity of the automaton allowed for a maximum likelihood estimation of each transition probability. This algorithm, can be easily adapted to infer a k-TSS DPFBA, $\mathcal{BA}_k$, generating a stochastic k-TSS *bi-language* by considering an *extended* alphabet of *bi-strings* $\Gamma \subseteq (\Sigma^{\leq m} \times \Delta^{\leq n})$. Example 4.1 shows the way to infer a k-TSS DPFBA $\mathcal{BA}_k$ that generates a k-TSS *bi-language* containing a previously defined sample R^+.

Example 4.1. *Let $\Sigma = \{a, b\}$ and $\Delta = \{1, 0\}$ be two finite alphabets and let $\Gamma \subseteq (\Sigma^{\leq m} \times \Delta^{\leq n})$ be the extended alphabet such as: $\Gamma = \{(a : 1), (aa : 11), (b : 0), (bb : 00)\}$. Let now R^+ be a positive sample set of a stochastic k-TSS bi-language $\mathcal{B}$ consisting of strings in Γ^* such that: $R^+ = \{(a : 1), (b : 0), (aa : 11), (a : 1)(a : 1), (aa, 11)(b : 0), (a : 1)(a : 1)(b : 0), (a : 1)(b : 0)(b : 0), (a : 1)(bb : 00)\}$*
Then for $k = 3$
$I_3 = \{(a : 1), (b : 0), (aa : 11), (a : 1)(a : 1), (aa : 11)(b : 0), (a : 1)(b : 0), (a : 1)(bb : 00)\}$
$P_{I_k} = \{0.125, 0.125, 0.125, 0.25, 0.125, 0.125, 0.125\}$
$F_3 = \{(a : 1), (b : 0), (aa : 11), (a : 1)(a : 1), (aa : 11)(b : 0), (a : 1)(b : 0), (b : 0)(b : 0), (a : 1)(bb : 00)\}$
$P_{f_k} = \{1, 1, 1, 0.5, 1, 0.5, 1, 1\}$
The inferred bi-automaton $\mathcal{BA}_3$ is represented as:

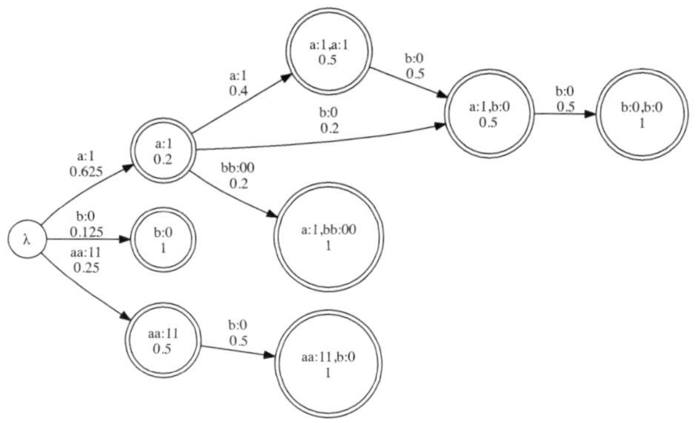

where each state $q \in Q_k$ is labelled by a bi-string $(\tilde{s}_1 : \tilde{t}_1 \ldots \tilde{s}_i : \tilde{t}_i) \in \Gamma^i$ $i < k$ along with the probability $P_f(q)$ and each edge is labelled by a pair $\tilde{s}_i : \tilde{t}_i \in \Gamma$ such that $(q, \tilde{s}_i : \tilde{t}_i, q') \in \delta_k$ along with the probability $P_k(q, \tilde{s}_i : \tilde{t}_i, q')$.

5 Inference of k-TSS bi-automata for machine translation

In Section 3 we have propose to compute the joint probability distribution $P(\mathbf{s}, \mathbf{t})$ through some stochastic *bi-automaton* according to definitions in Section 2. Then in Section 4 we have shown how to get an stochastic k-TSS *bi-automaton* from a positive sample set of *bi-strings*. Thus, we can now propose a technique for the inference of stochastic k-TSS *bi-automata* for machine translation purposes based on GIATI methodology, which takes advantage of theoretical background previously (Casacuberta and Vidal, 2004) (Vidal et al., 2005b) (Torres and Casacuberta, 2011).

Given a finite sample set $\mathcal{S}^+$ of strings pairs $(\mathbf{s}, \mathbf{t}) \in \Sigma^* \times \Delta^*$ from a bilingual (*parallel*) corpus then

- **Step 1**: Given a pair of strings $(\mathbf{s}, \mathbf{t})$ get a *bi-string* $\mathbf{z} \in \Gamma^*$ according to some particular alignment and segmentation procedures. As a result, the sample set $\mathcal{S}^+$ of bilingual sentences $(\mathbf{s}, \mathbf{t}) \in \Sigma^* \times \Delta^*$ is transformed into a set $\mathcal{R}^+$ of *bi-strings* $\mathbf{z} \in \Gamma^*$.

$$\mathcal{S}^+ \subseteq \Sigma^* \times \Delta^* \rightarrow \mathcal{R}^+ \subseteq \Gamma^*$$

- **Step 2**: From the set of *bi-strings* $\mathcal{R}^+ \subseteq \Gamma^*$ infer the k-TSS DPFBA $\mathcal{BA}_k$ generating a stochastic k-TSS *bi-language* that includes $\mathcal{R}^+$.

$$\mathcal{R}^+ \subseteq \Gamma^* \rightarrow \mathcal{BA}_k : \mathcal{R}^+ \subseteq \mathcal{B}_{\mathcal{BA}_k}$$

5.1 Step 1- Segmentation

The goal of this step is to get a corpus of *bi-strings* from a bilingual corpus. Let $(\mathbf{s}, \mathbf{t}) : \mathbf{s} \in \Sigma^*, \mathbf{t} \in \Delta^*$ be a pair of strings in $\mathcal{S}^+$ such that each string $\mathbf{s} \in \Sigma^*$ and each string $\mathbf{t} \in \Delta^*$ is a sequence of substrings $\tilde{s}_i$ and $\tilde{t}_i$. Then a *segmentation* procedure is required to get a *bi-string* $\mathbf{z} \in \Gamma^* : \mathbf{z} = (\tilde{s}_1, \tilde{t}_1) \ldots (\tilde{s}_{|\mathbf{z}|}, \tilde{t}_{|\mathbf{z}|})$ such that string $\mathbf{s}$ is a sequence of substrings $\tilde{s}_i$ and string $\mathbf{t}$ is a sequence of substrings $\tilde{t}_i$. The *segmentation* is *monotone* if $\mathbf{s} = \tilde{s}_1 \ldots \tilde{s}_{|\mathbf{z}|}$ and $\mathbf{t} = \tilde{t}_1 \ldots \tilde{t}_{|\mathbf{z}|}$.

Then a relation between substrings $\tilde{s}_i \in \Sigma^*$ and substrings $\tilde{t}_i \in \Delta^*$ need also be defined. This relation was called *alignment* in (Kornai, 2008) and depends on the the application task. In this context the aim of the *alignment* is to synchronize sequences of features from two different finite alphabets (Kornai, 1995). Correspondences between source and target strings could be complex, could include long-distance and/or not consecutive associations, etc, such that the choice of a suitable *alignment* is a difficult problem to be solved. One way to deal with this problem in the machine translation framework is the use of statistical *alignments* models (Brown et al., 1993) (Och and Ney, 2003).

The choice of an adequate alignment/segmentation procedure is also related with the parsing procedure based on the *bi-automaton*. In the translation procedure, the target sentence $\hat{\mathbf{t}}$ is obtained as the concatenation of target substrings matching a given source sentence that also consists of a sequence of source substrings. A monotonic segmentation guaranties that the procedure to transform pairs of strings in $\mathcal{S}^+$ into *bi-strings* in Γ^* is reversible.

Example 5.1. *Let* $\Sigma = \{a, b\}$ *and* $\Delta = \{0, 1\}$ *be two finite alphabets. Let now* $\mathcal{S}^+$ *be a bilingual corpus of translations consisting in pairs of strings* $(\mathbf{s}, \mathbf{t})$ *such that* $\mathbf{s} \in \Sigma^*$ *and* $\mathbf{t} \in \Delta^*$ *and* $\mathcal{S}^+ = \{(a, 1), (b, 0), (aa, 11), (aab, 110), (aab, 110)\}$. *From this corpus we can obtain, among others, the following alignments:*

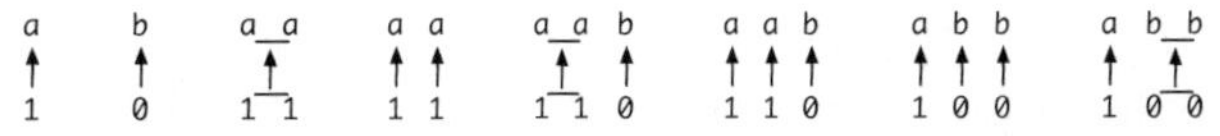

From these alignments we get the alphabet of bi-strings $\Gamma = \{(a : 1), (aa : 11), (b : 0), (bb : 00)\}$. *Thus the positive sample set* R^+ *consisting of bi-strings in* Γ^* *is:* $R^+ = \{(a : 1), (b : 0), (aa : 11), (a : 1)(a : 1), (aa, 11)(b : 0), (a : 1)(a : 1)(b : 0), (a : 1)(b : 0)(b : 0), (a : 1)(bb : 00)\}$

Let us to note that symbols of the general form $(\tilde{s}_i : \tilde{t}_i)$, relate strings in Σ^m, $m \geq 0$ with strings in Δ^n, $n \geq 0$. Alternatively, some machine translation models deal with pairs $(s_i : \tilde{t}_i)$ where the relation is established between symbols $s_i \in \Sigma \cup \{\lambda\}$ and strings $\tilde{t}_i \in \Delta^n$, $n \geq 0$. In such a case, the *bi-string* is defined as composed by pairs $(s_i : \tilde{t}_i) \in (\Sigma \cup \{\lambda\} \times \Delta^n)$, $n \geq 0$.

5.2 Step 2 - Inferring a k-TSS DPFBA

Next, a stochastic finite-state *bi-automaton*, such as the one defined in Section 4, is inferred from the corpus of *bi-stings* $\mathcal{R}^+$. In particular we propose the inference of a k-TSS DPFBA $\mathcal{BA}_k$. To this end, the inference algorithm for k-TSS DPFA summarized in (Torres and Casacuberta, 2011) and then extended to get k-TSS DPFBA in Section 4 need to be applied. Example 4.1 shows the k-TSS DPFBA inferred from the positive sample set R^+ get in Example 5.1

Notice that in this case a smoothed model is required since the model has to generate any *bi-string* $\mathbf{z} \in \Gamma^*$ with a non-zero probability, even for *bi-strings* not in the stochastic *bi-language* generated by the inferred *bi-automaton*. Specific smoothing schemas has been proposed for stochastic k-TSS automata for speech recognition purposes in (Torres and Varona, 2001) and in (Llorens et al., 2002). Under a back-off scheme, these techniques adjust the maximum likelihood estimation of transition probabilities to recursively obtain probabilities to be assigned to *unseen* combinations of strings from models with decreasing the value of k, i.e. less accurate (Torres and Varona, 2001) (Llorens et al., 2002). These procedures are now straightforward extended to get *smoothed* k-TSS DPFBA. However let us to note that this procedure does not assign a non-zero probability to *bi-strings* in Γ^* which does not consists of sequences of *extended* symbols in Γ. Thus, it does not guarantee that any target string $\mathbf{t} \in \Delta^*$ could be obtained (with either high or small probability) as a liable translation of a given source string. To this end the smoothing should be applied to get a non-zero probability for any pair $(\mathbf{s}, \mathbf{t}) \in (\Sigma^* \times \Delta^*)$. This problem is similar to the one of smoothing transducers, which is still an open problem (Llorens et al., 2002).

The k-TSS DPFBA $\mathcal{BA}_k$ models the joint probability distribution $P(\mathbf{s}, \mathbf{t})$ for machine translation purposes. Thus the string $\hat{\mathbf{t}} = \tilde{t}_1 \ldots \tilde{t}_{|\mathbf{z}|}$ that corresponds to the source sequence $\mathbf{s} = \tilde{s}_1 \ldots \tilde{s}_{|\mathbf{z}|}$, given $Pr_{\mathcal{BA}_k}(\mathbf{s}, \mathbf{t})$ can be directly obtained parsing with the *bi-automaton* using Equation 5 according to the procedure described in Section 3.1. As a consequence this procedure does not need any final step aimed to transform back extended symbols into pairs of strings in $\Sigma^* \times \Delta^*$ since any SFST is inferred. Thus, the morphism theorems which are the basis of the classical GIATI methodology (Casacuberta and Vidal, 2004) are not now required.

6 Conclusions and future work

Machine translation can be viewed as the problem of computing the joint probability distribution of some *bi-language* inferred from a bilingual corpus. In such a context, we have proposed to represent translation models by stochastic regular *bi-languages*. To this end we have provided some specific definitions. Moreover, stochastic *bi-automata* can directly obtain the target string corresponding to a given source string.

On the other hand, we have specifically considered the stochastic k-TSS *bi-languages* to model joint probability distributions. The morphism theorem relating stochastic local languages and stochastic regular languages can now be extended to stochastic k-TSS *bi-languages* through a corollary. Moreover, stochastic k-TSS *bi-automaton* can also be inferred from a positive sample set through an extension of the inference algorithm for classical stochastic k-TSS languages.

With this basis we have reformulated the GIATI methodology to infer stochastic stochastic k-TSS *bi-languages* for machine translation purposes, which takes advantage of the knowledge about stochastic k-TSS languages and their application to natural language tasks. Moreover, the finite-state formalism allows easy integration of other automata representing target language models or acoustic models in speech translation tasks. However, the monotonic segmentation does not allow to deal with long-distance alignments which is a problem when the distance between the pair of languages is large. On the other hand smoothing techniques dealing with any pair of strings need also to be further explored.

Finally let us notice that relationship between stochastic k-TSS *bi-languages* and a subclass of stochastic regular translations, i.e. between stochastic k-TSS *bi-automata* and a subclass of stochastic finite state transducers, is going to be explored in the future.

Acknowledgments.

We would like to acknowledge support for this work to the Spanish Ministry of Science and Innovation under the Consolider Ingenio 2010 programme (MIPRCV CSD2007-00018), grant TIN2008-06856-C05-01 and grant TIN2009-14511; to the the Basque Government under grant GIC10/158 IT375-10 and to the Generalitat Valenciana under grant Prometeo/2009/014.

References

S. Bangalore and G. Riccardi. 2002. Stochastic finite-state models for spoken language machine translation. *Machine Translation*, 17(3):165–184.

J. Berger and C. Pair. 1978. Inference for regular bi-languages. *Journal of Computer and System Sciences*, 16(1):100–122.

J. Berstel. 1979. *Transductions and context-free languages*. B.G. Teubner Verlag, Stuttgart.

G. Blackwood, A. de Gispert, J. Brunning, and W. Byrne. 2009. Large-scale statistical machine translation with weighted finite state transducers. In *Proceeding of the 2009 conference on Finite-State Methods and Natural Language Processing*, pages 39–49, Amsterdam, The Netherlands, The Netherlands. IOS Press.

P. F. Brown, S. A. Della Pietra, V. J. Della Pietra, and R. L. Mercer. 1993. The mathematics of statistical machine translation: Parameter estimation. *Computational Linguistics*, 19(2):263–311.

F. Casacuberta and C. de la Higuera. 2000. Computational complexity of problems on probabilistic grammars and transducers. In A.L. Oliveira, editor, *Grammatical Inference: Algorithms and Applications*, volume 1891 of *Lecture Notes in Computer Science*, pages 15–24. Springer-Verlag. 5th International Colloquium Grammatical Inference -ICGI2000-. Lisboa. Portugal. Septiembre.

F. Casacuberta and E. Vidal. 2004. Machine translation with inferred stochastic finite-state transducers. *Computational Linguistics*, 30(2):205–225.

F. Casacuberta and E. Vidal. 2007. Learning finite-state models for machine translation. *Machine Learning*, 66(1):69–91.

I. Galiano and E. Segarra. 1993. The application of k-testable languages in the strict sense to phone recognition in automatic speech recognition. In *Proceedings of the IEE Colloquium of Grammatical Inference. Theory, Applications and Alternatives*. IEE.

P. García and E. Vidal. 1990. Inference of k-testable languages in the strict sense and application to syntactic pattern recognition. *IEEE Transactions on Pattern Analysis and Machine Intelligence*, 12(9):920–925.

P. García, E. Vidal, and F. Casacuberta. 1987. Local languages, the succesor method, and a step towards a general methodology for the inference of regular grammars. *IEEE Transactions on Pattern Analysis and Machine Intelligence*, 9(6):841–845.

J. González and F. Casacuberta. 2009. GREAT: a finite-state machine translation toolkit implementing a Grammatical Inference Approach for Transducer Inference (GIATI). In *Proceedings of the EACL Workshop on Computational Linguistics Aspects of Grammatical Inference*, pages 24–32, Athens, Greece, March 30.

V. Guijarrubia and M.I. Torres. 2010. Text and speech based phonotactic models for spoken language identification of basque and spanish. *Pattern Recognition Letters*, 31(6):523–532.

R. Justo and M.I. Torres. 2009. Phrase classes in two-level language models for asr. *Pattern Analysis and Applications*, 12:427–437.

K. Knight and Y. Al-Onaizan. 1998. Translation with finite-state devices. In *Lecture Notes in Computer Science*, volume 1529, pages 421–437. Springer-Verlag.

A. Kornai. 1995. *Formal Phonology*. Outstanding Dissertations in Linguistics. Garland Publishing, NewYork.

A. Kornai. 2008. *Mathematical Linguistics*. Advanced Information and Knowledge Processing. Springer, Cambridge, MA - USA.

D. Llorens, J.M. Vilar, and F. Casacuberta. 2002. Finite state language models smoothed using n-grams. *International Journal of Pattern Recognition and Artificial Intelligence*, 16(3):275–289.

J.B. Mariño, R. E. Banchs ans J.M. Crego, A.de Gispert, P. Lambert, J.A.R. Fonollosa, and M.R. Costa-juss. 2006. N-gram based machine translation. *Computational Lingustics*, 32(4):527–549.

F. Och and H. Ney. 2003. A systematic comparison of various statistical alignments models. *Computational Linguistics*, 29(1):19–51.

J. Oncina, P. García, and E. Vidal. 1993. Learning subsequential transducers for pattern recognition interpretation tasks. *pami*, 15(5):448–458.

C. Pair and A. Quere. 1968. Définition et etude des bilangages réguliers. *Information and Control*, 13(6):565–593.

A. Pérez, M.I. Torres, and F. Casacuberta. 2008. Joining linguistic and statistical methods for Spanish-to-Basque speech translation. *Speech Communication*, 50:1021–1033.

E. Segarra. 1993. *Una aproximación Inductiva a la Comprensión del Discurso Continuo*. Ph.D. thesis, Universidad Politécnica de Valencia. Advisors: Dr. P. García and Dr. E. Vidal.

K. Shankar, Y. Deng, and W. Byrne. 2005. A weighted finite state transducer translation template model for statistical machine translation. *Natural Language Engineering*, 12:35–75, December.

C. E. Shannon. 1948. A mathematical theory of communication. *Bell Systems Technical Journal*, 27(3):379–423, July.

M. Inés Torres and F. Casacuberta. 2011. Stochastic k-tss languages. Technical report, PR&Speech Technologies Group, Depto. Electricidad y Electrónica, Universidad del País Vasco, April.

M. I. Torres and A. Varona. 2001. k-tss language models in speech recognition systems. *Computer, Speech and Language*, 15(2):127–149.

E. Vidal, F. Thollard, C. de la Higuera, F. Casacuberta, and R. Carrasco. 2005a. Probabilistic finite-state machines - part I. *IEEE Transactions on Pattern Analysis and Machine Intelligence (PAMI)*, 27(7):1013–1025.

E. Vidal, F. Thollard, C. de la Higuera, F. Casacuberta, and R. Carrasco. 2005b. Probabilistic finite-state machines - part II. *IEEE Transactions on Pattern Analysis and Machine Intelligence (PAMI)*, 27(7):1025–1039.

Measuring the confusability of pronunciations in speech recognition

Panagiota Karanasou
LIMSI/CNRS
Université Paris-Sud
pkaran@limsi.fr

François Yvon
LIMSI/CNRS
Université Paris-Sud
yvon@limsi.fr

Lori Lamel
LIMSI/CNRS
lamel@limsi.fr

Abstract

In this work, we define a measure aimed at assessing how well a pronunciation model will function when used as a component of a speech recognition system. This measure, *pronunciation entropy*, fuses information from both the pronunciation model and the language model. We show how to compute this score by effectively composing the output of a phoneme recognizer with a pronunciation dictionary and a language model, and investigate its role as predictor of pronunciation model performance. We present results of this measure for different dictionaries with and without pronunciation variants and counts.

1 Introduction

As explained in (Strik & Cucchiarini, 1999), pronunciation variations can be incorporated at different levels in ASR systems: the lexicon, the acoustic model, the language model. At the acoustic level, context dependent phone modeling captures the phone variations within particular contexts. At the lexicon level, a lexicon with alternative pronunciations is used. At the language model (LM) level, the inter-word pronunciation variations are handled with grammar network, statistical LMs or multi-word models.

The growing interest in automatic transcription of Conversational Speech (CTS) increases the need for modeling pronunciation variation. Indeed, there is a large number of possible pronunciation variants occurring in spontaneous speech; these variants often extend beyond single speech sounds (modeled by the acoustic model) and reach up to whole words or word tuples. Not even context-dependent acoustic models for sub-word units (like phonemes) are able to cover pronunciation variants of this kind (Kipp *et al*, 1997). Thus, pronunciation variation is usually modeled by enumerating appropriate pronunciations for each word in the vocabulary using a pronunciation lexicon.

However, when adding alternative pronunciations to a lexicon, there is always the potential of introducing a detrimental amount of confusability. The homophone (words that sound the same but are written differently) rate increases, which means that these additional variants may not be helpful to the recognition performance (Tsai *et al*, 2001). A typical example in English is the word *you*: the received pronunciation is */yu/* and is chosen when one single variant is used; modeling some variation requires to consider the pronunciations */yu/* and */yc/*, which both occur in our multiple pronunciation dictionary. The latter pronunciation (*/yc/*), in the phrase *you are* is easily confused with */ycr/*, the pronunciation of *your*. Such confusions, in particular when they involve frequent words, can cause a degradation of the ASR system as more alternatives are added.

A lot of work has been carried out on the generation of pronunciation and pronunciation variants independently of the speech (g2p conversion, p2p conversion) or in a task specific framework using surface pronunciations generated from a phoneme recognizer or including acoustic and language model information. However, most works lack a sense of how added alternative pronunciations will affect the overall decoding process. For example, some

Proceedings of the 9th International Workshop on Finite State Methods and Natural Language Processing, pages 107–115,
Blois (France), July 12-15, 2011.

of the confusability introduced by the pronunciation model is compensated by the LM. Thus, a method for quantifying the confusion inherent in a combined acoustic-lexical system is needed. A confusability measure traditionally used to measure the uncertainty residual to a system is entropy. Specifically in an ASR system, lexical entropy measures the confusability introduced by an LM. In some previous works, lexical entropy not only takes the LM scores into account, but also integrate the scores of the acoustic and pronunciation models (Printz & Olsen, 2000). In (Wolff *et al*, 2002), the authors consider as a measure of the pronunciation confusability the entropy of the variant distribution, but they do not take into account the language model. Our aim is to integrate pronunciation model and language model information into a single framework for describing the confusability. Especially incorporating language model information would provide a more accurate reflection of the decoding process, and hence a more accurate picture of the possible lexical/acoustic confusions (Fosler-Lussier *et al*, 2002). The idea is then to introduce a measure inspired by the proposed formulation in (Printz & Olsen, 2000) but in a somewhat reverse fashion. Instead of measuring the "true" disambiguation capacity of the LM by taking acoustic similarities into account, we aim at measuring the actual confusability introduced in the system by the pronunciation model, taking also into account the LM. We call this measure *pronunciation entropy*.

To compute this measure, we will decompose the decoding process in two separate parts: the acoustic decoding on the one hand, the linguistic decoding on the other hand. Given an input signal, a phoneme recognizer is first used to obtain a sequence of phonemes; the rest of the decoding process is realized using a set of Finite State Machines (FSMs) modeling the various linguistic resources involved in the process. Doing so allows us to measure the confusability incurred by the acoustic decoder for fixed linguistic models; or, conversely, to assess the impact of adding more pronunciations, for fixed acoustic and language models. This latter scenario is especially appealing, as these measurements do not require to redecode the speech signal: it thus become possible to try to iteratively optimize the pronunciation lexicon at a moderate computational cost. Experiments are carried out to measure the confusability introduced by single and multiple pronunciation dictionaries in an ASR system, using the newly introduced pronunciation entropy.

The remainder of the paper is organized as follows. Section 2 describes the necessary Finite State Tranducers (FSTs) background. Section 3 presents the FST decoding and details the new confusability measure. Sections 4 and 5 present the recognition experiments and the pronunciation entropy results. The paper concludes with a discussion of the results and of some future work in Section 6.

2 Background

2.1 Generalities

In the last decade, FSTs have been shown to be useful for a number of applications in speech and language processing (Mohri *et al*, 1997). FST operations such as composition, determinization, and minimization make manipulating FSTs both effective and efficient.

Weighted transducers (resp. automata) are finite-state transducers (resp. automata) in which each transition carries some weight in addition to the input and output (resp. input) labels. The interpretation of the weights depends on the algebraic structure of the semiring in which they are defined.

A *semiring* is a system $(\mathbb{K}, \oplus, \otimes, \bar{0}, \bar{1})$ containing the weights $\mathbb{K}$ and the operators $\oplus$ and $\otimes$, such that: $(\mathbb{K}, \oplus, \bar{0})$ is a commutative monoid with $\bar{0}$ as the identity element for $\oplus$; $(\mathbb{K}, \otimes, \bar{1})$ is a monoid with $\bar{1}$ as the identity element for $\otimes$; $\otimes$ distributes over $\oplus$: for all a, b, c in $\mathbb{K}$: $(a \oplus b) \otimes c = (a \otimes c) \oplus (b \otimes c)$ and $c \otimes (a \oplus b) = (c \otimes a) \oplus (c \otimes b)$, and $\bar{0}$ is an anihilator for $\otimes : \forall a \in \mathbb{K}, a \otimes \bar{0} = \bar{0} \otimes a = \bar{0}$. When manipulating weighted tranducers, the $\otimes$ and $\oplus$ operators are used to combine weights in a serial and parallel fashion, respectively. A semiring is idempotent if for all $a \in \mathbb{K}, a \oplus a = a$. It is commutative when $\otimes$ is commutative.

The real semiring $(\mathbb{R}, +, \times, 0, 1)$ is used when the weights represent probabilities. The semirings used in this work are the log semiring, the entropy semiring, as well as a new, defined for computational reasons, log-entropy semiring. The log semiring is defined as $(\mathbb{R} \cup [-\infty, \infty], -\log(\exp(-x) + exp(-y)), +, \infty, 0)$. It is isomorphic to the real semiring via the negative-log mapping and is used in practice for numerical stability.

A *weighted finite-state transducer* T over a semiring $\mathbb{K}$ is an 8-tuple $T = (\Sigma, \Delta, Q, I, F, E, \lambda, \rho)$ where: Σ is the finite input alphabet of the transducer; Δ is the finite output alphabet; Q is a finite set of states; $I \subseteq Q$ the set of initial states; $F \subseteq Q$ the set of final states; $E \subseteq Q \times (\Sigma \cup \{\epsilon\}) \times (\Delta \cup \{\epsilon\}) \times \mathbb{K} \times Q$ a finite set of transitions; $\lambda : I \rightarrow \mathbb{K}$ the initial weight function; and $\rho : F \rightarrow \mathbb{K}$ the final weight function mapping F to $\mathbb{K}$.

A *weighted automaton* $A = (\Sigma, Q, I, F, E, \lambda, \rho)$ is defined in a similar way simply by omitting the output labels. The weighted transducers and automata considered in this paper are assumed to be trimmed, i.e. all their states are both accessible and co-accessible. Omitting the input (resp. output) labels of a weighted transducer T results in a weighted automaton which is said to be the output (resp. input) projection of T.

Using the notations of (Cortes *et al*, 2006), if $e = (q, a, b, q')$ is a transition in E, $p(e) = q$ (resp. $n(e) = q'$) denotes its origin (resp. destination) state, $i(e) = a$ its input label, $o[e] = b$ its output label and $w(e) = E(e)$ its weight. These notations extend to paths: if π is a path in T, $p(\pi)$ (resp. $n(\pi)$) is its initial (resp. ending) state and $i(\pi)$ is the label along the path. We denote by $P(q, q')$ the set of paths from q to q' and by $P(q, x, y, q')$ the set of paths for q to q' with input label $x \in \Sigma^*$ and output label $y \in \Sigma^*$. The path from an initial to a final state is a successful path. The output weight associated by a weighted transducer T to a pair of strings $(x, y) \in \Sigma^* \times \Sigma^*$ is denoted by $T(x, y)$ and is obtained by $\otimes$-summing the weights of all successful paths with input label x and output label y:

$$T(x, y) = \bigoplus_{\pi \in P(I,x,y,F)} \lambda(p[\pi]) \otimes w[\pi] \otimes \rho(n[\pi]) \tag{1}$$

$T(x, y) = \bar{0}$ when $P(I, x, y, F) = \emptyset$.

The *composition* of two weighted tranducers T_1 and T_2 with matching input and output alphabet Σ, is a weighted transducer denoted by $(T_1 \circ T_2)$ when the semiring is commutative and when the sum:

$$(T_1 \circ T_2)(x, y) = \sum_{z \in \Sigma^*} T_1(x, z) \otimes T_2(z, y) \tag{2}$$

is well-defined and in $\mathbb{K}$ for all x, y.

2.2 Entropy Semiring

The entropy $H(p)$ of a probability mass function p defined over a discrete set X is defined as (Cover & Thomas, 1991):

$$H(p) = -\sum_{x \in X} p(x) logp(x), \tag{3}$$

where, by convention, $0log0 = 0$. This definition can be extended to probabilistic automata which define distributions over sets of strings. We call an automaton probabilistic if for any state $q \in Q$, the sum of the weights of all cycles at q is well-defined and in $\mathbb{K}$ and $\sum_{x \in \Sigma^*} A(x) = 1$. A probabilistic automaton such that at each state the weights of the outgoing transitions and the final weight sum to one, is a stochastic automaton. The entropy of A can be written as:

$$H(A) = -\sum_{x} A(x) logA(x), \tag{4}$$

where $A(x)$ is the output weight associated by an automaton A to an input string $x \in \Sigma^*$.

The expectation (or entropy) semiring is defined in (Eisner, 2001) as $(\mathbb{K}, \oplus, \otimes, (0, 0), (1, 0))$, where $\mathbb{K}$ denotes $(\mathbb{R} \cup [-\infty, \infty]) \times (\mathbb{R} \cup [-\infty, \infty])$. For weight pairs (a_1, b_1) and (a_2, b_2) in $\mathbb{K}$, the $\oplus$ and $\otimes$ operations are defined as follows:

$$(a_1, b_1) \oplus (a_2, b_2) = (a_1 + a_2, b_1 + b_2) \tag{5}$$

$$(a_1, b_1) \otimes (a_2, b_2) = (a_1 a_2, a_1 b_2 + a_2 b_1) \tag{6}$$

The entropy of A defined in equation (4) can be seen as a single-source shortest distance for an automaton defined over the entropy semiring (Cortes *et al*, 2006) with weights $(w, -wlogw)$ where $w \in \mathbb{R}$. If the sum of the weights of all paths from any state $p \in Q$ to any state $q \in Q$ is well-defined, the shortest distance from p to q is:

$$d[p, q] = \bigoplus_{\pi \in P(p,q)} w[\pi]. \tag{7}$$

Thus, the shortest distance from the initial states to the final states for the probabilistic automaton A with weights $(w, -wlogw)$ in $\mathbb{K}$ will be:

$$\begin{aligned} d[I, F] &= (\sum_{x} A(x), -\sum_{x} A(x) logA(x)) & (8) \\ &= (1, H(A)). & (9) \end{aligned}$$

3 A new confusability measure

3.1 ASR decoding with FSTs

The recognition process can be modeled with a sequence of weighted finite-state transducers (WFSTs) (Pereira & Riley, 1996). An abstract representation of the Viterbi decoding process of the present work can be given as:

$$\hat{W} = bestpath(A \circ P \circ L \circ G), \quad (10)$$

where $\hat{W}$ is the sequence of words corresponding to the best recognition hypothesis. A is the phoneme hypothesis lattice generated by the phoneme recognizer, P is an FST that contains a mapping from phonemes to the phonemic lexical representation of each word, L is the pronunciation model FST, containing a mapping from each phonemic lexical representation to the corresponding word, G is the language model finite state automaton (FSA), which contains n-gram statistics, and $\circ$ is the composition operator. Constraining the model by the pronunciation and the language models means that only words that are part of complete paths in the decoding will be counted as confusions. In this work, the FSTs and FSAs will be manipulated using the open-source toolkit OpenFst (Allauzen *et al*, 2007).

3.2 Decomposing the acoustic and linguistic modeling

In a first place, a phoneme recognizer generates the phoneme hypothesis lattice A from the speech signal. These phonemes are the input in the following process of consecutive compositions. The phoneme lattices are generated by the ASR system without taking into account the pronunciation nor the language model during decoding. The aim is to decompose the decoding parts in order to better evaluate the influence of the pronunciation model in the decoding process. The acoustic scores are considered stable and independent of the linguistic (pronunciation and language) confusability and thus are omitted. No time information is kept. The pronunciation model will automatically segment the phoneme sequences in pronunciations, and consequently in words.

The FST P representing the set of valid pronunciations in our lexicon (see Section 4) is then constructed; it takes as input a sequence of phonemes

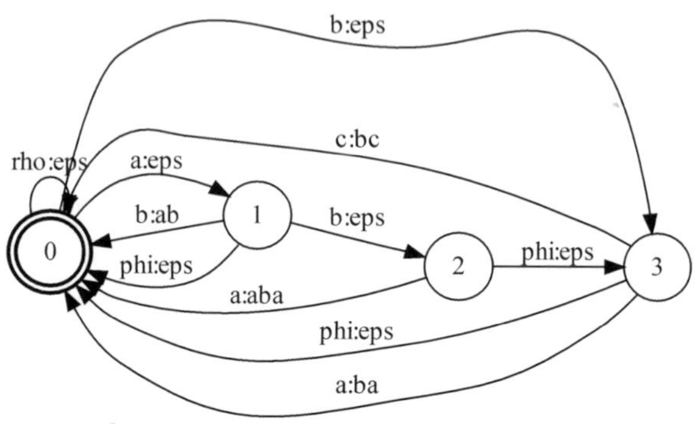

Figure 1: Expansion of the topology of the P FST with phi matchers that consume the phonemes inserted between valid pronunciations

and returns the sequence of corresponding phonemic lexical representation (pronunciation). P is composed with each phoneme lattice. In order to account for insertions of phonemes between valid pronunciations, the topology of P is slightly expanded. This expansion simulates a simple error recovery strategy consisting in deleting superfluous phonemes in a left to right fashion. Fig. 1 illustrates this expansion on a simple example, with the use of failure transitions implemented with the so-called *phi-matchers* and *rho-matchers*. Each state in P corresponds to the prefix of an actual pronunciation: whenever we reach a state from which no continuation is possible, a phi-transition allows to reach the state corresponding to a trimmed prefix, from which the first phoneme has been deleted. This simple error recovery strategy is applied recursively. A rho-loop is finally used in the initial state, which is also the final state, in case the first or last phonemes of a sequence do not permit to complete a known pronunciation. Assume, for instance, that we reach state 2 in P (see Fig. 1), and that the following symbol is 'c', for which no transition exists. The phi-transition will then allow to move to state 3, and continue the prefix 'bc'.

Next, the FST L representing the pronunciation dictionary with pronunciations as inputs and words as outputs is constructed. Its weights are the conditional probabilities of a pronunciation given a word.

When no pronunciation probabilities are available, a uniform distribution over the probabilities of pronunciations of each word is applied. This FST is composed with each phoneme-pronunciation FSTs $A \circ P$ resulting from the previous composition.

A final composition is made with the FSA G that models the backoff language model, with word probabilities as weights. G is constructed as described in (Riccardi *et al*, 1996; Allauzen *et al*, 2003). This results in FSTs with phonemes as input and words as output, which are projected to the output and determinized. Then, the arc weights of each FST are normalized per state, i.e. scaled such that the probability of arcs leading out of a state (plus the probability of state finality) sums to 1 for each state. A general weight-pushing algorithm in the log semiring (Mohri *et al*, 1997) is applied for the normalization and the weights in the new stochastic FSA are converted to the desired posterior probabilities given the pronunciations. What is calculated is the conditional probability $p(w \mid a)$ of all the word sequences that can be transcribed as a and, thus, are competitors:

$$p(w \mid a) = \frac{p(a \mid w)p(w)}{\sum_{w \in W} p(a \mid w)p(w)}. \tag{11}$$

3.3 Definition of pronunciation entropy

In order to have a measure of the confusability of the pronunciation lexicon, the entropy of the posterior probability $p(w \mid a)$ that combines the pronunciation model and the language model information is computed. As described in Section 2.2, calculating appropriately the shortest distance on the entropy semiring can result in the desired entropy. However, the entropy semiring must have components in the real semiring in order to calculate the entropy correctly, but even real numbers of double precision are not stable enough for large lattices. Thus, an expectation semiring with components on the log semiring is needed. That is why we define a new semiring, the log-expectation (or log-entropy) semiring, changing the $\oplus$ and $\otimes$ operators as well as the identities of the semiring. In this new semiring $(\mathbb{K}, \oplus, \otimes, (\infty, 0), (0, 0))$, $\mathbb{K}$ denotes $(\mathbb{R} \cup [-\infty, \infty]) \times (\mathbb{R} \cup [-\infty, \infty])$ and the operations $\oplus$ and $\otimes$ on weight pairs (a_1, b_1) and (a_2, b_2) in $\mathbb{K}$, are defined as:

$$(a_1, b_1) \oplus (a_2, b_2) = (-log(exp(-a_1) + exp(-a_2)), b_1 + b_2) \tag{12}$$

$$(a_1, b_1) \otimes (a_2, b_2) = (a_1 + a_2, exp(-a_1)b_2 + exp(-a_2)b_1) \tag{13}$$

When working on the log-entropy semiring, each negative log arc weight w is replaced by the new weight $(w, w * exp(-w))$. Then, the shortest distance from the initial to the final state is calculated as explained in Section 2.2. Some experiments were realised on small exemplar lattices with real arc weights and the entropy was calculated directly with the entropy semiring, already defined in OpenFst. However, for larger lattices the use of the log and the log-entropy semirings was required in order to keep the numerical stability.

4 Phoneme Recognition Configuration

The phoneme recognizer used in these experiments makes use of continuous density HMMs with Gaussian mixtures for acoustic modeling. The acoustic models are gender-dependent, speaker-adapted, and Maximum Likelihood trained on about 500 hours of audio data. They cover about 30k phone contexts with 11600 tied states. Unsupervised acoustic model adaptation is performed for each segment cluster using the CMLLR and MLLR techniques prior to decoding. It suffices to say that the phone labels that are produced at that stage are deterministically mapped to the corresponding phonemes, which constitute the actual labels in the phoneme lattice. The recognition dictionary is a simple lexicon made up of the same list of phonemes used to represent pronunciations in the word lexicon. A unigram phoneme-based language model was also constructed to respond to the demands of the system for language modeling, but its weight was set to zero during the decoding phase. A phoneme lattice is thus generated after a single decoding pass, with no pronunciation model nor language model information included. The lattices are pruned so as to limit them to a reasonable size. To circumvent the fact that a lattice does not always finish with an end-of-phrase symbol, which can be the case because of segmentation based on time, an end-of-phrase symbol is added before the final state of each lattice.

The FST approach described in Section 3 is applied for word decoding. A 4-gram word LM is used, trained on a corpus of 1.2 billion words of texts from various LDC corpora (English Gigaword, Broadcast News (BN) transcriptions, commercial transcripts), news articles downloaded from the web, and assorted audio transcriptions. The recognition word list contains 78k words, selected by interpolation of unigram LMs trained on different text subsets as to minimize the out-of-vocabulary (OOV) rate on set of development texts. The recognition dictionary used as a baseline is the LIMSI American English recognition dictionary with 78k word entries with 1.2 pronunciations per word. The pronunciations are represented using a set of 45 phonemes (Lamel & Adda, 1996). This dictionary is constructed with extensive manual supervision to be well-suited to the needs of an ASR system. Other dictionaries with and without counts and variants were also tested, as described in the next section.

A part of the Quaero (www.quaero.org) 2010 development data was used in the recognition experiments. This data set covers a range of styles, from broadcast news (BN) to talk shows. Roughly 50% of the data can be classed as BN and 50% broadcast conversation (BC). These data are considerably more difficult than pure BN data. The part of the Quaero data that was used resulted in 285 lattices generated by the phoneme recognizer. This is a sufficient number of lattices to have statistically significant results that can be generalized. The FST-based decoding is applied to these lattices. Table 1 summarizes some of the characteristics of the lattices and FSTs used in the composition process: the average number of states and arcs of the lattices A and of the phonemes-to-pronunciations FST P, of the pronunciations-to-words FST L and of the 4-gram word LM FSA G. Their size indicates that we are working in a real ASR framework with FSMs of large size. Thus, there is an important computational gain by the fact that the FST approach permits to change a part of the decoding without repeating the whole process.

Table 1: *Average number of states and arcs in the lattices*

Num.	A	P	L	G
States	303	180,833	2	83,367,599
Arcs	353	503,234	171,272	200,322,203

5 Pronunciation Entropy Results

The presented pronunciation entropy is an average of the entropy calculated on the FSAs of the word sequences generated after the application of the FST decoding on the output lattices of the phoneme recognizer. The pronunciation entropy is calculated for the baseline dictionary with and without frequency of occurrence counts, as well as for the "longest" baseline (keeping only the longest pronunciation per word in the original recognition dictionary) and the "most frequent" baseline (keeping only the most frequent pronunciation per word in the original recognition dictionary based on counts collected on the training data). The higher order language model (LM) used in the decoding of the word recognition experiments is a 4-gram.

In Table 2, the pronunciation entropy is presented when 2-, 3- and 4-gram LMs are used for the FST-based decoding. As expected, as the order of the LM diminishes, the entropy increases. The results when the order of the LM diminishes warrant some more thoughts. The difference in entropy even between the use of 4-gram and 2-gram is smaller than expected. The decoding is actually restricted by the given lexicon, that does not permit pronunciations, and thus words, to be correctly recognized if there is an error in the phoneme sequence. Deletions, insertions and substitutions of phonemes are ignored, with the exception of insertions between valid pronunciations. By manual observation of the best word hypotheses and their comparison with the corresponding references, it was thus noticed that not many long sequences of words are correctly recognized and, consequently, the impact of using a longer n-gram is relatively limited.

It is worth staying a bit longer in Table 2 to compare the pronunciation entropy of the baselines which contain one or more pronunciations per word (upper part of the table) and the single-pronunciation baselines (lower part of the table). The entropy is lower in the single pronunciation baselines, and its lowest score is observed when the "longest" baseline is used. The fact that its entropy is lower even

Table 2: *Pronunciation entropy on baselines*

4g LM	3g LM	2g LM
Baseline with uniform probabilities		
4.003	4.025	4.025
Baseline with counts		
4.065	4.083	4.108
Baseline longest with uniform probs		
3.013	3.024	3.022
Baseline mostfreq with uniform probs		
3.669	3.689	3.756

compared with the "most frequent" baseline, which is also a single-pronunciation baseline, may be explained by the fact that the most frequent pronunciations represent better the spoken terms that can be often easily confused. Especially in spontaneous speech, some function words are often pronounced similar to other function words and may not be easily distinguished by the LM. This is particularly a problem for frequent words that are easy to insert, delete or substitute.

A final observation from Table 2, comparing "Baseline with uniform probabilities" and "Baseline with counts", can be that pronunciations with counts do not reduce confusability. It is normal not to see a lot of changes because in any case the majority of words has only one pronunciation and thus probability 1 which do not change when counts are added. In addition, counts are not available for all words, but only for those observed in the training data. When no counts are available, uniform probabilities are applied. Thus, finally there are no great differences between the dictionary with counts and the dictionary without counts. Moreover, it could be that counts only for a few words create an inconsistency that explains the light deterioration of the pronunciation entropy.

The increase in entropy is much greater when more pronunciations are added in the dictionary as can be seen in Tables 3 and 4. The n-best pronunciations are added in the "longest" and the "most frequent" baselines. The M1, M2 and M5 in these tables correspond to the 1-, 2- and 5-best pronunciations generated automatically using Moses (Koehn *et al*, 2007) as a g2p converter, being trained on the baseline dictionary (with 1.2 pronunciations per word). Moses has been successfully used as a g2p converter for several languages, and for English it gives state-of-the-art results (Karanasou & Lamel, 2011). The results in Tables 3 and 4 are calculated with the 4-gram LM.

Table 3: *Pronunciation entropy with the 4-gram LM after adding n-best pronunciations, produced by a Moses-based g2p converter, to the "longest" baseline*

Training condition	M1	M2	M5
Multiple pronunciations	4.523	6.578	10.005
Baseline longest	3.013		

Table 4: *Pronunciation entropy with the 4-gram LM after adding Moses' n-best pronunciations to the "most frequent" baseline*

Training condition	M1	M2	M5
Multiple pronunciations	5.185	6.914	10.077
Baseline most frequent	3.669		

These results suggest that there can be a large influence of the pronunciation dictionary in the confusability of an ASR system, not sufficiently compensated by the language model. However, when adding as much alternative pronunciations some non-uniform probabilities should be used to moderate confusability. If not, the uniform probability contributed to each variant of a word with multiple pronunciations is lower. Thus, for highly probable words, since the system will have the tendency to choose them, the confusability will increase. But if the pronunciation probabilities are also taken into account, this confusability can be moderated, because a pronunciation of a word with lower probability and lower confusability (higher pronunciation probability) can be prefered from a pronunciation of a word with higher probability but lower pronunciation probability. We have started working on this direction and plan to see if our measure will actually improve when pronunciation probabilities are added to the decoding.

More confusability is observed when adding variants to the "most frequent" than to the "longest" baseline. This is consistent with the explanation given above supporting that the most frequent baseline presented more confusability than the longest baseline because it is closer to the real spoken terms that are often difficult to distinguish.

6 Conclusion and Discussion

A new measure of the confusability of the pronunciation model during the decoding phase in an ASR system, that integrates also language model information, was presented and results were reported using baseline dictionaries with one or more pronunciations per word, with and without counts, as well as on dictionaries extended with variants generated by a state-of-art data-driven method.

It is not straightforward to find a correlation between this work and ASR performance. The follow-up of this work will be to examine this correlation and propose a combined measure of confusability and accuracy for the selection of pronunciation variants and for the training of weights for the existing ones. What makes this procedure particularly complicated is the fact that confusable words are a non-negligible phenomenon of natural speech and ignoring them severely reduces the completeness of the dictionary, meaning that a consistent set of pronunciations is not necessarily connected with a pronunciation network of low perplexity.

A drawback of the work so far is that sequences obtained from the phoneme recognizer contain many errors. To avoid the problems caused by the low performance of the phoneme recognizer, some phoneme substitutions should be permitted. For this, a confusion matrix and a consensus representation could be useful.

Lastly, the pronunciation entropy introduced in this work is a measure of the confusability at the sentence level. It would be interesting to try and measure confusability at a sub-sentence level, such as at a word level using confusion networks, as the error rate of an ASR system is also calculated at a word level. At a more general sub-sentence level, some word-context could be taken into account to better model the cross-word confusability, because when adding many variants to an ASR system what is more important than the homophone rate in the dictionary, is to measure this rate in the data. In fact the homophone rate in the original recognition dictionary (baseline) is 1.16, while in the baseline "longest" is 1.10 and in the baseline "most frequent" is 1.15. When adding up to 5 pronunciation variants to the baseline "longest" or the baseline "most frequent", the homophone rate becomes 1.24 in both cases. All these rates are close to one another, so it seems that what mostly influences confusability are some frequent homophone words or word sequences.

Acknowledgments

This work is partly realized as part of the Quaero Programme, funded by OSEO, the French State agency for innovation and by the ANR EdyLex project. The authors wish to thank T. Lavergne for sharing his expertise on the OpenFst library.

References

Allauzen,C., Mohri, M. and Roark, B.. 2003. Generalized algorithms for constructing statistical language models. In *Proceedings of ACL*, volume 1, pages 40-47.

Allauzen, C., Riley, M., Schalkwyk, J., Skut, W. and Mohri, M.. 2007. OpenFst: a general and efficient weighted finite-state transducer library. In *Proceedings of CIAA*, pages 11-23.

Cortes, C., Mohri, M., Rastogi, A. and Riley, M. D.. 2006. Efficient Computation of the Relative Entropy of Probabilistic Automata. In *Proceedings of LATIN*, volume 3887, pages 323-336.

Cover, T.M. and Thomas, J. A.. 1991. Elements of Information Theory. John Wiley & Sons, inc., New York.

Eisner, J.. 2001. Expectation Semiring: Flexible EM for Learning Finite-State Transducers. In *Proceedings of FSMNLP*.

Fosler-Lussier, E., Amdal, I. and Kuo, H.-K. J. 2002. On the road to improved lexical confusability metrics. In *Proceedings of PMLA*, pages 53-58.

Karanasou, P. and Lamel, L.. 2011. Pronunciation Variants Generation Using SMT-inspired Approaches. In *Proceedings of ICASSP*.

Kipp, A., Weswnick, M.-B. and Schiel, F.. 1997. Pronunciation modeling applied to automatic segmentation of spontaneous speech. In *Proceedings of Eurospeech*, pages 1023-1026.

Koehn, P., Hoang H., Birch, A., Callison-Burch, C., Federico, M., Bertoldi, N., Cowan B., Shen, W., Moran, C., Zens, R., Dyer, C., Bojar, O., Constantin, A. and Herbst, E. 2007. Moses:Open source toolkit for statistical machine translation. In *Proceedings of ACL*, pages 177-180.

Lamel, L. and Adda, G.. 1996. On designing pronunciation lexicons for large vocabulary continuous speech recognition. In *Proceedings of ICSLP*.

Mohri, M., Riley, M. and Sproat, R.. 1997. Finite-state transducers in language and speech processing. In *Computational Linguistics*, volume 23-2, pages 269-311.

Pereira, F.C.N. and Riley, M.D.. 1996. Speech recognition by composition of weighted finite automata. In *Finite-State Language Processing*, pages 431-453.

Printz, H. and Olsen, P.. 2000. Theory and practice of acoustic confusability. In *Proceedings of ISCA ITRW ASR*, pages 77-84.

Riccardi, G., Pieraccini, R. and Bocchieri, E.. 1996. Stochastic automata for language modeling. In *Computer Speech and Language*, volume 10, pages 265-293.

Strik, H. and Cucchiarini, C.. 1999. Modeling pronunciation variation for ASR: A survey of the literature. In *Speech Communication*, volume 29, pages 225-246.

Tsai, M., Chou, F. and Lee, L.. 2001. Improved pronunciation modeling by inverse word frequency and pronunciation entropy. In *Proceedings of ASRU*, pages 53-56.

Wolff, M., Eichner, M. and Hoffmann, R.. 2002. Measuring the quality of pronunciation dictionaries. In *Proceedings of PMLA*, pages 117-122.

Fast Yet Rich Morphological Analysis

Mohamed Altantawy, Nizar Habash, and Owen Rambow
Center for Computational Learning Systems
Columbia University
New York, NY, USA
{mtantawy,habash,rambow}@ccls.columbia.edu

Abstract

Implementations of models of morphologically rich languages such as Arabic typically achieve speed and small memory footprint at the cost of abandoning linguistically abstract and elegant representations. We present a solution to modeling rich morphologies that is both fast and based on linguistically rich representations. In our approach, we convert a linguistically complex and abstract implementation of Arabic verbs in finite-state machinery into a simple precompiled tabular representation.

1 Introduction

Arabic is a morphologically rich and complex language, characterized by a combination of templatic and affixational morphemes, complex morphological, phonological and orthographic rules, and a rich feature system. Arabic morphological analysis and generation are important to many NLP applications such as machine translation (Habash, 2007; Kholy and Habash, 2010) and information retrieval (Aljlayl and Frieder, 2002). Much work has been done on Arabic morphological analysis and generation in a variety of approaches and at different degrees of linguistic depths.

There is a continuum of approaches which is characterized by its two poles: on one end, very abstract and linguistically rich representations and rules (often based on particular theories of morphology) are used to derive surface forms; while on the other end, simple and shallow techniques focus on efficient search in a space of precompiled (tabulated) solutions. The first type is typically implemented using finite-state technology and can be at many different degrees of sophistication and detail. An example of this type of implementation is the MAGEAD (Morphological Analysis and GEneration for Arabic and its Dialects) system (Habash et al., 2005; Habash and Rambow, 2006). This system, which we use as starting point in this paper, compiles abstract high-level linguistic information of different types to finite state machinery. The second type is typically not implemented in finite-state technology. Examples include the Buckwalter Arabic Morphological Analyzer (BAMA) (Buckwalter, 2004) and its extension ALMORGEANA (Habash, 2007). These systems do not represent the morphemic, phonological and orthographic rules directly at all, and instead compile their effect into the lexicon itself.

Numerous intermediate points exist between these two extremes (e.g., (Smrž, 2007)). The various approaches typically trade off different degrees of speed and memory (model size) for more abstract and elegant representations. Precompiled tabular systems usually have fast response time when implemented using hash tables. The cost of building the linguistic resources manually is the main drawback for this approach since such resources are prone to error and hard to debug and extend. Linguistically sophisticated systems are easier to understand and extend and they allow for modeling morphology without lexicons (to address unknown forms); however, with the complexity of some languages' morphology, the finite-state transducers (FSTs) tend to become extremely large, causing a significant deterioration in response time.

Proceedings of the 9th International Workshop on Finite State Methods and Natural Language Processing, pages 116–124,
Blois (France), July 12-15, 2011.

In this paper, we present a solution to the modeling of rich morphologies that combines the best of these two approaches. In previous work, we presented MAGEAD, a multi-tier finite-state implementation of Arabic morphology (Habash et al., 2005; Habash and Rambow, 2006; Altantawy et al., 2010). We improve the speed by automatically converting our FST-based MAGEAD system to a precompiled tabular implementation that preserves all of the rich linguistic information used in MAGEAD's design. The new system, MAGEAD-EXPRESS is not only much faster and smaller in size, but it also still allows linguistically based abstract changes and updates in its model. Furthermore, MAGEAD-EXPRESS produces complete linguistic analyses that include intermediate levels of representation, an advantage MAGEAD does not have readily in its output. The only disadvantage of MAGEAD-EXPRESS is its inability to produce analyses for unknown words (unlike MAGEAD).

The paper is organized as follows. We give a short introduction to Arabic morphology in section 2. The related work is discussed in section 3. We then present MAGEAD and MAGEAD-EXPRESS in sections 4 and 5 respectively. The extraction process of MAGEAD's linguistic information is discussed in section 6. Finally, the evaluation is presented in section 7.

2 Arabic Morphology

For an extensive discussion of Arabic morphology from a computational perspective, see (Habash, 2010); we give a short overview here. Arabic has a rich and complex morphology. This is due to its numerous linguistic features, such as gender, number, mood and case, and the existence of two types of morphemes: templatic and affixational (concatenative). **Templatic morphemes** come in three types that are equally needed to create a word stem: roots, patterns and vocalisms. The **root morpheme** is a sequence of typically three consonants (termed *radicals*) that signifies some abstract meaning shared by all its derivations. For example, the words كَتَبَ *kataba*[1] 'he wrote' and كَاتِب *kaAtib* 'writer' share the root morpheme (ك ت ب) *ktb* 'writing-related'. The **pattern morpheme** is an abstract template in which roots and vocalisms are inserted. The **vocalism morpheme** specifies which short vowels to use with a pattern. We represent the pattern as a string made up of numbers to indicate radical position, of the symbol *V* to indicate the position of the vocalism, and of pattern consonants (if needed) following (Habash et al., 2005). As an example, the word stem كَتَب *katab* is constructed from the root (ك ت ب) *ktb*, the pattern *1V2V3* and the vocalism *aa*. This is represented as ⟨ 1V2V3, ktb, aa ⟩. Arabic **affixes** can be **prefixes** such as (+سَ) *sa+* 'will', **suffixes** such as (هُم+) *+hum* 'they [masculine]' or **circumfixes** such as (نَ+ +تَ) *ta++na* '[imperfective subject 2nd person feminine plural]'. We do not distinguish between clitics and inflectional affixes in this paper. Multiple affixes can appear in a word. An Arabic word is constructed by first creating a word **stem** from templatic morphemes, then adding affixational morphemes. The process of combining morphemes involves a number of morphemic, phonological and orthographic rules that modify the form of the created word so it is not a simple interleaving or concatenation of its morphemic components. See example in section 4.

As in other languages, surface word forms in Arabic that differ only in inflectional morphology can be grouped into a lexicographic abstraction called a *lexeme*. A lexeme is usually represented by a conventionally chosen word form called the *lemma*, but it can also be represented by a stem and an inflectional class, and in Arabic (as in other Semitic languages), we can represent it as the set of radicals and an inflectional class. Thus, we can represent a morphological analysis of any Arabic word form in terms of its lexeme (i.e., radicals and inflectional class), and a set of feature-value pairs which the morphology of the word form represents. For example, the MSA verb وَلِيَدعُوه *waliyadςuwhu* 'and that they invite him' corresponds to the following lexeme-and-features representation:

[1]Arabic transliteration is in the HSB scheme (Habash et al., 2007): (alphabetically) *AbtθjHxdðrzsš SDTĎςγfqklmnhwy* and (additional symbols) ' ء, Â أ, Ǎ إ, Ā آ, ŵ ؤ, ŷ ئ, *ħ* ة, ý ى.

(1) [1d][2ς][3w][mbc:verb-I-au-tr]
[asp:I][vox:act][mod:s][per:3][gen:m][num:p]
[cnj:w][prt:l][pro:3MS]

This representation indicates (in order of symbols above) that the root radicals of the word are d-ς-w; that the verb belongs to a particular inflectional class called *I-au* and that it is transitive; that aspect is indicative; voice, active; mood, subjunctive; person, third; gender, masculine; number, plural; that it has the conjunction proclitic *w* 'and'; that it has particle proclitic *l* 'for/that'; and that it has a pronominal enclitic that is 3rd person masculine singular.

3 Related Work

There has been a considerable amount of work on Arabic morphological analysis; for an overview, see (Al-Sughaiyer and Al-Kharashi, 2004). The first large-scale implementation of Arabic morphology within the constraints of finite-state methods is that of Beesley et al. (1989) (the "Xerox system") with a 'detouring' mechanism for access to multiple lexica, which gives rise to other works by Beesley (1998) and Beesley and Karttunen (2000) and, independently, by Buckwalter (2004). Unlike the Xerox system, the Buckwalter Arabic Morphological Analyzer (BAMA) uses a hard-coded tabular approach with a focus on analysis into surface morphemes (discussed above). Buckwalter's work has been since extended to handle generation as well as the lexeme-and-features representation (ALMORGEANA, (Habash, 2007)) and functional morphology in Arabic (ELIXIR, (Smrž, 2007)).

Finite-state handling of templatic morphology has been demonstrated using a variety of techniques for several Semitic languages other than Arabic including Akkadian (Kataja and Koskenniemi, 1988), Syriac (Kiraz, 2000), Hebrew (Yona and Wintner, 2005), Amharic (Amsalu and Gibbon, 2005), and Tigrinya (Gasser, 2009). Kay (1987) proposes a framework for handling templatic morphology in which each templatic morpheme is assigned a tape in a multi-tape finite state machine, with an additional tape for the surface form. Kiraz (2000) extends Kay's approach and implements a multi-tape system for Modern Standard Arabic (MSA) and Syriac. The MAGEAD system (Habash et al., 2005; Habash and Rambow, 2006) extended Kiraz's work through a new implementation using AT&T finite state machine toolkit (Mohri et al., 2000) with an eye on handling morphology for Arabic and its dialects. In this work, we start with MAGEAD and address three of its weaknesses: its slowness, its size, and the absence of rich morphological information in its output despite of its presence in model specifications.

4 The MAGEAD System

4.1 MAGEAD's Representation of Linguistic Knowledge

MAGEAD relates (bidirectionally) a lexeme and a set of feature-value pairs to a surface word form through a sequence of transformations. In a generation perspective, the features are translated to abstract morphemes which are then ordered and expressed as concrete morphemes. The concrete templatic morphemes are interdigitated and affixes added, and finally morphological and phonological rewrite rules are applied.

MAGEAD defines the lexeme to be a triple consisting of a root and a **morphological behavior class (MBC)**. The MBC is characterized by the part-of-speech and the inflectional paradigm. For verbs, the inflectional paradigm is closely identified with the pattern and the transitivity. MAGEAD uses a representation of the morphemes which is independent of the specific variant of Arabic (Standard or dialect). These morphemes are referred to as **abstract morphemes** (AMs). For instance, in our example, the MBC [mbc:verb-I-au-tr] maps the two feature-value pairs [asp:I] and [vox:act] to the two AMs: [PAT_IV:I] and [VOC_IV:I-au-act].

The AMs are then ordered into the surface-order of the corresponding concrete morphemes. The ordering of AMs is specified in a **context-free grammar (CFG)**. This particular CFG is non-recursive and compiles to an FSA; we use a CFG and its non-terminals only for descriptive clarity. The ordered AMs for our example look like this:

(2) [CONJ:w][PREP:l][SUBJPRE_IV:3MP]
[d][ς][w][PAT_IV:I][VOC_IV:I-au-act]
[SUBJSUF_IV:3MP_Sub][OBJ:3MS]

The AMs are then translated to their corresponding variant-specific **concrete morphemes (CMs)**:

(3) wa+ li+ y+ ⟨V12V3,dςw,au⟩ +ū +hu

Next, the morphemic representation is obtained by interdigitating the templatic morphemes (root/vocalism/pattern):

(4) wa+ li+ y+ adςuw +ū +hu

MAGEAD has two types of rules. **Morphophonemic/phonological rules** map from the morphemic representation (4) to the phonological and orthographic representations. This includes default rules which copy the root and vocalism to the phonological and orthographic tiers, and specialized rules such as the rules that handle the hollow and defective verbs (our example is a defective verb, it has a glide */w/* in its final radical). Note that a simple concatenation of the morphemes in (4) will result in **/waliyadςuwūhu/* which is a wrong surface (phonological) form. In our example, a morphophonemic rule mandates assimilating the sequence */uw/* with the suffix */+ū/*. The phonological representation of our example is:

(5) wa+ li+ y+ adς +ū +hu

Orthographic rules rewrite only the orthographic representation. These include, for example, rules for using the Shadda (consonant doubling diacritic). In our example, the orthographic rule rewrites the verbal suffix long-vowel +ū as (+ـُوا) *+uwA* in a final position or as (+ـُو) *+uw* in medial position (i.e., when followed by a pronominal object as in our example). The orthographic representation is:

(6) wa+ li+ y+ adς +uw +hu

4.2 Implementation of MAGEAD in FSTs

MAGEAD follows Kiraz (Kiraz, 2000) in using a multi-tape analysis. The five tiers are used as follows: tier 1 (pattern and affixational morphemes), tier 2 (root), tier 3 (vocalism), tier 4 (phonological representation), and tier 5 (orthographic representation). In the generation direction, tiers 1 through 3 are always input tiers. Tier 4 is first an output tier, and subsequently an input tier. Tier 5 is always an output tier. All tiers are read or written at the same time, so that the rules of the multi-tier transducer are rules that scan the input tiers and, depending on the state, write to the output tier.

MAGEAD is implemented as a multi-tape finite state transducer layer on top of the AT&T two-tape finite state transducers (Mohri et al., 2000). Conversion from this higher layer (the **Morphtools format**) to the Lextools format (an NLP-oriented extension of the AT&T toolkit for finite-state machines (Sproat, 1995)) is done for different types of Lextools files such as rule files or context-free grammar files. A central concept here is that of the **multi-tier tokens** (MTT), which is a token which represents five tiers but which is compatible with Lextools. An MTT is a sequence $[T, R, V, P, O]$ where: *T* is a token from the pattern "template", *R* is a root radical, *V* is a vowel from the vocalism, *P* is a token from the phonological representation, and *O* is a letter from the orthographic representation. The first (or pattern) tier (*T*) is always required. The additional tiers can be left underspecified or empty (ε), which is both represented with the symbol 0. For example, the information in (3) is conceptually represented in the multi-tier system as follows (only the top three tiers are filled in since no processing has taken place yet):

In the implementation, each column becomes one MTT (i.e., a single symbol in the underlying FST), and the information in (7) is actually represented as follows:

(8) [w0000] [a0000] [+0000] [l0000] [i0000] [+0000] [y0000] [+0000] [V0a00] [1d000] [2ς000] [V0u00][3w000] [+0000] [ū0000] [+0000] [h0000] [u0000]

After applying phonological rules, the fourth (phonological) tier has been filled in in each MTT:

(9) [w00w0] [a00a0] [+0000] [l00l0] [i00i0] [+0000] [y00y0] [+0000] [V0aa0] [1d0d0] [2ς0ς0] [V0uu0][3w000] [+0000] [ū00ū0] [+0000] [h00h0] [u00u0]

Note that the last radical in the stem [3w000] did not map to the phonological layer due to the morphophonemic rules discussed in the previous section. In this fourth tier, this represents the phonological form /waliyadςuūhu/. Orthographic rules are then applied which write symbols into the fifth tier and to modify them, ultimately yielding *waliyadςuwhu*. Note that the fourth tier provides the (phonemic) pronunciation for the orthography in

(7)

Pattern Tier	w	a	+	l	i	+	y	+	V	1	2	V	3	+	ū	+	h	u
Radicals Tier	0	0	0	0	0	0	0	0	0	d	ς	0	w	0	0	0	0	0
Vocalism Tier	0	0	0	0	0	0	0	0	a	0	0	u	0	0	0	0	0	0
Phonological Tier	0	0	0	0	0	0	0	0	0	0	0	0	0	0	0	0	0	0
Orthographic Tier	0	0	0	0	0	0	0	0	0	0	0	0	0	0	0	0	0	0

the fifth tier. The orthographic tier always has diacritics; it differs from the phonological tier in terms of spelling conventions relating to the Ta-Marbuta, the Alif Maqsura, and the Hamza forms. This does not mean that as an analyzer, the system always requires diacritized input: the input to the analyzer can be fully diacritized, partially diacritized, or undiacritized, since the operational system includes a step of hypothesizing diacritics if they are absent.

4.3 Lexicon

One of the main design goals of MAGEAD was to be able to operate without a lexicon or with only a partial lexicon. The motivation is that despite the similarities between dialects at the morphological and lexical levels, it is hard to build a complete lexicon for every dialect. The lexicon in MAGEAD operates as a filter that is not part of MAGEAD's FSTs. After the morphological analyzer generates all morphologically possible analyses, the lexicon removes those analyses that do not correspond to lexical entries. Therefore, running MAGEAD without a lexicon comes at the cost of over-generation. We created another version of MAGEAD that has the lexicon compiled into its FST, we call this version MAGEAD-LEX. We will discuss MAGEAD-LEX in more details in Section 7.

5 MAGEAD-EXPRESS

Similar to MAGEAD, MAGEAD-EXPRESS is a morphological analyzer and generator for Arabic and its dialects that also analyzes to or generates from a lexeme and a set of linguistic feature-value pairs. MAGEAD-EXPRESS is composed of two parts: the **linguistic resources** and the **the morphological engine**. MAGEAD-EXPRESS's linguistic database follows the general structure of BAMA (Buckwalter, 2004) and ALMORGEANA (Habash, 2007). The main difference is that MAGEAD-EXPRESS's databases are extracted automatically from MAGEAD's FSTs. This section will give an overview on the structure of the linguistic information. Section 6 will go over the extraction process in detail.

An Arabic word can be viewed as a concatenation of three regions: a prefix, a suffix and a stem; only the prefix and suffix regions can be null. MAGEAD-EXPRESS's database consists of three lexicons, one for each word-region and three **compatibility tables** (CTs): prefix-stem, stem-suffix and prefix-suffix CT. Prefix and suffix lexicon entries cover all possible concatenations of Arabic prefixes/proclitics and suffixes/enclitics respectively. Similarly, the stem entries cover all possible stems for each lexeme. Each entry, in any of the lexicons, is *minimally* composed of four fields: undiacritized surface form, morphological category, diacritized surface form and morphological feature-value pairs associated with the entry. In our example وَلِيَدعُوهُ *waliyadςuwhu* 'and that they invite him', the prefix, stem and suffix entries are, respectively:

(10) wly pre-10 diac:waliy asp:I per:3 gen:m num:p cnj:w prt:l

(11) dς stem-60 diac:adς 1:d 2:ς 3:w mbc:verb-I-au-tr asp:I vox:act

(12) wh suf-23 diac:uwhu asp:I mod:s per:3 gen:m num:p pro:3MS

The CTs specify which morphological categories are allowed to co-occur. In our example, pre-10, stem-60, and suf-23 have to be three-way compatible to generate our example verb. Because the CTs are built automatically in MAGEAD-EXPRESS, the name of a category is nothing but a unique identifier; unlike BAMA/ALMORGEANA's categories that have human-interpretable meanings.

MAGEAD-EXPRESS utilizes the morphological analysis/generation engine of ALMORGEANA as it complies with the two main general specifications of MAGEAD **analysis/generation** to/from **a lexeme and feature-value pairs**. In analysis, the word is segmented into all possible sets of prefix, stem and suffix strings. In a valid segmentation, the strings should exist in their corresponding lexicons and their categories should be compatible. Generation is similar to analysis but instead of matching on surface forms, the matching occur on the features. For a valid generation, the surface forms corresponding to the compatible sets of features of each word part are then concatenated to form the final word form.

6 Extracting MAGEAD-EXPRESS Tables from MAGEAD FSTs

In this section, we present how we extract the linguistic information from MAGEAD's FSTs and present it in a tabular format compatible with MAGEAD-EXPRESS as descried in section 5. The extraction process takes place in an incremental fashion where more information is added to the initial tables in each step.

Creating the Initial AM Tables: MAGEAD's context-free grammar (CFG) automaton (introduced in Section 4.1) encodes all the possible combinations of abstract morphemes (AMs) that are compatible. We start by listing all possible AM combinations. For instance, the AM combination responsible for the analysis or generation of our example, وَلِيَدْعُوهُ *waliyadςuwhu* 'and that they invite him', is as in (2). We separate the prefixes, stems and suffixes into three different tables by composing the list with appropriate FST filters that delete un-needed AMs. We also restrict the entries in the stem-AM table to the set of lexemes that exists in MAGEAD's lexicon. Each AM subsequence receives a compatibility category, which is computed as follows. First, we populate three compatibility tables (CTs): prefix-stem, stem-suffix and prefix-suffix that specify compatibility of the AM subsequences. We cluster the prefixes into sets whose member are all compatible with the exact same sets of stems and suffixes; the set is assigned an automatically generated compatibility category name. The same happens to stems and suffixes. Finally, we augment the entries of the prefix-AM, stem-AM and suffix-AM tables with their compatibility categories.

For example, the AM sequence in (2) would contribute the following three AM subsequences (paired with their compatibility categories) to the prefix-AM, stem-AM and suffix-AM tables, respectively:

(13) pre-AM-1 [CONJ:w][PREP:l]
[SUBJPRE_IV:3MP]

(14) stem-AM-1 [1d][2ς][3w][PAT_IV:I]
[VOC_IV:I-au-act]

(15) suf-AM-14 [SUBJSUF_IV:3MP_Sub]
[OBJ:3MS]

Creating the Morphemic Tables: Each AM subsequence in the prefix-AM, stem-AM and suffix-AM tables is composed with the abstract morpheme-to-concrete morpheme transducer that is responsible for translating the AM to their equivalent CM represented in multi-tier tokens (MTTs). Also, the AMs are composed with the abstract morpheme-to-feature transducer that maps the AMs to their linguistic features. This results in a new set of tables that also includes the morphemic representation and the corresponding set of the linguistic feature-value pairs. There is no change in categories in this phase. Each entry in any of the morphemic tables has four columns ordered as: CM, compatibility category, AM, feature-value pairs. Examples of the tables are as follows for prefix, stem and suffix, respectively:

(16) [w0000][a0000][+0000][l0000][i0000][+0000]
[y0000][+0000] pre-AM-1 [CONJ:w]
[PREP:l][SUBJPRE_IV:3MP] [asp:I]
[per:3][gen:m][num:p][cnj:w][prt:l]

(17) [V0a00][1d000][2ς000][V0u00][3w000]
stem-AM-1 [1d][2ς][3w][PAT_IV:I]
[VOC_IV:I-au-act] [1:d][2:E][3:w]
[mbc:verb-I-au-tr][asp:I][vox:act]

(18) [+0000][ū0000][+0000][h0000][u0000]
suf-AM-14 [SUBJSUF_IV:3MP_Sub]
[OBJ:3MS] [asp:I][mod:s][per:3][gen:m]
[num:p][pro:3MS]

Creating the Surface Form Tables: The CM of prefixes, stems and suffixes cannot be converted separately to their surface form because there are morphemic, phonological and orthographic rules that target interactions among them. At this stage we use the AM categories to form all possible morphemic representations in our tables. So for our example, the morphemic representation is (8). The morphemic representations are then composed with MAGEAD's generation FST where the morphemic, phonological and orthographic rules are applied. We also keep track of the word parts to be able to divide the surface form later to prefix, stem and suffix by using +'s to mark the boundaries. The result of this operations is as follows:

(19) waliy+ adς +uwhu

Applying the rules creates new surface forms that require new categories. For example, as discussed earlier, the verbal suffix long-vowel +ū is rewritten as (ـُوا+) *+uwA* in a final position or as (ـُو+) *+uw* in a medial position. These two new surface forms need two new categories because they are no longer compatible with everything +ū was compatible with. The surface forms and the new categories are then added to the entries in the morphemic tables and a new set of surface-form tables is created (prefix, stem, and suffix, respectively):

(20) waliy pre-10 [w0000][a0000][+0000][l0000][i0000][+0000][y0000][+0000] pre-AM-1 [CONJ:w][PREP:l][SUBJPRE_IV:3MP] [asp:I][per:3][gen:m][num:p][cnj:w][prt:l]

(21) adς stem-60 [V0a00][1d000][2ς000] [V0u00][3w000] stem-AM-1 [1d][2ς] [3w] [PAT_IV:I][VOC_IV:I-au-act] [1:d] [2:E][3:w][mbc:verb-I-au-tr][asp:I][vox:act]

(22) uwhu suf-23 [+0000][ū0000][+0000] [h0000][u0000] suf-AM-14 [SUBJSUF_IV:3MP_Sub][OBJ:3MS] [asp:I] [mod:s][per:3][gen:m][num:p][pro:3MS]

In a final step, we put these tables in the appropriate format for ALMORGEANA as described in section 5.

7 Evaluation

MAGEAD-EXPRESS uses MAGEAD's linguistic resources; therefore its lexical coverage should be identical to that of MAGEAD. We do not evaluate MAGEAD's coverage here; for more information about MSA and Levantine verb coverage, see (Habash and Rambow, 2006) and for MSA nouns, see (Altantawy et al., 2010). In this section, we evaluate the conversion of MAGEAD's linguistic resources for MSA Verbs from their FST representation to the tabular representation used by MAGEAD-EXPRESS. We also report on time performance and memory usage of MAGEAD-EXPRESS versus MAGEAD.

Both MAGEAD and MAGEAD-EXPRESS are bidirectional systems. It is sufficient to evaluate them either in analysis or generation mode. For the purpose of this evaluation, we opted to do the generation mode only. The goal of this evaluation is to ensure that given any lexeme from MAGEAD's lexicon paired with a plausible set of linguistic feature-value pairs, both MAGEAD and MAGEAD-EXPRESS will generate the same surface forms.

MAGEAD's verb lexicon contains 8,960 lexemes, each of which has either 1,092 inflected surface forms if the lexeme is for an intransitive verb or 14,196 if transitive (accepts pronominal object clitics). Since it is too time-consuming to test all the 8,960 lexemes, we create a representative sample of lexemes to serve as an evaluation dataset. We cluster MAGEAD's lexicon into 611 lexeme groups. Each group represents an MBC with a particular root type that triggers a particular set of rewrite rules. Each lexeme group is assigned an **iconic lexeme** (IL) that represents the group. The 611 ILs (240 intransitive and 371 transitive) are used as our evaluation dataset. Each IL in the evaluation dataset is paired with all possible combinations of feature-value pairs and then fed to both MAGEAD and MAGEAD-EXPRESS. The surface forms generated by both systems were identical in all cases. This validates the correction of our conversion process.

We now evaluate the time and memory requirements of MAGEAD-EXPRESS against MAGEAD. For the sake of this evaluation, we also created another version of MAGEAD that has the lexicon compiled into its FST; we call this version MAGEAD-LEX. Table 7 compares MAGEAD-EXPRESS to both MAGEAD-LEX and MAGEAD. MAGEAD-LEX is restricted by the lexicon and thus can not operate on any lexemes that are not in the lexicon (unlike MAGEAD but like MAGEAD-EXPRESS). MAGEAD is the only system among these three that can run without a lexicon. MAGEAD-EXPRESS is the only system among the three that allows easy access to intermediate representations such as those appearing in (20)-(22), i.e., AMs and CMs.

	MAGEAD-EXPRESS	MAGEAD-LEX	MAGEAD
Embedded lexicon	Yes	Yes	No
Can run without a lexicon	No	No	Yes
Intermediate representations in output	Yes	No	No
Time to build	30mins (MAGEAD) + 48hrs	30mins (MAGEAD) + 30mins	30mins
Time to analyze 10K verbs (batches of 1,000)	68 secs	100 secs	3,985 secs
Time to analyze 1 verb	3.5 secs	4.5 secs	2.1 secs
Time to analyze 1 verb online (client-server)	0.00679 secs	No	No
Size of machines	7MB	388MB	Not Composable 13M⊙14M⊙583K

Table 1: Comparing MAGEAD-EXPRESS, MAGEAD-LEX, and MAGEAD. All reported times are CPU seconds.

In terms of time to build, MAGEAD takes 30 mins to compile (MAGEAD-LEX takes an hour), and then MAGEAD-EXPRESS takes around 48 hours to extract its tables from MAGEAD's FSTs.

As for time performance, we created a list of 10,000 verbs collected randomly from the list of surface forms generated in the extraction evaluation. We measure the time MAGEAD-EXPRESS takes to finish analyzing the 10,000 verbs (in ten batches of 1,000 verbs each) against the time taken by MAGEAD and MAGEAD-LEX. As Table 7 shows, MAGEAD-EXPRESS is 1.5 times as fast as MAGEAD-LEX and 58 times faster than MAGEAD. We next compute the average speed of analyzing one verb at a time offline (using all 10,000 verbs). In this scenario, MAGEAD is the fastest due to the overhead time (3.4 secs) that MAGEAD-EXPRESS needs to load its tables into memory. Of course, MAGEAD-EXPRESS is the only system among the three systems that can operate in a client-server setup where it loads its lexicons once into memory. In such setup, MAGEAD-EXPRESS is more than 300 times faster than MAGEAD.

As for memory requirements, MAGEAD-EXPRESS requires about 7MB to store its tables into memory. When the tables get loaded in memory, MAGEAD-EXPRESS does not require additional resources. On the other hand, MAGEAD consists of three FSTs that are composed with the input in an online fashion, see Table 7 for sizes. In fact, we could not compose any two of MAGEAD's three FSTs into a bigger FST on our 64GB memory machine. However, MAGEAD-LEX is much smaller than MAGEAD because it is only restricted to the lexicon. MAGEAD-LEX's FSTs are composed into one big FST of size 388MB. The amount of memory needed by MAGEAD depends mainly on the size of the input. For 1 verb to be analyzed, the input is composed with MAGEAD's three FSTs and the result is an FST of size 10KB, and for a batch of 10, 100, and 1,000 verbs the resulting FST is of size 113KB, 1.7MB, and 13MB, respectively.

8 Conclusion

In this paper, we introduced MAGEAD-EXPRESS, a lexicon-based morphological analyzer and generator for Arabic and its dialects. MAGEAD-EXPRESS extracts its linguistic knowledge automatically from MAGEAD. As a result, MAGEAD-EXPRESS still benefits from the level of abstraction with which the linguistic information is encoded in MAGEAD's FSTs, while being much faster than MAGEAD. Both systems are bidirectional and analyze to and generate from a lexeme and a set of linguistic feature-value pairs. MAGEAD's main advantage over MAGEAD-EXPRESS, is its ability to work without a lexicon or with a partial lexicon. In ongoing work, we are studying how we can combine the two system to build a more extensive system. The main idea is to port MAGEAD as a back-off mechanism to deal with the out-of-vocabulary words that are not in the lexicon. Although we only demonstrate the FST-table conversion idea on Arabic, we believe it is applicable to other languages with comparable benefits (depending on the language's morphological complexity).

References

Imad Al-Sughaiyer and Ibrahim Al-Kharashi. 2004. Arabic Morphological Analysis Techniques: A Comprehensive Survey. *Journal of the American Society for Information Science and Technology*, 55(3):189–213.

Muhammed Aljlayl and Ophir Frieder. 2002. On Arabic Search: Improving the Retrieval Effectiveness via a Light Stemming Approach. In *Proceedings of ACM Eleventh Conference on Information and Knowledge Management, Mclean, VA*, pages 340–347.

Mohamed Altantawy, Nizar Habash, Owen Rambow, and Ibrahim Saleh. 2010. Morphological analysis and generation of arabic nouns: A morphemic functional approach. In *Proceedings of the International Conference on Language Resources and Evaluation, LREC. Valletta, Malta*.

Saba Amsalu and Dafydd Gibbon. 2005. Finite state morphology of Amharic. In *International Conference on Recent Advances in Natural Language Processing (RANLP)*, pages 47–51, Borovets.

Kenneth Beesley and Lauri Karttunen. 2000. Finite-state non-concatenative morphotactics. In *acl00*, Hong Kong, China.

Kenneth Beesley, Tim Buckwalter, and Stuart Newton. 1989. Two-level finite-state analysis of Arabic morphology. In *Proceedings of the Seminar on Bilingual Computing in Arabic and English*, page n.p.

Kenneth Beesley. 1998. Arabic morphology using only finite-state operations. In M. Rosner, editor, *Proceedings of the Workshop on Computational Approaches to Semitic Languages*, pages 50–7, Montereal.

Tim Buckwalter. 2004. Buckwalter arabic morphological analyzer version 2.0. LDC catalog number LDC2004L02, ISBN 1-58563-324-0.

Michael Gasser. 2009. Semitic morphological analysis and generation using finite state transducers with feature structures. In *Proceedings of the 12th Conference of the European Chapter of the ACL (EACL 2009)*, pages 309–317, Athens, Greece.

Nizar Habash and Owen Rambow. 2006. MAGEAD: A Morphological Analyzer and Generator for the Arabic Dialects. In *Proceedings of the Conference of the Association for Computational Linguistics*, Sydney, Australia.

Nizar Habash, Owen Rambow, and George Kiraz. 2005. Morphological Analysis and Generation for Arabic Dialects. In *Proceedings of the ACL Workshop on Computational Approaches to Semitic Languages*, Ann Arbor, Michigan.

Nizar Habash, Abdelhadi Soudi, and Tim Buckwalter. 2007. On Arabic Transliteration. In A. van den Bosch and A. Soudi, editors, *Arabic Computational Morphology: Knowledge-based and Empirical Methods*. Springer.

Nizar Habash. 2007. Arabic Morphological Representations for Machine Translation. In Antal van den Bosch and Abdelhadi Soudi, editors, *Arabic Computational Morphology: Knowledge-based and Empirical Methods*. Kluwer/Springer.

Nizar Habash. 2010. *Introduction to Arabic Natural Language Processing*. Morgan & Claypool Publishers.

Laura Kataja and Kimmo Koskenniemi. 1988. Finite state description of Semitic morphology. In *COLING-88: Papers Presented to the 12th International Conference on Computational Linguistics*, volume 1, pages 313–15.

Martin Kay. 1987. Nonconcatenative Finite-State Morphology. In *Proceedings of the Conference of the European Chapter of ACL (EACL-87)*, Copenhagen, Denmark.

Ahmed El Kholy and Nizar Habash. 2010. Orthographic and Morphological Processing for English-Arabic Statistical Machine Translation. In *Actes de Traitement Automatique des Langues Naturelles (TALN)*, Montreal, Canada.

George Kiraz. 2000. Multi-tiered nonlinear morphology using multi-tape finite automata: A case study on Syriac and Arabic. *Computational Linguistics*, 26(1):77–105.

Mehryar Mohri, Fernando C. N. Pereira, and Michael Riley. 2000. The design principles of a weighted finite-state transducer library. *Theoretical Computer Science*, 231:17–32, January.

Otakar Smrž. 2007. *Functional Arabic Morphology. Formal System and Implementation*. Ph.D. thesis, Charles University in Prague, Prague, Czech Republic.

Richard Sproat. 1995. Lextools: Tools for finite-state linguistic analysis. Technical Report 11522-951108-10TM, Bell Laboratories.

Shlomo Yona and Shuly Wintner. 2005. A finite-state morphological grammar of Hebrew. In *Proceedings of the ACL Workshop on Computational Approaches to Semitic Languages*, pages 9–16, Ann Arbor, Michigan.

An Open-Source Finite State Morphological Transducer for Modern Standard Arabic

Mohammed Attia, Pavel Pecina, Antonio Toral, Lamia Tounsi and Josef van Genabith
School of Computing,
Dublin City University, Dublin, Ireland
`http://computing.dcu.ie`
`{mattia, ppecina, atoral, ltounsi, josef}@computing.dcu.ie`

Abstract

We develop an open-source large-scale finite-state morphological processing toolkit (AraComLex) for Modern Standard Arabic (MSA) distributed under the GPLv3 license.[1] The morphological transducer is based on a lexical database specifically constructed for this purpose. In contrast to previous resources, the database is tuned to MSA, eliminating lexical entries no longer attested in contemporary use. The database is built using a corpus of 1,089,111,204 words, a pre-annotation tool, machine learning techniques, and knowledge-based pattern matching to automatically acquire lexical knowledge. Our morphological transducer is evaluated and compared to LDC's SAMA (Standard Arabic Morphological Analyser).

1 Introduction

Due to its complexity, Arabic morphology has always been a challenge for computational processing and a hard testing ground for morphological analysis technologies. A lexicon is a core component of any morphological analyser (Dichy and Farghaly, 2003; Attia, 2006; Buckwalter, 2004; Beesley, 2001). The quality and coverage of the lexical database determines the quality and coverage of the morphological analyser, and limitations in the lexicon will cascade through to higher levels of processing.

In this paper, we present an approach to automatically construct a corpus-based lexical database for Modern Standard Arabic (MSA), focusing on the problem that existing lexical resources tend to include obsolete lexical entries no longer attested in contemporary use. The database is used as the lexical component of a large-scale finite state morphological analyser. We specify the morpho-syntactic features and inflection paradigms that need to be explicitly stated for the morphological analyser and show how this information can be learned through machine learning techniques. We explain how broken plural forms are extracted from the corpus using Levenshtein Distance and pattern matching. We report the results of our experiments and evaluate and compare our system against LDC's SAMA (Standard Arabic Morphological Analyser) (Maamouri et al., 2010) showing a substantial reduction of the number of analyses per input word due to avoiding obsolete interpretations no longer present in MSA.

This paper is structured as follows. In the introduction, we differentiate between MSA, the focus of this research, and Classical Arabic (CA) which is a historical version of the language. We also give a brief account of the current state of Arabic morphological analysis and outline the structure of the Arabic morphological system, showing what layers and tiers are involved in word derivation and inflection. Section 2 explains the methodology in constructing our morphological analyser and the lexical database. Section 3 presents the results obtained so far in building and extending the lexical database by using our MSA data-driven filtering method and machine learning techniques. We outline how broken plurals are extracted and handled in our morphology. In Section 4, we evaluate the morphology, and finally, Section 5 gives the conclusion.

[1] http://sourceforge.net/projects/aracomlex/

Proceedings of the 9th International Workshop on Finite State Methods and Natural Language Processing, pages 125–133,
Blois (France), July 12-15, 2011.

1.1 Modern Standard Arabic vs. Classical Arabic

Modern Standard Arabic (MSA), the subject of our research, is the language of modern writing, prepared speeches, and the language of the news. It is the language universally understood by Arabic speakers around the world. MSA stands in contrast to both Classical Arabic (CA) and vernacular Arabic dialects. CA is the language which appeared in the Arabian Peninsula centuries before the emergence of Islam and continued to be the standard language until the medieval times. CA continues to the present day as the language of religious teaching, poetry, and scholarly literature. MSA is a direct descendent of CA and is used today throughout the Arab World in writing and in formal speaking (Bin-Muqbil, 2006).

MSA is different from Classical Arabic at the lexical, morphological, and syntactic levels (Watson, 2002; Elgibali and Badawi, 1996; Fischer, 1997). At the lexical level, there is a significant expansion of the lexicon to cater for the needs of modernity. New words are constantly coined or borrowed from foreign languages while many words from CA have become obsolete. Although MSA conforms to the general rules of CA, MSA shows a tendency for simplification, and modern writers use only a subset of the full range of structures, inflections, and derivations available in CA. For example, Arabic speakers no longer strictly abide by case ending rules, which led some structures to become obsolete, while some syntactic structures which were marginal in CA started to have more salience in MSA. For example, the word order of object-verb-subject, one of the classical structures, is rarely found in MSA, while the relatively marginal subject-verb-object word order in CA is gaining more weight in MSA. This is confirmed by Van Mol (2003) who quotes Stetkevych (1970) as pointing out the fact that MSA word order has shifted balance, as the subject now precedes the verb more frequently, breaking from the classical default word order of verb-subject-object. Moreover, to avoid ambiguity and improve readability, there is a tendency to avoid passive verb forms when the active readings are also possible, as in the words نُظِّمَ 'to be organised'. Instead of the passive form, the alternative syntactic construction تَمَّ 'performed/done' + verbal noun is used, تَمَّ تَنظِيمُهُ 'lit. organising it has been done / it was organised'.

To our knowledge, apart from Van Mol's (2003) study of the variations in complementary particles, no extensive empirical studies have been conducted to check how significant the difference between MSA and CA is either at the morphological, lexical, or syntactic levels.

1.2 The Current State of Arabic Morphological Analysis

Existing Arabic lexicons are not corpus-based (as in a COBUILD approach (Sinclair, 1987)), but rather reflect historical and prescriptive perspectives, making no distinction between entries for MSA and CA (Classical Arabic). Therefore, they tend to include obsolete words not in contemporary use.

The Buckwalter Arabic Morphological Analyzer (BAMA) (Buckwalter, 2004) is a *de facto* standard tool which is widely used in the Arabic NLP research community. The latest version of BAMA is renamed SAMA version 3.1 (Maamouri et al., 2010), and it contains 40,648 lemmas. However, SAMA suffers from a legacy of heavy reliance on older Arabic dictionaries, particularly Wehr's Dictionary (Wehr and Cowan, 1976). We estimate that about 25% of the lexical items included in SAMA are outdated based on our data-driven filtering method presented in Section 3.2.

Therefore, there is a strong need to compile a lexicon for MSA that follows modern lexicographic conventions (Atkins and Rundell, 2008) in order to make the lexicon a reliable representation of the language and to make it a useful resource for NLP applications dealing with MSA. Our work represents a further step to address this critical gap in Arabic lexicography and morphological analysis. We use a large corpus of more than one billion words to automatically create a lexical database for MSA.

1.3 Arabic Morphotactics

Arabic morphology is well-known for being rich and complex. Arabic morphology has a multi-tiered structure where words are originally derived from roots and pass through a series of affixations and clitic attachments until they finally appear as surface forms. Morphotactics refers to the way mor-

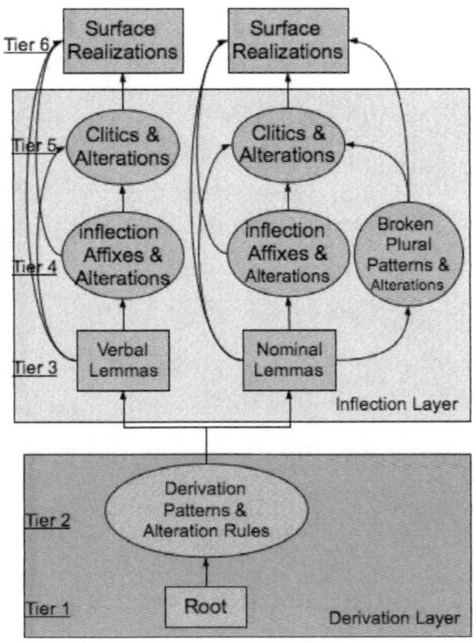

Figure 1: The Multi-tier Structure of the Arabic Morphology.

phemes combine together to form words (Beesley, 1998; Beesley and Karttunen, 2003). Generally speaking, morphotactics can be concatenative, with morphemes either prefixed or suffixed to stems, or non-concatenative, with stems undergoing internal alterations to convey morpho-syntactic information (Kiraz, 2001). Arabic is considered as a typical example of a language that employs both concatenative and non-concatenative morphotactics. For example, the verb اِستَعمَلوها 'they-used-it' and the noun وَالاستَعمَالَات 'and-the-uses' both originate from the root عمل.

Figure 1 shows the layers and tiers embedded in the representation of the Arabic morphological system. The derivation layer is non-concatenative and opaque in the sense that it is a sort of abstraction that affects the choice of a part of speech (POS), and it does not have a direct explicit surface manifestation. By contrast, the inflection layer is more transparent. It applies concatenative morphotactics by using affixes to express morpho-syntactic features. We note that verbs at this level show what is called 'separated dependencies' which means that some prefixes determine the selection of suffixes.

2 Methodology

In this section, we explain the techniques and standards we follow in the construction of our lexical resource.

2.1 Using Finite State Technology for Arabic

One of our objectives for constructing the lexical resource is to build a morphological analyser and generator using bidirectional finite state technology (FST). FST has been used successfully in developing morphologies for many languages, including Semitic languages (Beesley and Karttunen, 2003). There are a number of advantages of this technology that makes it especially attractive in dealing with human language morphologies; among these are the ability to handle concatenative and non-concatenative morphotactics, and the high speed and efficiency in handling large automata of lexicons with their derivations and inflections that can run into millions of paths.

The Xerox XFST System (Beesley and Karttunen, 2003) is a well-known finite state compiler, but the disadvantage of this tool is that it is a proprietary software, which limits its use in the larger research community. Fortunately, there is an alternative, namely Foma, (Hulden, 2009), which is an open-source finite-state toolkit that implements the Xerox lexc and xfst utilities. We have developed an open-source morphological analyser for Arabic using the Foma compiler allowing us to share our morphology with third parties. The lexical database, which is being edited and validated, is used to automatically extend and update the morphological analyser, allowing for greater coverage and better capabilities.

Arabic words are formed through the amalgamation of two tiers, namely root and pattern. A root is a sequence of three consonants and the pattern is a template of vowels (or vowels with consonants) with slots into which the consonants of the root are inserted. This process of insertion is called interdigitation (Beesley, 2001). An example is shown in Table 1.

Root	درس **drs**		
Pattern	$R_1aR_2aR_3a$	$R_1aR_2R_2aR_3a$	$R_1\bar{a}R_2iR_3$
POS	V	V	N
Stem	d a r a s a 'study'	d a r r a s a 'teach'	d ā r i s 'student'

Table 1: Root and Pattern Interdigitation.

There are three main strategies for the development of Arabic morphological analysers depending on the initial level of analysis: root, stem or lemma. In a root-based morphology, such as the Xerox Arabic Morphological Analyser (Beesley, 2001), analysing Arabic words is based on a list of roots and a list of patterns interacting together in a process called interdigitation, as explained earlier. In a stem-based morphology, such as SAMA (Buckwalter, 2004; Maamouri et al., 2010), the stem is considered as a base form of the word. A stem is a form between the lemma and the surface form. One lemma can have several variations when interacting with prefixes and suffixes. Such a system does not use alteration rules and relies instead on listing all stems (or form variations) in the database. For example, in SAMA's database, the verb شَكَرَ *šakara* 'to thank' has two entries: شَكَرَ *šakara* for perfective and شْكُر *škur* for the imperfective. In a lemma-based morphology, words are analysed at the lemma level. A lemma is the least marked form of a word, that is the uninflected word without suffixes, prefixes, proclitics, or enclitics. In Arabic, this is usually the perfective, 3rd person, singular verb, and in the case of nouns and adjectives, the singular indefinite form. Other inflected forms are generated from the lemma through alteration rules.

In our implementation of the Arabic finite state transducer, we use the lemma as the base form. We believe that a lemma-based morphology is more economical than the stem-based morphology as it does not list all form variations and relies on generalised rules. It is also less complex than the root-based approach and less likely to overgenerate (Dichy and Farghaly, 2003; Attia, 2006). This leads to better maintainability and scalability of our morphology.

In an XFST finite state system, lexical entries along with all possible affixes and clitics are encoded in the lexc language which is a right recursive phrase structure grammar (Beesley, 2001; Beesley and Karttunen, 2003). A lexc file contains a number of lexicons connected through what is known as "continuation classes" which determine the path of concatenation. Example (1) gives a snapshot of some verbs in our lexc file. The tags are meant to provide the following information:

- The multi-character symbol `^ss^` stands for stem start, and `^se^` for stem end.
- The flag diacritic `@D.V.P@` means "disallow the passive voice", and `@D.M.I@` means "disallow the imperative mood".
- `Transitive` and `Intransitive` are used as the continuation classes for verbs.

```
(1) LEXICON Verbs
^ss^شَكَرَ['thank']^se^                  Transitive;
^ss^فَرِحَ['be-happy']^se^@D.V.P@        Intransitive;
^ss^أَمَرَ['order']^se^@D.M.I@           Transitive;
^ss^قَالَ['say']^se^                     Intransitive;
```

Similarly, nouns are added by choosing from a set of continuation classes which determine what path of inflection each noun is going to select, as shown in example (2) (gloss is included in square brackets for illustration only). These continuation classes (13 in total) are based on the facts in Table 2, which shows the inflection choices available for Arabic nouns according to gender (masculine or feminine) and number (singular, dual or plural).

```
(2) LEXICON Nouns
+m+human^ss^مُعَلِّم['teacher']^se^        FMduFduFplMpl;
+m+human^ss^طَالِب['student']^se^          FMduFduFpl;
+m+nonhuman^ss^كِتَاب['book']^se^          Mdu;
+f+nonhuman^ss^بَقَرَة['cow']^se^          DuFpl;
```

With inflections and concatenations, words usually become subject to changes or alterations in their forms. Alterations are the discrepancies between underlying strings and their surface realisations (Beesley, 1998), and alteration rules are the rules that relate the surface forms to the underlying forms. Alteration rules are expressed in finite state systems using XFST replace rules of the general form shown in (3).

```
(3) a -> b || L _ R
```

The rule states that the string `a` is replaced with the string `b` when `a` occurs between the left context `L` and the right context `R`. In Arabic, long vowels, glides and the glottal stop are the subject of a great deal of phonological (and consequently orthographical) alterations like assimilation and deletion. Many of the challenges an Arabic morphological analyser

	Masculine Singular	Feminine Singular	Masculine Dual	Feminine Dual	Masculine Plural	Feminine Plural	Continuation Class
1	مُعَلِّم *muʿallim* 'teacher'	مُعَلِّمَة *muʿallimat*	مُعَلِّمَان *muʿallimān*	مُعَلِّمَتَان *muʿallimatān*	مُعَلِّمُون *muʿallimuwn*	مُعَلِّمَات *muʿallimāt*	F-Mdu-Fdu-Mpl-Fpl
2	طَالِب *ṭālib* 'student'	طَالِبَة *ṭālibat*	طَالِبَان *ṭālibān*	طَالِبَتَان *ṭālibatān*	-	طَالِبَات *ṭālibāt*	F-Mdu-Fdu-Fpl
3	تَحضِيرِيّ *taḥḍiyriyy* 'preparatory'	تَحضِيرِيَّة *taḥḍiyriyyat*	تَحضِيرِيَّان *taḥḍiyriyyān*	تَحضِيرِيَّتَان *taḥḍiyriyyatān*	-	-	F-Mdu-Fdu
4	-	بَقَرَة *baqarat* 'cow'	-	بَقَرَتَان *baqaratān*	-	بَقَرَات *baqarāt*	Fdu-Fpl
5	تَنَازُل *tanāzul* 'concession'	-	-	-	-	تَنَازُلَات *tanāzulāt*	Fpl
6	-	ضَحِيَّة *ḍaḥiyyat* 'victim'	-	ضَحِيَّتَان *ḍaḥiyyatān*	-	-	Fdu
7	مَحض *maḥḍ* 'mere'	مَحضَة *maḥḍat*	-	-	-	-	F
8	اِمتِحَان *imtiḥān* 'exam'	-	اِمتِحَانَان *imtiḥānān*	-	-	اِمتِحَانَات *imtiḥānāt*	Mdu-Fdu
9	طَيَّار *ṭayyār* 'pilot'	-	-	-	.tayyAruwn	-	Mdu-Mpl
10	كِتَاب *kitāb* 'book'	-	كِتَابَان *kitābān*	-	-	-	Mdu
11	دِيمُقرَاطِيّ *diymuqrāṭiyy* 'democrat'	-	-	-	دِيمُقرَاطِيُّون *diymuqrāṭiyyuwn*	-	Mpl
12	خُرُوج *ḫuruwǧ* 'exiting'	-	-	-	-	-	NoNum
13	مَبَاحِث *mabāḥiṯ* 'investigators'	-	-	-	-	-	Irreg_pl

Table 2: The Arabic Inflection Grid and Continuation Classes.

faces are related to handling these issues. In our system there are about 130 replace rules to handle alterations that affect verbs, nouns, adjectives and function words when they undergo inflections, or when they are attached to affixes and clitics.

2.2 Using Heuristics and Statistics from a Large Corpus

For the construction of a lexicon for MSA, we take advantage of large and rich resources that have not been exploited in similar tasks before. We use a corpus of 1,089,111,204 words, consisting of 925,461,707 words from the Arabic Gigaword corpus fourth edition (Parker et al., 2009), in addition to 163,649,497 words from news articles we collected from the Al-Jazeera web site.[2]

We pre-annotate the corpus using MADA (Roth et al., 2008), a state-of-the-art tool for morphological processing. MADA combines SAMA and SVM classifiers to choose the best morphological analysis for a word in context, doing tokenisation, lemmatisation, diacritisation, POS tagging, and disambiguation. MADA is reported to achieve high accuracy (above 90%) for tokenisation and POS tagging tested on the Arabic Penn Treebank, but no evaluation of lemmatisation is reported. We use the annotated data to collect statistics on lemma features and use machine learning techniques, described in Section 3.2.2, in order to extend a manually constructed seed lexicon (Attia, 2006). We also use the annotated data to extract a list of broken plurals, as described in Section 3.3.

3 Results to Date

In this section, we present the results obtained so far in building and extending the lexical database.

[2]http://aljazeera.net/portal. Collected in January 2010.

3.1 Building Lexical Resources

There are three key components in the Arabic morphological system: root, pattern, and lemma. In order to accommodate these components, we create four lexical databases: one for nominal lemmas (including nouns and adjectives), one for verb lemmas, one for word patterns, and one for root-lemma lookup. From a manually created MSA lexicon (Attia, 2006) we construct a seed database of 5,925 nominal lemmas and 1,529 verb lemmas. At the moment, we focus on open word classes and exclude proper nouns, function words, and multiword expressions which are relatively stable and fixed from an inflectional point of view.

We build a database of 490 Arabic patterns (456 for nominals and 34 for verbs) which can be used as indicators of the morphological inflectional and derivational behaviour of Arabic words. Patterns are also powerful in the abstraction and coarse-grained categorisation of word forms.

3.2 Extending the Lexical Database

In extending our lexicon, we rely on Attia's manually-constructed finite state morphology (Attia, 2006) and the lexical database in SAMA 3.1 (Maamouri et al., 2010). Creating a lexicon is usually a labour-intensive task. For instance, Attia took three years in the development of his morphology, while SAMA and its predecessor, Buckwalter's morphology, were developed over more than a decade, and at least seven people were involved in updating and maintaining the morphology.

Our objective here is to automatically extend Attia's finite state morphology (Attia, 2006) using SAMA's database. In order to do this, we need to solve two problems. First, SAMA suffers from a legacy of obsolete entries and we need to filter out these outdated words, as we want to enrich our lexicon only with lexical items that are still in current use. Second, our lexical database and the FST morphology require features (such as humanness for nouns and transitivity for verbs) that are not provided by SAMA, and we want to automatically induce these features.

3.2.1 Lexical Enrichment.

To address the first problem, we use a data-driven filtering method that combines open web search engines and our pre-annotated corpus. Using frequency statistics[3] from three web search engines (Al-Jazeera,[4] Arabic Wikipedia,[5] and the Arabic BBC website[6]), we find that 7,095 lemmas in SAMA have zero hits. Frequency statistics from our corpus show that 3,604 lemmas are not used in the corpus at all, and 4,471 lemmas occur less than 10 times. Combining frequency statistics from the web and the corpus, we find that there are 29,627 lemmas that returned at least one hit in the web queries and occurred at least 10 times in the corpus. Using a threshold of 10 occurrences here is discretionary, but the aim is to separate the stable core of the language from instances where the use of a word is perhaps accidental or somewhat idiosyncratic. We consider the refined list as representative of the lexicon of MSA as attested by our statistics.

3.2.2 Feature Enrichment.

To address the second problem, we use a machine learning classification algorithm, the Multilayer Perceptron (Haykin, 1998). The main idea of machine learning is to automatically learn complex patterns from existing (training) data and make intelligent decisions on new (test) data. In our case, we have a seed lexicon (Attia, 2006) with lemmas manually annotated with classes, and we want to build a model for predicting the same classes for each new lemma added to the lexicon. The classes (second column in Table 3) for nominals are continuation classes (or inflection paths), the semantico-grammatical feature of humanness, and POS (noun or adjective). The classes for verbs are transitivity, allowing the passive voice, and allowing the imperative mood. From our seed lexicon we extract two datasets of 4,816 nominals and 1,448 verbs. We feed these datasets with frequency statistics from our pre-annotated corpus and build the statistics into a vector grid. The features (third column in Table 3) for nominals are number, gender, case and clitics; for verbs, number, gender, person, aspect, mood, voice and clitics. For the implementation of the machine learning algorithm, we use the open-source application Weka

[3]Statistics were collected in January 2011.
[4]http://aljazeera.net/portal
[5]http://ar.wikipedia.org
[6]http://www.bbc.co.uk/arabic/

No.	Classes	Features	P	R	F
	Nominals				
1	Continuation Classes: 13 classes	number, gender, case, clitics	0.62	0.65	0.63
2	Human: yes, no, unspecified		0.86	0.87	0.86
3	POS: noun, adjective		0.85	0.86	0.85
	Verbs				
4	Transitivity: transitive, intransitive	number, gender, person, aspect, mood, voice, clitics	0.85	0.85	0.84
5	Allow passive: yes, no		0.72	0.72	0.72
6	Allow imperative: yes, no		0.63	0.65	0.64

Table 3: Results of the Classification Experiments.

version 3.6.4.[7] We split each dataset into 66% for training and 34% for testing. We conduct six classification experiments to provide the classes that we need to include in our lexical database. Table 3 gives the results of the experiments in terms of precision, recall, and f-measure.

The results show that the highest f-measure scores are achieved for 'Human', 'POS', and 'Transitivity'. Typically one would assume that these features are hard to predict with any reasonable accuracy without taking the context into account. It was surprising to obtain such good prediction results based only on statistics on morphological features alone. We also note that the f-measure for 'Continuation Classes' is comparatively low, but considering that here we are classifying for 13 classes, the results are in fact quite acceptable. Using the machine learning model, we annotate 12,974 new nominals and 5,034 verbs.

3.3 Handling Broken Plurals

In our seed morphology (Attia, 2006), we have 950 broken plurals which were collected manually and clearly tagged. In SAMA, however, broken plurals are rather poorly handled. SAMA does not mark broken plurals as "plurals" either in the source file or in the morphology output. There is no straightforward way to automatically collect the list of all broken plural forms from SAMA. For example, the singular form جَانِب *ǧānib* "side" and the broken plural جَوَانِب *ǧawānib* "sides" are analysed as in (4) and (5) respectively.

```
(4) <lemmaID>jAnib_1</lemmaID>
    <voc>jAnib</voc> <pos>jAnib/NOUN</pos>
    <gloss>side/aspect</gloss>

(5) <lemmaID>jAnib_1</lemmaID>
    <voc>jawAnib</voc> <pos>jawAnib/NOUN</pos>
    <gloss>sides/aspects</gloss>
```

The only tags that distinguish the singular from the broken plural form is the gloss (or translation) and voc (or vocalisation). We also note that MADA passes this problem on unsolved, and broken plurals are all marked with `num=s`, which means that the number is singular. We believe that this shortcoming can have a detrimental effect on the performance of any syntactic parser based on such data.

To extract broken plurals from our large MSA corpus (which is annotated with SAMA tags), we rely on the gloss of entries with the same LemmaID. We use Levenshtein Distance which measures the similarity between two strings. For example, using Levenshtein Distance to measure the difference between "sides/aspects" and "side/aspect" will give a distance of 2. When this number is divided by the length of the first string, we obtain 0.15, which is within a threshold (here set to <0.4). Thus the two entries pass the test as possible broken plural candidates. Using this method, we collect 2,266 candidates. We believe, however, that many broken plural forms went undetected because the translation did not follow the assumed format. For example, the word حَرب *ḥarb* has the translation "war/warfare" while the plural form حُرُوب *ḥuruwb* has the translation "wars".

To validate the list of candidates, we use Arabic word pattern matching. For instance, in the above example, the singular form (vocalisation) follows the pattern `fAEil` (or the regular expression `.A.il`) and the plural form follows the pattern `fawAEil` (or `.awA.i.`). In our manually developed pattern database we have `fawAEil` as a possible plural pattern for `fAEil`. Therefore, the matching succeeds, and the candidate is considered as a valid broken plural entry. We compiled a list of 135 singular patterns that choose from a set of 82 broken plural patterns. The choice, however, is not free, but

[7] http://www.cs.waikato.ac.nz/ml/weka/

Morphology	No. of Lemmas	General News		Semi-Literary	
		Coverage	Rate per word	Coverage	Rate per word
AraComLex 1.0	10,799	79.68%	1.67	69.37%	1.62
AraComLex 2.0	28,807	86.89%	2.10	85.14%	2.09
AraComLex 2.1	30,587	87.13%	2.09	85.73%	2.08
SAMA	40,648	88.13%	5.32	86.95%	5.30

Table 4: Coverage and Rate Per Word Test Results.

each singular form has a limited predefined set of broken plural patterns to select from. From the list of 2,266 candidates produced by Levenshtein Distance, 1,965 were validated using the pattern matching, that is 87% of the instances. When we remove the entries that are intersected with our 950 manually collected broken plurals, 1,780 forms are left. This means that in our lexicon now we have a list of 2,730 broken plural forms.

There are some insights that can be gained from the statistics on Arabic plurals in our corpus. The corpus contains 5,570 lemmas which have a feminine plural suffix, 1,942 lemmas with a masculine plural suffix (of these 1,273 forms intersect with the feminine plural suffix), and about 1,965 lemmas with a broken plural form. This means that the broken plural formation in Arabic is as productive as the regular plural suffixation. Currently, we cannot explain why the feminine plural suffix enjoys this high preference, but we can point to the fact that masculine plural suffixes are used almost exclusively with the natural gender, while the feminine plural suffix, as well as broken plurals, are used liberally with the grammatical gender in addition to the natural gender.

4 Morphology Evaluation

In this section, we test the coverage and rate per word (or the average number of analyses per word) in our morphological analyser compared to an earlier version (the baseline) and SAMA. We build a test corpus of 800,000 words, divided into 400,000 of what we term as Semi-Literary text and 400,000 for General News texts. The Semi-Literary texts consist of articles collected from columns, commentaries, opinions and analytical essays written by professional writers who tend to use figurative and metaphorical language not commonly used in ordinary news. This type of text exhibits the characteristics of literary text, especially the high ratio of word tokens to word types: out of the 400,000 tokens there are 60,564 types. The General News text contrasts with the literary text in that the former has a lower ratio of word tokens to word types: out of the 400,000 tokens there are 42,887 types.

Table 4 compares the results of coverage and rate per word for AraComLex 2.1 against the baseline (AraComLex 1.0), that is the morphology originally developed in (Attia, 2006); AraComLex 2.0, which does not contain the broken plural extension; and LDC's SAMA version 3.1.

The results show that for the Semi-Literary text, we achieve a considerable improvement in coverage for AraComLex 2.1 over the baseline, increasing from 69.37% to 85.73%, that is 16.36% absolute improvement. However, for the General News text, we achieve less improvement: from 79.68% to 79.68% coverage, that is 7.45% absolute improvement.

Compared to SAMA, AraComLex 2.1 has 1.00% (absolute) less coverage on General News, and 1.22% (absolute) less coverage on the Semi-Literary text. However, the rate per word is significantly lower in AraComLex (2.08) than in SAMA (5.30). We assume that the lower rate of ambiguity in AraComLex is mainly due to the fact that we excluded obsolete words and morphological analyses from our lexical database.

5 Conclusion

We build a large-scale open-source finite state transducer for MSA (AraComLex) distributed under the GPLv3 license. We start off with a manually constructed lexicon of 10,799 MSA lemmas and automatically extend it to 30,587 lemmas, carefully excluding obsolete entries and analyses that are not attested in contemporary data, that is a large MSA corpus containing more than one billion words. We successfully use machine learning to predict morpho-syntactic features for newly acquired words. We also use Levenshtein Distance and Arabic word pattern matching to extract broken plurals. Evaluation results show that our transducer has coverage similar to SAMA, but at a significantly reduced average rate of analysis per word, due to avoiding outdated entries and analyses.

Acknowledgments.

This research is funded by Enterprise Ireland (PC/09/037), the Irish Research Council for Science Engineering and Technology (IRCSET), and the EU projects PANACEA (7FP-ITC-248064) and META-NET (FP7-ICT-249119).

References

Atkins, B. T. S. and Rundell, M. 2008. *The Oxford Guide to Practical Lexicography*. Oxford University Press.

Attia, M. 2006. An Ambiguity-Controlled Morphological Analyzer for Modern Standard Arabic Modelling Finite State Networks. In: Challenges of Arabic for NLP/MT Conference, The British Computer Society, London, UK.

Beesley, K. R. 1998. Arabic Morphological Analysis on the Internet. In: The 6th International Conference and Exhibition on Multilingual Computing, Cambridge, UK.

Beesley, K. R. 2001. Finite-State Morphological Analysis and Generation of Arabic at Xerox Research: Status and Plans in 2001. In: The ACL 2001 Workshop on Arabic Language Processing: Status and Prospects, Toulouse, France.

Beesley, K. R., and Karttunen, L. 2003. Finite State Morphology: CSLI studies in computational linguistics. Stanford, Calif.: Csli.

Bin-Muqbil, M. 2006. Phonetic and Phonological Aspects of Arabic Emphatics and Gutturals. Ph.D. thesis in the University of WisconsinMadison.

Buckwalter, T. 2004. Buckwalter Arabic Morphological Analyzer (BAMA) Version 2.0. Linguistic Data Consortium (LDC) catalogue number LDC2004L02, ISBN1-58563-324-0.

Dichy, J., and Farghaly, A. 2003. Roots & Patterns vs. Stems plus Grammar-Lexis Specifications: on what basis should a multilingual lexical database centred on Arabic be built? In: The MT-Summit IX workshop on Machine Translation for Semitic Languages, New Orleans.

Elgibali, A. and Badawi, E. M. 1996. *Understanding Arabic: Essays in Contemporary Arabic Linguistics in Honor of El-Said M. Badawi*. American University in Cairo Press, Egypt.

Fischer, W. 1997. *Classical Arabic*. In: *The Semitic Languages*. London: Routledge.

Haykin, S. 1998. *Neural Networks: A Comprehensive Foundation (2 ed.)*. Prentice Hall.

Hulden, M. 2009. Foma: a finite-state compiler and library. In: Proceedings of the 12th Conference of the European Chapter of the Association for Computational Linguistics (EACL '09). Stroudsburg, PA, USA.

Kiraz, G. A. 2001. *Computational Nonlinear Morphology: With Emphasis on Semitic Languages*. Cambridge University Press.

Maamouri, M., Graff, D., Bouziri, B., Krouna, S., and Kulick, S. 2010. LDC Standard Arabic Morphological Analyzer (SAMA) v. 3.1. LDC Catalog No. LDC2010L01. ISBN: 1-58563-555-3.

Parker, R., Graff, D., Chen, K., Kong, J., and Maeda, K. 2009. Arabic Gigaword Fourth Edition. LDC Catalog No. LDC2009T30. ISBN: 1-58563-532-4.

Roth, R., Rambow, O., Habash, N., Diab, M., and Rudin, C. 2008. Arabic Morphological Tagging, Diacritization, and Lemmatization Using Lexeme Models and Feature Ranking. In: Proceedings of Association for Computational Linguistics (ACL), Columbus, Ohio.

Sinclair, J. M. (ed.). 1987. *Looking Up: An Account of the COBUILD Project in Lexical Computing*. London: Collins.

Stetkevych, J. 1970. *The modern Arabic literary language: lexical and stylistic developments*. Publications of the Center for Middle Eastern Studies, No. 6. Chicago and London: University of Chicago Press.

Van Mol, M. 2003. *Variation in Modern Standard Arabic in Radio News Broadcasts, A Synchronic Descriptive Investigation in the use of complementary Particles*. Leuven, OLA 117.

Watson, J. 2002. *The Phonology and Morphology of Arabic*, New York: Oxford University Press.

Wehr, H. and Cowan, J. M. 1976. Dictionary of Modern Written Arabic, pp. VII-XV. Ithaca, N.Y.: Spoken Language Services.

Recognition and Translation of Arabic Named Entities with NooJ Using a New Representation Model

Héla Fehri
Laboratory MIRACL, University of Sfax
Route Tunis Km 10 B.P 242, Sakiet Ezziet
3021 Sfax
hela.fehri@fss.rnu.tn

Kais Haddar
Laboratory MIRACL, University of Sfax
Route Tunis Km 10 B.P 242, Sakiet Ezziet
3021 Sfax
kais.haddar@fss.rnu.tn

Abdelmajid Ben Hamadou
Laboratory MIRACL, University of Sfax
Route Tunis Km 10 B.P 242, Sakiet Ezziet 3021 Sfax
abdelmajid.benhamadou@isimsf.rnu.tn

Abstract

Recognition and translation of named entities (NEs) are two current research topics with regard to the proliferation of electronic documents exchanged through the Internet. The need to assimilate these documents through NLP tools has become necessary and interesting. Moreover, the formal or semi-formal modeling of these NEs may intervene in both processes of recognition and translation. Indeed, the modeling task makes more reliable the constitution of linguistic resources, limits the impact of linguistic specificities and facilitates transformations from one representation to another. In this context, we propose an approach of recognition and translation based on a representation model of Arabic NEs and a set of transducers resolving morphological and syntactical phenomena. The representation model is based on the feature structure independent of lexical categories.

Keywords: Representation Model, NE' recognition, NE' translation, Transducer, Local grammar.

1 Introduction

Recognition and translation of NEs are two current research topics with regard to the proliferation of electronic documents exchanged through the Internet. The need to assimilate these documents through NLP tools has become necessary and interesting.

Furthermore, the formal or semi-formal modeling of NEs can be involved in recognition and translation processes. This modeling task allows the constitution of more reliable linguistic resources. Indeed, such a modeling can represent all the constituents of a NE in a standard manner and limit the impact of linguistic specificities. In fact, a formal representation of Arabic NEs can help, firstly, in the identification of dictionaries and grammars required for any NLP application and, secondly, in the use of advanced linguistic methods of translation (i.e., transfer or pivot method). This abstraction level favors the reuse of certain linguistic resources.

Proceedings of the 9th International Workshop on Finite State Methods and Natural Language Processing, pages 134–142,
Blois (France), July 12-15, 2011. ©2011 Association for Computational Linguistics

The elaboration of a formal and generic representation of an NE is not an easy task because, on the one hand, we have to find a representation that takes into consideration the concept of recursion and length of NE. In fact, a NE can be formed by other NEs. So, its length is not known in advance. On the other hand, the representation to be proposed should also contain a sufficient number of features that can represent any NE independently of the domain and grammatical category. In other words, the same features must satisfy all types of NE.

Transducers (eventually local grammars) can resolve many problems of the NEs and should respect hierarchy types of NEs. However the connection between these transducers to obtain a deep analysis isn't a trivial task. So, a linguistic platform like NooJ can help us to do this kind of analysis.

It is in this context that the present work is situated. In fact, the main objective is to propose an approach of recognition and translation of Arabic NEs based on a representation model, a set of bilingual dictionaries and a set of transducers resolving morphological and syntactical phenomena related to the Arabic NEs and implemented with the linguistic platform NooJ. To reach our objective, we have to offer a representation model that takes into account the notion of recursion of NEs. We have also to specify features that describe any NE independently of the domain. Finally, the representation should be compatible with the linguistic platform NooJ (Silberztein, 2004) chosen for the implementation.

In this paper, we present, firstly, a brief overview of the state-of the art. Then, we detail our proposed representation model. After that, we give a general idea of our resources construction and their implementation in the linguistic platform NooJ. Finally, the paper concludes with some perspectives.

2 Related Work

Research on NEs revolves around two complementary axes: the first involves the typing of NEs while the second concerns the identification and translation of NEs. As for the identification, the tagging and the translation of NEs, they have been implemented for multiple languages based on different approaches: linguistic (Coates-Stephens, 1993), statistic (Borthwick et al., 1998) and hybrid (Mikheev et al., 1998) approaches. In what follows, we focus on the linguistic approach used for NE processing.

Regarding the recognition of NEs, we cite the work presented in (Friburger, 2002). This work allows the extraction of proper names in French. The proposed method is based on multiple syntactic transformations and some priorities that are implemented with transducers. We can cite also the work described in (Mesfar, 2007). The elaborated method is applied on a biomedical domain. Other Arabic works are dealing with the recognition of elliptical expressions (Hasni et al., 2009), compound nouns (Khalfallah et al., 2009), broken plurals (Ellouze et al., 2009) and most important categories in Arabic script (Shaalan and Raza, 2009). All these works that use the linguistic platform NooJ can be integrated in the NE processing.

Other works have been dedicated to the translation of different structure (e.g., NE) from one language to another. We can cite the work presented in (Barreiro, 2008) dealing with the translation of simple sentences from English to Portuguese. Additionally, the work of (Wu, 2008) provides a noun translation of French into Chinese. The elaborated prototype tests a limited corpus of 600 French nouns and is experimented with NooJ.

The literature review shows that the already proposed translation approaches are not well specified (e.g., lack of abstraction and genre). Each one addresses a particular phenomenon without taking into account other phenomena. We should also mention that there are few works that proposed a modeling of NEs for explicitly representing the effects of meaning within the NE and explaining phenomena like synecdoche and the metonymy (Poibeau, 2005). However, these works don't treat the concept of embedded NEs which is very important and can help to implement the recognition and the translation process of NEs.

Furthermore, all translations using NooJ platform adopt a semi-direct approach of translation, in which the recognition task is combined with that of translation. Thus, the reuse of such work has become limited, which does not promote multilingualism.

3 Proposed Model for Representing Arabic NEs

The model that we propose is used to formalize and to identify Arabic NEs. This model is inspired by formalisms based on structural features like Head-driven Phrase Structure Grammar (Pollard and Sag, 1994). Its features are inspired from the concepts "Head and Expansion" introduced by (Bourigault, 2002). The essential characteristics of the feature structure of the proposed model are:

- an element of the structure can be atomic or complex,
- an internal structure of an element is defined by its attributes and values.

In what follows, we describe the structure and features of our proposed model.

3.1 Structure and Features of the Proposed Model

Each NE has a type and is composed of two parts: one is essential and the other is extensional. The essential part is also a NE and has itself essential and extensional parts. This proves the recursion for an NE. The type of a NE "Type_EN" is usually indicated by a trigger word. The essential part is represented by the feature "Tête_EN" (head of NE) and the trigger word is represented by the feature "Mot_declencheur". The extensional part represents the final form that composes the NE. It does not admit a type because it is preceded by a lexical item "Element_EN" (element of NE) (e.g., preposition, special character). Then, it can not be considered as a NE but it can contain a NE. Its existence or non-existence doesn't affect the well-formation of the NE. This part is represented by the feature "Fin_EN" (end of NE).

The value of the feature "Tête_EN" can be atomic or structured. If it is structured, then it is composed by the features "Mot_déclencheur", "Tête_EN", "Fin_EN" and "Type_EN". The "Mot_déclencheur" value is simple or composed. Indeed, the trigger word can be formed by a word or a sequence of words. It can also be empty. The "Fin_EN" value can be atomic or structured. If it is structured, then it is composed by the features "Element_EN", "Tête_EN" and "Fin_EN". It can also be empty. The feature "Type_EN" value is always simple or composed but not empty. In fact, it represents one of the categories identified in the NE hierarchy. The "Element_EN" value is always simple. The structure can be equipped with a set of principles allowing the well-formed construction and the evaluation of NE-representation.

3.2 Principles of the Proposed Model

For the presented model, two principles should be satisfied and are useful in the recognition phase. These principles are used to indicate whether a NE is well-formed or not.

Saturation Principle: A structure is called *saturated* if it can be considered as a well-formed NE. That means, it consists of a NE head ("Tête_EN") whose value is not empty. Figure 1 describes an example of a formal representation that satisfies a saturation principle.

El *Riadh* الرياض

Tête_EN	الرياض
Fin_EN	ϕ
Type_EN	Ville

Figure 1: Representation of the word الرياض *el Riadh*

In Figure 1, the value of the feature "Type_EN" is atomic; it is not empty. Thus, a word *الرياض Riadh* is considered as a NE whose type is *Ville.*

Non-saturation Principle: A structure is called *unsaturated* if it is not a NE and can be completed to become a NE. That means, it is formed only by a NE end (*"Fin_EN"*) or if the value of the feature "Tête_EN" is empty. For example, in the word بالرياض *bi Riadh,* the value of the feature "Tête_EN" is empty because this word doesn't have a type. Thus, this word cannot be considered as a NE. It doesn't satisfy the saturation principle. However, it should be noted that this word can contain a NE.

The two mentioned principles allow us to avoid ambiguity between a NE-word (or set of words) and a non NE-word.

3.3 Illustrative Example

In this section, we give an example that explains how to construct NE representation. So, Figure 2 gives a formal representation of the NE *ملعب الملك عبد العزيزالدولي بالرياض Malaab el malik Abd el Aziz el doali bil Riadh*, *King Abd el Aziz international stadium in Riadh*. In this NE, the word بالرياض *bil Riadh* has the function of place complement. Its purpose is just to elaborate on the NE. Consequently, its elimination doesn't affect the well-formation of this NE. That's why it will be presented by the feature "Fin_EN" as follows: "Elément_EN" equals ب *bi* and "Tête_EN" equals الرياض *Riadh*. Let's note the word الرياض *Riadh* has its proper type without the particle ب *bi*. For this reason, it will be a simple value of the feature "Tête_EN". However, the rest of the NE ملعب الملك عبد العزيز الدولي *Malaab el malik Abd el Aziz el doali* has in turn its proper type. It will hence be described by the feature "Tête_EN" which will be structured because this NE contains supplementary words. In our NE, the supplementary word is the adjective الدولي *el doali* which has the same role as the place complement بالرياض *bil Riadh*. Therefore, it will be put in the "Fin_EN". Moreover, the word ملعب *malaab* plays the role of trigger word. What is left is the NE الملك عبد العزيز *el malik Abd el Aziz* whose type is person name. In this NE, the word الملك *el malik* also plays the role of trigger word. But, the NE عبد العزيز *Abd el Aziz* has a type of first name. So, it will be represented by the feature "Tête_EN" as a simple value since عبد العزيز *Abd el Aziz* doesn't contain any supplement word. Therefore, the mentioned NE is represented in our model as follow:

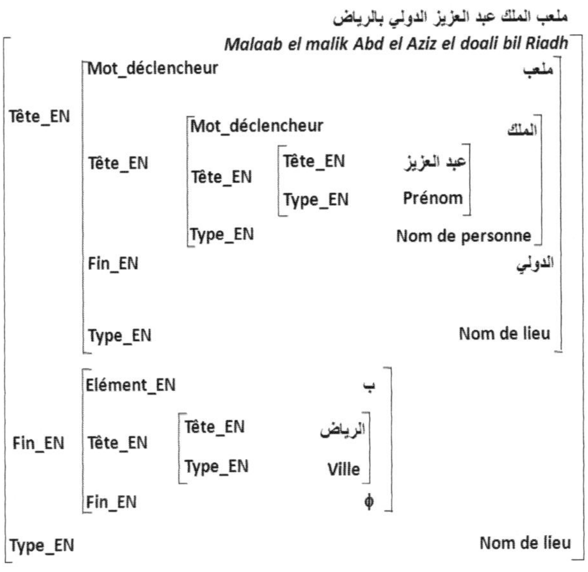

Figure 2: Example of a NE representation

In Figure 2, the saturation principle is determined. In fact, the value of the "Tête_EN" feature is not empty.

Let's note that the proposed representation is applicable independently of the domain. In fact, having conducted a study of the location names, we noticed that all their NEs have the same structure whatever the domain is.

3.4 Word-to-word Translation Representation

Word-to-word translation consists to translate each feature value composing a NE structure representation. This translation is done with bilingual dictionaries without any risk of information loss. Figure 3 represents an example of this phase.

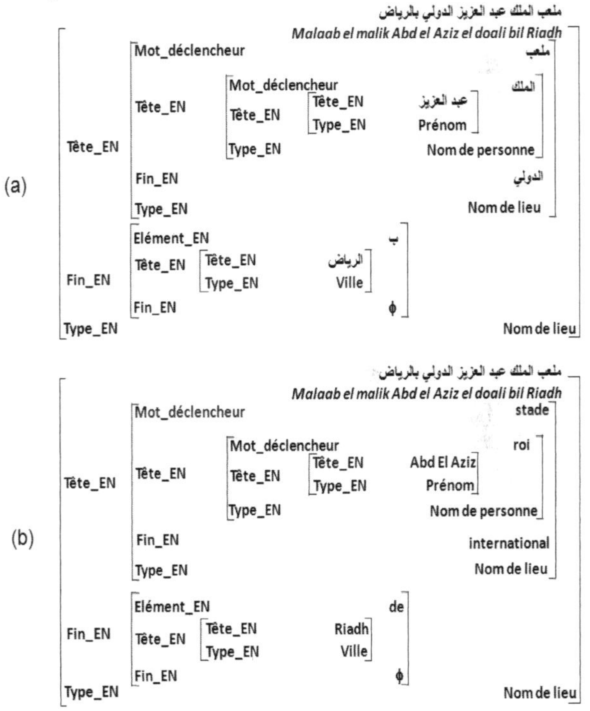

Figure 3: Example of a word-to-word translation of NE structure

As shown in Figure 3 ((a) and (b)), the word ملعب *malaab stadium* is translated to *stade*, the word *الملك el malik king* to *roi*, the adjective *الدولي el doali international* to *international and* the preposition ب *bi in* to *de*. It is obvious that types keep the same value whatever the language is.

Let's note that the representation of a word-to-word translation is not sufficient to generate a well formed NE in the target language. In fact, the translation of the NE in Figure 3 (a) ملعب الملك عبد العزيزالدولي بالرياض Malaab el malik Abd el Aziz el doali bil Riadh gives in Figure 3 (b) the sequence of words "stade du roi Abd el Aziz international à Riadh" representing an ill-formed NE because it doesn't respect the specificities of the target language. Therefore, readjustment rules are necessary and should be associated in translation process.

4 NooJ Implementation of the Set of Transducers

The NooJ implementation of our system requires two phases process: recognition of Arabic NEs and translation in which a transliteration process is integrated. Each phase requires the construction of its proper transducers.

4.1 Phase of Recognition

The proposed representation model helps us to identify the necessary resources for the recognition and translation of NEs. In fact, each structured feature "Tête_EN" containing not empty features, other than the feature "Type_EN", is transformed into a local grammar (*place name*, *person name*, ...); whereas, each elementary NE (value of "Tête_EN" feature is atomic) will be transformed into a dictionary (*city name*, ...).

From the NE representation in the considered model, we have created the following transducer:

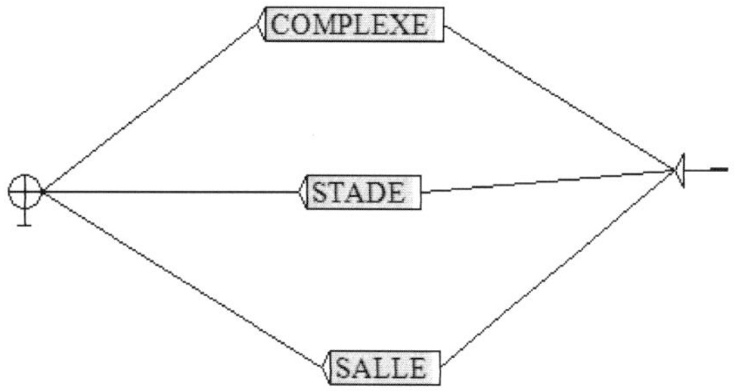

Figure 4: Main transducer of NE' recognition

The transducer of Figure 4 contains three sub-graphs. Each sub-graph represents a category identified in the NE hierarchy, especially in the category of *Place name*. This grammar allows recognition of NEs. Each path of each sub-graph represents a rule extracted in the study corpus.

In the recognition phase, we have solved the problems related to the Arabic language (e.g., agglutination) establishing morphological grammars built into the platform NooJ. This phase contains 19 graphs respecting the local grammars identified in the study corpus.

4.2 Phase of Translation

The implementation of the translation phase involves two steps as illustrated in Section 4.4: a step of word-to-word translation and another more detailed taking into account the readjustment rules and following the specificities of the target language (in our case the French language). In what follows, we describe resources designed to these two steps.

Word-to-word Translation: To implement the word-to-word translation in the platform NooJ, we built a syntactic grammar allowing the translation of each word composing a NE with the exception of words not found in dictionaries, or can not be translated (number, special character, etc.). This grammar takes as input the NE list extracted by the transducer of Figure 4 allowing the recognition. It is described by the transducer of Figure 5.

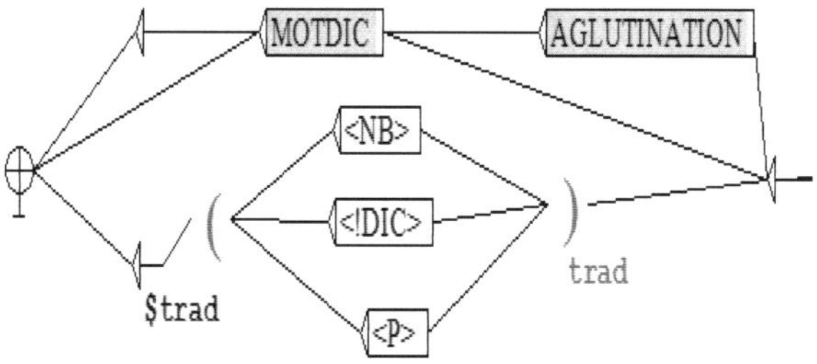

Figure 5: Transducer of word-to-word translation

The transducer of Figure 5 takes into account, in a NE, the words that keep the same values in the target language. These words can correspond to a number <NB>, a special character <P> or a word not existing in designed dictionaries <!DIC>. The sub-graph MOTDIC treats the rest of the words (existing in dictionaries) which require a specific treatment. For example, if the word to translate is a first name, then it keeps the same value in the source language; this word will be treated in the transliteration process (Fehri et al., 2009).

Translation with Readjustments: Several readjustment rules must be applied to improve the word-to-word translation step. These rules have essentially a relationship with the order of the words composing a NE and with the agglutination. For instance, on the one hand, if a NE in the source language contains an adjective then we have to know whether this adjective belongs to the trigger word or to the noun that comes just before. For example, in the NE ملعب المدينة الدولي *malaab el madina el doali stadium of ground city*, the adjective الدولي *el doali ground* is singular and masculine, the trigger word ملعب *malaab stadium* is also singular and masculine, but the noun المدينة *el madina city* is singular and feminine. We can deduce that the adjective الدولي *el doali* belongs to the trigger word ملعب *malaab* and not to the noun المدينة *el madina* that comes just before. On the other hand, if a NE in the source language contains a noun then some rules are applied to solve the problem of contracted forms in Arabic. For example, in the NE ملعب الملك فهد *malaab el malik Fahd*, the noun الملك *el malik* is singular, masculine and definite by the letter ال *el*, so when we translate this noun we should add the preposition "du" before it. Thus, we obtain *stade du roi Fahd* (international stadium of Fahd) and not *stade roi Fahd* (international stadium Fahd).

Readjustment rules are made with syntactic local grammars in NooJ. These grammars intervene after the word-to-word translation phase. In what follows, we give an idea about transliteration process integrated in translation phase.

Transliteration process: The transliteration is done after having executed all the transducers allowing the NE' recognition and translation (word-to-word translation or with readjustments). In fact, it consists in transliterating all the non-translated words which are written in the source language (Arabic characters) using the appropriate resources. In this process, we consider rules respecting the chosen transliteration system *El Qalam* and also the transformation rules. These rules are implemented with NooJ morphological transducers. The transliteration is preceded by a voweling phase to avoid some problems. So, the word is voweled before its transliteration. However, the connection between a vowel transducer and transliteration transducer can not be done in NooJ; that is why, we resort to use noojapply. Noojapply is a command-line program which can be called either directly from a "shell" script, or from more sophisticated programs written in PERL, C++, JAVA, etc. In our work, we use C#. The transliteration step is detailed in (Fehri et al., 2009).

5 Experimentation and Evaluation

The experimentation of our resources is done with NooJ. As mentioned above, this platform uses (syntactic and morphological) local grammars already built. Table 1 gives an idea about dictionaries which we added to the resources of NooJ. In addition to the dictionaries mentioned in Table 1, we use other dictionaries existing in NooJ like dictionary of adjectives, nouns and first names (Mesfar, 2008).

Dictionaries	Number of inputs	Annotation in the dictionary
Player Names	18000	N+Joueur
Team Names	5785	N+Equipe
Sport Names	337	N+Sport
Capital and country Names	610	N+Topony me
Personality Names	300	N+Perso
Trigger words	20	N+Dec
Functions Names	100	N+Fonction

Table 1: Added dictionaries

To these dictionaries, we add some entries related to the sport domain. We also add French translations of all entries in all mentioned dictionaries. Let's note that the first name dictionary remains monolingual because its entries can be transliterated. To experiment and evaluate our work, we have applied our resources to two types of corpus: sport and education corpora. We started with sport domain since it is the subject of our study corpus.

5.1 Experimentation of Recognition Phase

To evaluate the recognition phase, we have applied our resources to a corpus formed by 4000 texts of sport domain (different of the study corpus). This corpus is collected from various newspapers (e.g., Assabah, al Anwar, al chourou9, al ahram) and Wikipedia. It contains 180000 NEs belonging to different categories of sport domain (e.g., player name, name of sport, sports term). In these

NEs, there are 40000 NEs belonging to the category *place name*. These NEs are manually identified using NooJ queries. The obtained result is given in the NooJ concordance table of Figure 6.

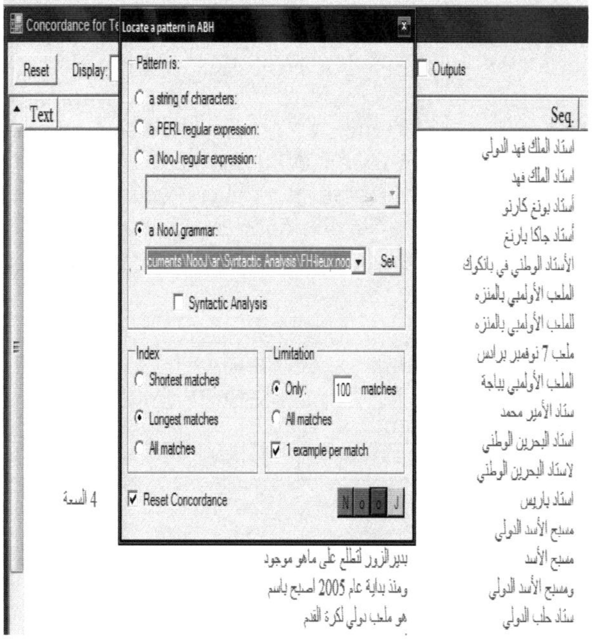

Figure 6: Concordance table of NE' recognition in the sport domain

Let's note that a NE is detected if it satisfies one of the paths described by the transducer of Figure 4. Indeed, a transducer is characterized by an initial node and one or many end nodes. If multiple paths are verified, we maintain the longest one. The obtained results are interpreted by calculating the following metrics: Precision, Recall and F-measure. Results are illustrated in Table 2.

The values of measures in Table 2 show that there are some problems that are not yet resolved. Some problems are related to the lack of standards for writing proper names (e.g., *el hamza*). This causes a silence. Other problems are related to Arabic specific concepts as metaphor. For example, we can find a NE in a text composed of a trigger word specific to the sport domain followed by a famous person name followed by a city as ملعب الأسد بسوريا *Malaab el Assad bi Souriya* (*stadium al Assad in Syria*). The context where this NE appears is not in the objective to cite a stadium name but to show the skills of *President al-Assad* in the cited subject. Such problems are rare but cause the noise.

	Precision	**Recall**	**F-measure**
Newspaper texts (Sport domain) 4000 texts (94,5 Mo)	98%	90%	94%

Table 2: Obtained results

As indicated above, we have also applied our resources to the education domain. We have collected a corpus composed of 300 texts containing university institution names. The performance measure of the obtained results gives 98% of precision, 70% of recall and 82% of F-measure. We deduce that the silence is increased. This is caused by the incompleteness of specific dictionaries to this domain and lack of some paths in the developed transducers. So our resources are applicable regardless of the domain, provided that we use the same features adopted in dictionaries we have built. It is evident that for reasons specific to the domain, we should sometimes add other paths and other sub-graphs, but we do not have to redo everything.

5.2 Experimentation of Translation Phase

The translation phase is applied to the extracted Arabic NEs during the recognition phase. Note that erroneous results are inherited. Therefore, heuristics filtering are necessary before the translation process. The obtained results of the translation phase are illustrated in Figure 7. As shown in this figure, the proper problems of this phase involve multiple translations that can be assigned to a word. For example, the selected lines in Figure 7 represent the NE' translation ملعب مدينة الباسل الرياضية بدرعا *malaab madinat el bacel el riadhiya bi deraa stadium of city Bacel sportive in Deraa*. In this NE, the word مدينة *madina* can be translated to the word "cité" *city* or "ville" *country*. NooJ displays all possibilities. In this case, the adjective can resolve this ambiguity. In fact, the adjective الرياضية *el riadhiya sportive* is generally related to the city and not to the country. Let's note that the word "باسل" *Bacel* remains in the source language because it is a first name, so it will be transliterated later.

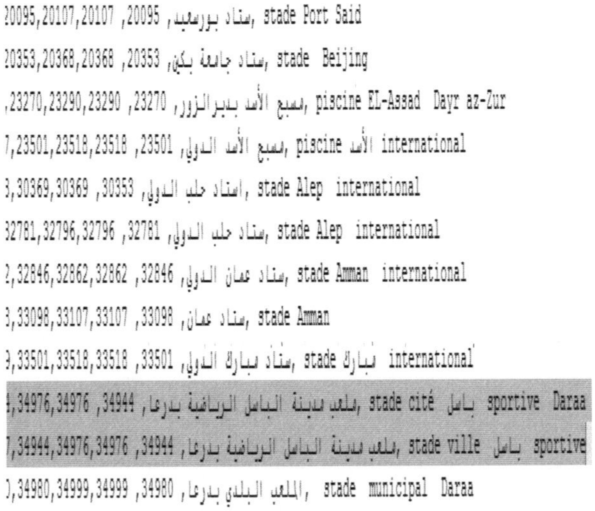

Figure 7: Extract of results of word-to-word translation

To get a finer translation, we applied the readjustment rules that take into account the order of the constituents of NEs and the agreement of the adjective with the noun for which it is associated.

Our method provides 97% of well translated NEs while ensuring the specificities of the target language. The obtained result is promising and shows that there are some problems. These problems are related to the multiple translations assigned to a toponym (e.g., تونس *tounis* can be translated in *Tunis* or *Tunisia*).

After this evaluation, we remark that the proposed representation model facilitates the construction of the linguistic resources with the platform NooJ and the transformation from the semi-direct translation to transfer one. Indeed, we have separated the NE-recognition of their translation. In addition, it helps the promotion to the reuse of the needed local grammars. In fact, it is sufficient to change the inputs (i.e., dictionaries, morphological grammars) of the syntactic grammars for the desired results. Thus, for example, if we want to translate Arabic NE to another language other than French, the recognition module can be reused with some modifications if necessary (related to the specificities of the domain). Moreover, if we want to translate NEs from any language into French, also translation module can be reused. Indeed, this module addresses the specificities of the French language.

6 Conclusion and Perspectives

In this paper, we have proposed an approach for recognition and translation of Arabic NEs (eventually NEs from other languages) based on a representation model, a set of bilingual dictionaries and a set of transducers resolving morphological and syntactical phenomena related to the Arabic NEs. Besides, we have described the representation model structure, its features and principles that should be satisfied. We have also given an experimentation and evaluation on the sports and education domains proving that our resources can be reused independently of the domain. The experimentation and the evaluation are done in the linguistic platform NooJ. The obtained results are satisfactory.

As perspectives, we try to improve our representation model by introducing other features related to the semantics. Furthermore, we are currently identifying heuristics filtering enabling finer NE translation.

References

Barreiro A. 2008. Port4NooJ: an open source, ontology-driven Portuguese linguistic system with applications in machine translation. NooJ'08, Budapest.

Borthwick A. Sterling J. Agichtein, E. and Grishman R. 1998. NYU: Description of the MENE Named Entity System as used in MUC-7. In Proc. of the Seventh Message Understanding Conference (MUC-7).

Bourigault D. 2002. UPERY : un outil d'analyse distributionnelle étendue pour la construction d'ontologies à partir de corpus. TALN.

Coates-Stephens S. 1993. The Analysis and Acquisition of Proper Names for the Understanding of Free Text. In Computers and the Humanities, Kluwer Academic Publishers, Vol. 26(5-6), Hingham, MA, p. 441-456.

Ellouze S. Haddar K. and Abdelwahed A. 2009. Etude et analyse du pluriel brisé avec la plateforme NooJ. Tozeur, Tunisia.

Fehri, H. Haddar K. and Ben Hamadou A. 2009. Translation and Transliteration of Arabic Named Entities. LTC Conference, Pologne, pp 275-279.

Friburger N. 2002. Reconnaissance automatique des noms propres. PhD thesis, university of François Rabelais.

Hasni E. Haddar K. and Abdelwahed A. 2009. Reconnaissance des expressions elliptiques arabes avec NOOJ. In proceedings of the 3rd International Conference on Arabic Language Processing (CITALA'09) sponsored by IEEE Morocco Section, 4-5 May 2009, Rabat, Morocco, pp 83-88.

Khalfallah F. Haddar K. and Abdelwahed A. 2009. Construction d'un dictionnaire de noms composes en arabe. In proceedings of the 3rd International Conference on Arabic Language Processing (CITALA'09) sponsored by IEEE Morocco Section, 4-5 May 2009, Rabat, Morocco, pp111-116.

Mesfar S. 2007. Named Entity Recognition for Arabic Using Syntactic grammars. NLDB 2007 Paris, 28-38.

Mesfar S. 2008. Analyse morpho-syntaxique automatique et reconnaissance des entités nommées en arabe standard.: Thesis, November 2008, University of Franche-Comté.

Mikheev A. Grover C. and Moens M. 1998. Description of the LTG system used for MUC -7. In Proc. of 7th Message Understanding Conference (MUC-7), http://www.itl.nist.gov/iad/ 894.02/ related_projects/muc/.

Poibeau, T. 2005. Sur le statut référentiel des entités nommées. Laboratory of data processing of Paris North – CNRS and University Paris 13.

Pollard C. and Sag I.A. 1994. Head-Driven Phrase Structure Grammar. Published by the press in the University of Chicago, Edition Golgoldmittu, Chicago, LSLI.

Shaalan K. and Raza H. 2009. NERA: Named Entity Recognition for Arabic. Published in Journal of the American Society for Information Science and Technology, Volume 60 Issue 8.

Silberztein M. 2004. NooJ : an Object-Oriented Approach. In INTEX pour la Linguistique et le Traitement Automatique des Langues. C. Muller, J. Royauté M. Silberztein Eds, book of the MSH Ledoux. Presses University of Franche-Comte, pp. 359-369.

Wu M. 2008. La traduction automatique français-chinois pour les groupes nominaux avec NooJ. Budapest.

Author Index